SALVAGE

#7
TOWARDS THE PROLETAROCENE

AUTUMN / WINTER 2019

Contents

SALVAGE EDITORIAL COLLECTIVE

The Tragedy of the Worker: Towards the Proletarocene

How should we dream of this place without us?—
The sun mere fire, the leaves untroubled about us,
A stone look on the stone's face?
                    Richard Wilbur, 'Advice to a Prophet'

Life exists in Vernadskian space. A globe, twenty-five kilometres deep, from the oceanic abyss to the outer limit of the troposphere. A biosphere, to the destruction of which, humanity is witness, and of which, perpetrator.

This biosphere is a contingent product of an improbable and rare chemical interaction, in conditions that amounted to a cosmic fluke, in no way inferable from the original state of the planet in the Hadean Eon. Somehow, whether by the work of 'black smokers' in the oceanic depths, or by an Oparin-style, solar and lightning-induced catalysis of protobiotic compounds, or by means of some other gradient of chemicals, heat and density, geochemistry became biochemistry. Emergence. Inorganic chemical processes began to self-replicate, gathering energy and atoms from their environment, and adapting to environmental pressures. Once formed, the first life forms depended, as Vernadsky put it, on 'radiations that pour upon the earth', causing 'the matter of the biosphere' to collect and redistribute solar energy, converting into 'free energy capable of doing work on Earth'.

For two billion years of life, Earth was inhabited solely by single-celled organisms, bacteria and archaea. Sophisticated swimming creatures, they were able to swim, metabolise sugars, avoid toxins, and produce nitrous oxides. (By comparison, our most advanced robotics have struggled to match this level of intelligent, adaptive behaviour, and may even now only be reaching, as Rodney Brooks puts it, the phase of 'Cambrian intelligence'.) They were distinctly symbiotic creatures, routinely sharing genetic material, effectively accessing to a single gene pool.

This is the 'microcosmos' from which, as Lynn Margulis argues, all life has evolved, in which all life exists. The cell, of which the bacterium is the original template, is the engine, the mechanism by which energy is converted into life. The 'web of life' is microbial, because the microbe is the primordial engine for the transformation of energy.

More complex animals exhibit similarly symbiotic propensities as did their archaic forebears: termites host tiny organisms in their digestive tracts, coral feed with the assistance of tiny plant cells living in their flesh, humans are colonised by microbiota. The mitochondria of modern cells have their own DNA, reflecting the cell's origins in a process of bacterial symbiogenesis. Margulis goes so far as to speculate that the ancestors of brain cells were spirochetes, fast-moving killer bacteria consumed and absorbed in a defensive move by slower archaea. Humanity is thus 'a symbiotically evolving, globally interconnected, technologically enhanced, microbially based system'.

Capitalism subsumes these life-processes, these flows of energy, these microbial dependencies, within its own molecular flow. It subordinates them to the homogenising frame of value-production: M-C-M'. A regime of creative-destructive accumulation that is as inexhaustible as biospheric resources are finite.

> Since their inception the bourgeois class has been waiting
> for the flood.
>
> Theodore Adorno, *Minima Moralia*

Capitalism, like certain bacteria, like the death-drive, is immortal. It has its limits and crises but, perversely, seems to *thrive* on these. Unlike the multi-species life-systems powering it, the only *terminal* limit to capital's perpetual augmentation is, if driven toward from within, external: either revolution or human extinction; communism, or the common ruin of the contending classes.

Long ago, both Max Weber and Walter Benjamin pointed out an occulted religious foundation in capitalist civilisation. As Michael Löwy points out, Benjamin, by defining capitalism as a cultic religion, went much farther than Weber in identifying a Puritan/Capitalist guilt-driven imperative to accumulate. 'The duration of the cult,' for Benjamin, 'is permanent'. There are 'no days which are not holidays', and 'nothing has meaning that is not immediately related to the cult'.

In what sense is capitalism a cult? What are its rituals, its fetishes? Those of investment, speculating, buying and selling. It has no dogma other than those 'real abstractions', as Alfred Sohn-Rethel put it, entailed by its rituals. In Sohn-Rethel's words, the act of commodity-exchange is the key exemplar of a social action governed by an abstraction of which the participants have no consciousness. The buyer may be concerned only with the sensuous particularities of the commodity, the needs it fills, but behaves in the moment of exchange as though what matters is the quantity of exchange-value embedded in it. Ritual action determines dogma; social being, that is, determines consciousness.

Capitalist theology instates, not dogma, but unyielding imperatives governing action. 'Accumulate, accumulate! That is Moses and the prophets!', Marx sarcastically withered in *Capital*. Accumulation is, for capital, an imperative and not an option. To exist as a unit of capital in conditions of universal competition, is to accumulate or die. As long, therefore, as there is labour-power to exploit and, in Jason W Moore's term, 'cheap nature' to appropriate, capital will augment itself. This very bifurcation of life into the exploitable and the appropriable, which Moore identifies as the foundation of a 'Cartesian dualism' unsustainably counterposing 'Nature' to 'Society', is not dogma but *programme*. It is related to a distinctive move of capitalist theology, currently given right-Evangelical sanction by Calvin Beisner and the Cornwall Declaration, to disavow in practice the existence of inherent physical limits. It posits, in its action, the Earth as limitless cornucopia over which humans have dominion, and from which limitless accumulation must be extracted.

This disavowal, this 'real abstraction', is the social basis of capitalist *implicatory denial*: the seemingly evidence-proof conviction of capitalist states that capitalogenic climate change can be remedied by means, and according to systems, that guarantee its perpetuation. The capitalocentric purview is commonly, but mistakenly, identified with the anthropocentrism of ancient and medieval monotheisms. Here, however, it is clearly *not* the Anthropos that stands at the centre, as though appointed by God to steward the garden of Earth. At the centre is the ritual: that unconditional imperative to accumulate. And insofar as this imperative drives 'adorers', as Benjamin put it, to the horizon of human extinction, capitalism can – must – be described as a death cult.

Fossil capital is but one modality of the death cult, albeit a paragon. The 'externalities' of capital – climate chaos, biosphere destruction, resource depletion, topsoil erosion, ocean acidification, mass extinction, the accumulation of chemical, heavy metal, biological and nuclear wastes – extend far beyond the specific catastrophe of a carbonised atmosphere. Capitalism is a comprehensive system of work-energetics. The food industry, which powers waged labour, and is key to the shifting value of labour-power itself, is as central to the deterioration of the biosphere as is fossil-fuelled transit. Nonetheless, the continuing decision for fossil fuels as a solution to the energy demands of capitalist production, for all the growing denial of climate-change denial among the anti-vulgarian ruling class, for all their concerned mouth music, is an exemplary case of the capitalist imperative of competitive accumulation at work.

As Andreas Malm has fiercely and beautifully argued, capitalism did not settle for fossil fuels as a solution to energy scarcity. The common assumption that fossil energy is an *intrinsically* valuable energy resource worth competing over, and fighting wars for is, as geographer Matthew Huber argues, an example of fetishism. At the onset of steam power, water was abundant, and cheaper to use even with its fixed costs, than coal. The hydraulic mammoths powered by water wheels required far less human labour to convert to energy, and were far more energy-efficient. Even today, only a third of the energy in coal is actually converted in the industrial processes dedicated thereto: the only thing that is efficiently produced is carbon dioxide. On such basis, the striving for competitive advantage by capitalists seeking maximum market control 'should' have favoured renewable energy.

Capital, however, preferred the spatio-temporal profile of stocks due to the internal politics of competitive accumulation. Water use necessitated communal administration, with its perilously collectivist implications. Coal, and later oil, could be transported to urban centres, where workers were acculturated to the work-time of capitalist industry, and hoarded by individual enterprises. This allowed individual units of capital to compete more effectively with one another, secured the political authority of capital and incorporated workers into atomised systems of reproduction, from transport to heating.[*]

Thus, locked in by the short-termist imperatives of competitive accumulation, fossil capital assumed a politically privileged position within an emerging world capitalist ecology. It monopolised the supply of energy for dead labour, albeit in a highly inefficient way.

This is the tragedy of the worker. That, as avatar of a class in itself, she was put to work for the accumulation of capital, from capitalism's youth, amid means of production not of her choosing, and with a telos of ecological catastrophe. That thus even should the proletariat become a class *for* itself, and even if it does so at a point of history where the full horror of the methods of fossil capitalism is becoming clear, it would – will – inherit productive forces

---

[*] This argument is made beautifully and in full in Andreas Malm's *Fossil Capital.*

11

inextricable from mass, trans-species death. This does not preclude systemic, planet-wide transformation. Particularly given the inevitably uneven global growth of class consciousness and resistance, however, and the concomitant embattledness of any reformist, let alone revolutionary, power on the global stage, it does ensure that it faces extraordinary barriers. As will become clear.

As of 2015, estimates suggested that humanity produced a total of 15.5 trillion watts of energy each year, of which a considerable 29 per cent was not used. At an average of 2000 watts per person (rising to 10,000 watts in the core capitalist economies), the majority was used for industry, commerce and transit, with only 22 per cent for household consumption. Some 90 per cent of this output was powered by fossil fuels: oil, coal, gas. This monopoly, enabling superprofits as monopolies do, ensured that fossil capital would always realise profit margins far higher than the industrial average. It has, in Malm's term, become worth a 'planet of value'. Each fossil fuel plant represents decades of investment awaiting realisation.

To avert planetary disaster is to inflict an Earth-sized blow on capitalist industry. It is to choose between burning a planet of value, and burning the planet itself. But the death cult is so strong, so pervasive, that, against all resistance, the choice has already been made.

> I look out on the earth ... lo, all is chaos;
> I look at heaven ... its light is gone;
> I look out on the mountains ... they are trembling;
> And all the hills are swaying!
>
> Jeremiah 4: 23-26

Apocalypse has begun. The button has been pushed. Humanity is already committed to irreversible climate change. Climate activists are, in Richard Wilbur's phrase, 'mad-eyed from stating the obvious'. To understand the scale of what faces us, and the way it ramifies into every corner of our lives, is to marvel that we aren't having emergency meetings in every city, town and village every week.

SALVAGE

WWW.SALVAGE.ZONE

THIS POSTCARD HAS BEEN PRINTED TO ACCOMPANY

THE SEVENTH ISSUE OF *SALVAGE*, IN AUTUMN / WINTER 2019.

SALVAGE 7 – AUTUMN/WINTER 2019

TOWARDS THE PROLETAROCENE

Salvage is – still – a journal of revolutionary arts and letters.

'Hope must be abandoned before it can be salvaged,' we wrote at the time of our launch in 2015. Now that it appears hope is to be so salvaged – cautiously, urgently, warily, exuberantly – we are embarking on a modest relaunch, a consolidation of our operations, online and in-print.

This insert is accompaniment to *Salvage #7: Towards the Proletarocene*, our Autumn/Winter issue of 2019. This is our relaunch issue, and the first to appear according to our new bi-annual schedule.

Our previous issues have all included a pamphlet entitled 'Perspectives', outlining various national and international phenomena and forces we consider particularly salient at time of publication, and the position of the *Salvage* editorial collective thereto. In future issues we intend to return to this practice. But for this relaunch issue, in place of our synoptic overview, we offer a special, extended in-depth editorial essay. This piece, 'The Tragedy of the Worker: Towards the Proletarocene', opens the issue itself.

Future issues will, of course, include the familiar elements: essays, visual art, poetry and fiction, as well as the perspectives – and a postcard. The journal may continue to vary somewhat in length, but the quality of its contents will be constant.

We are also excited to announce the launch of our newly revamped website, at www.salvage.zone.

Subscriptions are now available directly through the website, where readers can also log in to amend subscription details, get early access to our recently inaugurated monthly online editorial essays, and download PDFs of all our back issues. Essays from the print edition will continue to be posted online in the weeks after their print publication, as will online-exclusive content. Fiction, poetry and visual art will remain exclusive to the print edition.

The subscription rates are £25 per year for two issues for UK readers, and £30 per year for those elsewhere. All subscription prices include postage.

If you would like to support *Salvage* financially, and are able to help us grow, you can sign up for a 'Comrade' subscription for £10 a month or £50 per year.

If you *really* want to support us – and if you can afford to be generous – you can sign up for a 'Solidarity' subscription, at £20 a month or £100 per year. And as an inadequate if heartfelt token of our gratitude, we will send you a *Salvage* Christmas card.

We are glad to announce new distribution networks in both North America and the UK and Europe, which means you should see us in all good bookshops. If *Salvage* is not in your favourite bookshop, please ask them to order it! In the UK and Europe, we are distributed by Central Books, and in North America, by Penguin Random House.

This relaunch is possible only because of the generosity of those who have supported us online, at www.patreon.com. It will remain possible to support us there, but in this, our new phase, we would be particularly grateful to those who can if you support us via our own website www.salvage.zone, not least so as to deny Silicon Valley their slice.

We extend thanks and solidarity to all our readers, and the promise of shared worthwhile work to come.

– *Salvage* Editorial Collective, October 2019

'THUS AN IMAGE OF *SEHNSUCHT* THAT
EVOLVED FROM DESPAIR — EXTREME
CONDITIONS PRODUCE EXTREME UTOPIAS.'

- IRMTRAUD MORGNER

We are, increasingly, out of time. In the capitalist *untimelich*, the time of the living and the time of the dead, human history and the history of inorganic sediments, collide. 'Millions of years of concentrated solar energy', as Huber calls it, have been released in an historical blink of an eye, only to rebound just as fast: the Deep Time equivalent of an asteroid strike. The cyclical time of seasons turns freakish, leaving us uneasily sweating in the clammy mid-winter. Spring comes too early, hurricane-force winds and flash floods break the October calm, polar ice melts while temperate zones are plunged into polar winter. The Arctic burns, boreal forests turned to charred sticks. The Greenland ice sheet melts even in winter. Antarctic sea ice has suddenly and drastically contracted in recent years. The polar vortex wanders, perturbed, and the mid-West freezes. In a parody of Revelations, Mediterranean storms rain fish on the island of Malta. Stochastic weather events accumulate. Birds fall dead from the sky. The progression of geological deep time, with its periods, eras and epochs speeds up so rapidly that it precipitates a crisis in the temporal order itself: spinning so fast, we may as well be standing still. The progressive time of human civilization, reduced to the endless accumulation of stuff, collapses into nonsense. The cycle of ice ages, a necessary condition for human evolution, melts away for eternity.

The sixth mass extinction, signalled by what one study calls 'biological annihilation', is underway. The oceans, which produce roughly half of the oxygen we breathe, are acidifying, and are swept by heatwaves, says a recent study, 'like wildfire'. Coral reefs, home to a quarter of marine life, are bleaching. Insect biomass collapses, with forty per cent of all species undergoing drastic decline. The bees, that once we believed saved, are disappearing eight times faster than are mammals, birds or reptiles. Without their pollination work, 70 per cent of the crops that feed 90 per cent of the planet will fail.

The question of human survival is inextricable from that of what sort of humans we should be. By 2070, MIT research says, the new norm for 'many billions' of people will be impossibly high temperatures that will kill less fit people and make outdoors work impossible. Half a billion will experience temperatures that would 'kill even healthy people in the shade within six hours'. The Arctic, that 'congealed sea' discovered by Pytheas, a breathing 'mixture like sea-lung', will be gone by, on conservative estimates by 2040. Last year, the usually snow-bowed woodlands circling this uncanny sea-continent burned more fiercely than ever. Precise metrics of the scale of what will unfold are to be determined, not least by class struggle, but there is no longer, if there ever was, a choice between adaptation and mitigation.

So adapt. But to what? Those species now going extinct were once well adapted. The widely accepted geo-logism, 'Anthropocene', is in one sense an obvious political evasion, diluting as it does the necessary focus on capital accumulation itself. Yet, of course, capitalism is something that the human species, and no other, does. And while there are unthinkably vast disparities in power and responsibility in the production of petro-modernity, the latter has had a proven – if, crucially, hardly irrevocable – popular base: the vatic rage of activists notwithstanding, no politician has been crucified for promising fuel tax cuts.

This fact can easily be weaponised by the Right. Of the recent protests of the gilets jaunes in France against declining wages and rising inequality and sparked by a rise in diesel tax later reversed by Macron faced by the scale of the protests, Trump tweeted that '[p]eople do not want to pay large sums of money ... in order to maybe protect the environment'.

In fact, however, and allowing that the movement is hardly monolithic, the French uprising has been characterised by a remarkable *refusal to refuse* to engage with questions of ecology, particularly compared, say, to the fuel-price protests in the UK in 2000 and 2005. Far from being characterised by ecological indifference, what has characterised much of the recent French protest is disagreement between those for whom talk of ecology comes too soon, and those for whom such talk is inextricable from social – class – justice. One example of the former is visible in the claim of the prominent activist Jerôme Rodriguez that '[e]ventually, when we obtain the first things, ecology will have its place'; of the latter, the words of another, François Boulot, that '[t]he social and ecological emergencies are inseparable', that '[w]e will not be able to operate the ecological transition without an equitable wealth redistribution'.

Rodriguez's rationale for his position, that 'nowadays, people aren't concentrated on this', is not supported by the superlative gilets jaunes slogans, 'End of the month, end of the world: same perpetrators, same fight', and 'More ice sheets, fewer bankers'. This refusal to compartmentalise is energising evidence of the new politicisation of the moment.

Still, that not everyone opposed to the fuel tax rise has been so assiduous in drawing the connections is in part because the dispersed, privatised accommodation and individualised trans-portation of modern life offer individualised, immediate-term and distinctively capitalist answer to specifically human strivings.

The concept of the Anthropocene is a tacit acknowledgment that the alienated labour of humanity has itself become a selective evolutionary pressure. It has already forced rapid adaptation in some species, where it has not resulted in extinction, as Bernard Kettlewell's experiments with peppered moths show. The besooting of tree bark in industrial areas became a powerful selective force, favouring darker moths, harder for birds to see and pick off. Now such pressures are coming for us, as powerful as the asteroid strike behind the Cretaceous-Paleogene mass extinction.

We are compelled to adapt to ourselves.

From this point of view, there is no difference between adap-tation and mitigation. To close the fossil fuel plants, to destroy a planet of value, or even, dare we hope, the value-form itself: are these not adaptations?

Of course, this is not what is generally meant by adaptation. Implicit is a Green Zone-style survivalism of the rich, explicitly touted are permanent adaptations of capitalism to the conse-quences of capitalism. The ideology of 'adaptation' has become the ideology of capitalism's triumph over all life.

> Nature is man's inorganic body. Nature is his body, with which he must remain in continuous interchange if he is not to die.
>
> Karl Marx, 'Estranged Labour'

Extinction is everyday. It is what there is to eat, wrapped in cling-film and sold from refrigerated shelves. We have lost half of all the mammals, birds, reptiles and fish on the planet over the last forty years.

This is neither random, nor naturally determined, but the creative-destructive act of humanity in its capitalist phase. It is our capitalist *Stoffwechsel*. As Kenneth Fish puts it in *Living Factories*, capitalism produces industrial systems that 'come themselves to approximate a force of nature infused with human purpose'. A massive metabolic entity, chewing up and spitting out at unprecedented rates: the agribusiness complex.

The Triassic-Permian 'great dying' was a megaphase change taking place through pulses lasting for tens of thousands of years, separated by interludes of hundreds of thousands of years, if not millions. The current mass extinction event is a megaphase change taking place in microphase time.

Mass extinction is punctuated by the production of what the environmentalist Jonathan Lymbery calls 'dead zones': the conversion of wild ecosystems into dead monocultures. In Sumatra, these dead zones are made by burning rainforest and, amid the stench of death, planting palm crop. The palm oil is used in foods and household items while the nut is used in animal feed. It is secured with barbed wire, and treated with poison, to prevent the crop from being eaten. Surviving animal life, and surrounding human communities, are pushed to the edges, to the brink of extinction. Agricultural workers are abused, underpaid, even enslaved. This is an example what Moore would call 'cheap food', where the 'value composition' of the goods, the amount of waged labour necessary to produce each item is 'below the systemwide average for all commodities'. In this case, a 'cheap nature' is produced by a distinctly capitalist form of territorialisation, wherein forestry is converted through deforestation into palm monoculture, while 'cheap labour' is secured partly through the dispossession of neighbouring human communities. More calories with less socially-necessary labour-time, is cheap food.

Cheap is not, of course, the same thing as efficient. Food production is, alongside fuel, a fulcrum of the capitalist organisation of work-energetics. It is one that, as with fossil fuels, wastes an incredible amount of the energy it extracts. Thirty per cent of cereals that are grown for human and animal consumption are wasted, according to the FAO. Almost half of all root crops, fruits and vegetables are wasted. To conclude from this grotesque squander that a 'more efficient' capitalism would 'solve the problem' of 'the environment' would be to fail to understand waste, capitalism and ecology: that the first is intrinsic to the second; that the second, whatever the degree to which it is inflected by the first, is inimical to the third.

Capitalism also directly undermines its own productivity, precisely through its industrially-produced biospheric destruction. According to the UN, for example, there are at most sixty harvests remaining before the world's soils are too exhausted to feed the planet. This edaphic impoverishment is a product, not a byproduct. It is the predictable, and long-predicted, consequence of intensive agriculture, over-grazing and the destruction of natural features (such as trees) that prevent erosion. Likewise, the death-drop of insect biomass, the decline of pollinating bees, are hastened by the extensive use of pesticides and fertilisers. Capitalist food production can only evade the problem – a problem, in its terms, of accumulation – either by establishing new 'cheap natures' through such means as deforestation, or by extracting rent from competitor producers through such means as intellectual property rights. For instance, the World Trade Organisation enforced property agreements outlawing the saving of seeds, thus sharply raising costs for farmers producing 70 per cent of the global food supply.

In response to environmentalist opposition, capitalism has a number of moves available to it. One, faced with direct class opposition, is outright repression, as in Brazil where agribusiness has formed an alliance with Jair Bolsonaro, to crush land rights activists as 'terrorists', the better to extend its dead zones. The skies of Sao Paulo have blackened this summer, the rainwater dark with soot as, amid a wave of rancher arson and a scale of racist violence against indigenous communities not seen since the dictatorship, the Amazon rainforest burned at record speed. This existential threat to life on earth was visible from outer space. Another, faced with consumerist pressure, is some variant or other of that chimerical 'green capitalism'. As Jesse Goldstein has documented, this has opened a profitable niche of capital accumulation, with minor energy-saving and 'clean' technologies being sold as world-saving innovations. It is also inseparable from capitalist imperialism.

In one respect, the struggles over the Arctic are unusual. The pivot of imperialism today is not direct political control of territory. It is, rather, a global, liberal property-rights regime, policed by everyone from the US Trade Representative to the European Commission, backed by the power of the US Treasury, the Federal Reserve and Wall Street, supported by capitalist classes from Paris to Beijing and secured by violence 'in the last instance'. Thus it falls to these institutions to elaborate a 'green capitalist' response to ecological crisis. As ever, the solution is predicated on 'sustainability'. In relation to the palm industry, the Roundtable on Sustainable Palm Oil (RSPO) exists to certify certain producers as sustainable. The RSPO is notorious with Greenpeace and Amnesty International for certifying companies engaged in deforestation, labour abuses and even slavery as 'sustainable'. Nonetheless, its certifying processes proved useful for the European Commission when it was challenged to find a 'politically feasible' solution to the palm oil crisis.

Even were the palm oil industry to be crushed in one legal blow, however, substantially the most likely result would be that capitalism would shift to another monoculture: rapeseed, or soybean. When one dead zone ceases to be productive, or politically feasible, capital permanently searches out others. The problem remains the death cult of capital accumulation, and its specific *Stoffwechsel*.

> The basis of optimism is sheer terror.
>
> Oscar Wilde

We live in Bad Hope. Capitalism produces *mauvais-espérer*, cognate of *mauvais-foi*, as rapidly as it does carbon emissions.

More pervasive than its literalist denialist cousin, and growing, is the *implicatory* denial of the 'adults in the room'; the 'green capitalism' that vocally 'believes in' anthropogenic climate change. – It shares with its cousin a grundnorm: that scientific knowledge must never threaten accumulation. Capitalism can very easily accommodate denial and denial-denial. As with so many issues, it is effortlessly virtuoso in instrumentalising apparent opposites.

The fact of 'Anthropocene' is no shock to capitalism. As Christophe Bonneuil and Jean-Baptiste Fressoz argue in *The Shock of the Anthropocene*, the danger posed by capital accumulation to the web of life has always been either partly known or knowable. There was no desire, on the part of capitalists or the managers of capitalist states, to investigate further until the future of the system itself was threatened. Until that point, the 'hockey stick' charts that now grace environmental literature were the basis for capitalist triumphalism. From approximately 1950, Ian Angus shows in *Facing the Anthropocene*, there is a sharp rise in atmospheric carbon dioxide and methane, surface temperature, marine fish capture, biosphere degradation, and ocean acidification. Deforestation begins to soar earlier, around 1900. Martin Gorke's study of mass extinction shows a similar hockey-stick curve, with an enormous spike in extinctions taking off after 1900. This was for a long time a *success story*: more industry, easier transportation, large urban populations, more domesticated land, more food on the plate, growing population.

The 'awakening' of recent decades has been marked by a series of false starts. In 1972, two years after the first 'Earth Day', the OECD proposed a green economy. Polluters would be expected to pay for their contamination of the environment. In 1987, the Brundtland Commission exhorted governments to embrace 'sustainable development'. The following year, the Intergovernmental Panel on Climate

Change was launched. In 1992, the Rio Earth Summit signalled the apparent beginnings of a global framework for climate mitigation. Five years later, the Kyoto Protocol agreed binding targets for the reduction of carbon emissions by participating states (the United States remaining stubbornly aloof), which came into effect in 2005. A decade later, countries across the world signed up to new emissions targets at the UN Framework Convention on Climate Change, in Paris. The agreement reprised the instruments of Kyoto, such as carbon trading and 'sustainable development' targets, but this time with US participation. At each step, a new beginning has been loudly pronounced.

And yet, with all this noisy global effort, it isn't even plausible to say that apocalypse has been deferred. The majority of carbon emissions in the entire history of humanity, as David Wallace-Wells starkly reports, have been produced *since* the Earth Summit in 1992. The reason: every supposed effort at mitigation has been designed almost as if it were intended to fail.

Liberal *bien-pensants* used to bewail the refusal of the US, especially under George W Bush, to participate in Kyoto. But for all this theatre, Kyoto was always-already a failure on its own grounds. Even where Kyoto participants achieved some nominal reductions, these took place for reasons that either had little to do with Kyoto, or that revealed Kyoto's hollowness. The cuts were largest in Ukraine, Lithuania and Latvia, largely as a result of the demolition of national industries by structural adjustment. The United Kingdom achieved cuts largely by dint of the one-off, unrepeatable feat of demolishing the coal industry, a feat undertaken largely to break organised labour. And many countries like Italy achieved nominal reductions simply by trading emissions with poorer countries.

The Kyoto Protocol endorsed the market approach. Rationing emissions by price enabled some capitalist states or industrial sectors to purchase more fossil-driven growth from those whose emissions were suppressed by low growth anyway. And it was purchased cheaply (and subject to collapsing prices, particularly after 2008), with deliberate oversupply making European carbon credits cheaper than 'junk bonds', as the *Economist* put it, by 2013.

Elsewhere, for example in Canada, Australia and New Zealand, carbon emissions increased dramatically.

The panacea of 'carbon trading' is a particularly cultic iteration of neoclassical economics, groping for the invisible hand for more than mere survival. 'Putting a price on carbon is the only prudent answer', then-Prime Minister of Australia Julia Gillard wrote almost a decade ago, 'because it unlocks one of the most powerful forces on earth – the genius of the free market. By resetting price signals, we will open the door to a new era of investment and innovation'. The truth is that such commodification is, was always, and has always been known to be by those with eyes to see, worse than nothing.

It has certainly made money for some: 'infested by corruption and non-transparency', in Steffen Böhm's words, carbon markets have created 'a lot of income for consultants, carbon brokers and project'. Grift aside, the system in its very essence bolsters big polluters. Daniel Tanuro and others have shown how '[c]arbon trading is a source of windfall profits for polluting sectors', that those profits 'generated by the quota system strengthen big carbon emitters that have a strategic interest in slowing or delaying climate change mitigation and in continuing to burn fossil fuels as long as possible'.

The faithful blame the failures of capitalism on inadequate capitalism: in 2012, the think tank Open Europe described the EU Greenhouse Gas Emissions Trading Scheme as 'botched central planning rather than a real market'. But that this market is real is precisely the problem. 'Part of the failures of carbon trading can be put down to neoclassical economic orthodoxy', as Rebecca Pearse puts it. Focusing on an Australian domestic scheme, but with more general pertinence, she describes how

> [c]arbon price signals are understood as a means to
> correct market failure. The excess greenhouse gases
> in the global atmosphere are understood as aberrant
> and unintended externalities of otherwise efficient
> markets. There is a tendency toward heroic expecta-
> tions about the effects of carbon price signals in our
> broken electricity markets and false assumptions

about the equivalence of different parts of the carbon
cycle. This understanding of climate change is ahis-
torical and asocial: it creates all sorts of problems
and blind spots in climate change practice. ... Perhaps
most importantly, the carbon market project rests on
the assumption states are able and willing to institute
carbon trading rules that deliver environmental goals,
as well as acceptable and profitable outcomes for all
relevant fractions of capital and citizens.

Of course it is always and only profit that will be prioritised. The
ecological 'assumptions' of such strategies are predicated on that
disavowed understanding. For Pearse, marketised climate policy
is precisely a 'displacement strategy ... aimed at deflecting or
deferring the climate crisis spatially ... materially ... and politically'
– and, we can add, *temporally*. But time is up.

Kyoto was an example of ideological reification on a grand
scale. The interconnected global processes through which the web
of life is converted into value, and atmospheric carbon, have been
represented as localisable objects for exchange in a lucrative global
market. At one stage, the *New York Times* looked forward to it being
the biggest market in the world, as it reached a global value of
$117bn. By 2020, subject to the violent vicissitudes of speculation,
it is possible it will be worth $1 trillion. But consider that the larg-
est single increase in carbon emissions from any country during the
Kyoto period was from China, which as a 'developing' economy was
exempted from the treaty. Most of the goods it produced, however,
were for export: services-driven economies had simply outsourced
much of their industrial base. Under the guise of a spurious geopolitical egalitarianism, hand-in-glove with a thin market utopianism,
Kyoto enabled capitalism's frantic, carbon-fuelled growth. The
same applies to the meat industry, which accounts for 15 per cent
of global emissions. Much of the meat consumed in Europe, for
example, is imported from Africa, the Americas and Asia.

Even the recent Paris Accords, feted as the last best hope for
the planet before Trump's sabotage, were committed by their own

estimates to warming of between 1.5 and 2 degrees above prein-dustrial temperatures. This is a plan not to avert, but for, disaster. The IPCC's Fourth Assessment Report suggested that 20-30 per cent of animal and plant species may go extinct if global average temperatures exceed 1.5 degrees above pre-industrial levels. A cataclysm at countless levels - including for the food chain. A rise of two degrees would severely raise the likelihood of 60 per cent of the populated surface of the earth being flooded.

The Paris objectives, relying on voluntary emissions targets thanks to a last-minute intervention by Obama, will not be met. They are supposed to be achieved by a combination of the failed carbon trading model and the use of 'energy efficiency'. The latter, something of a shibboleth for policy-makers since the 1990s, rests on the disproved assumption that the economical use of fuel reduc-es its consumption. Energy efficiency has become a benchmark of environmental regulation, and there has, indeed, been a sharp in-crease in the efficiency of electrical goods. And yet, of course, as the Jevons paradox predicts, this merely resulted in *more* consumption, efficiency sustaining the illusion of 'plenty'. Numerous studies look-ing at the measures incorporated in the Paris Accords expect them to lock in decades of emissions leading to global temperatures ris-ing by an average estimate 3.7 degrees by 2100. Hence these ac-cords being welcomed by Exxon and major coal firms. Hence BP's confidence, in lobbying the Trump administration for Arctic drilling rights, that they would be fully in accord with the Paris objectives.

No wonder that the IPCC currently expects 1.5 degrees of warming by 2030, with 3-4 degrees by 2100. Such warming would produce sufficient flooding, desertification and heat as to make large populated areas uninhabitable. And there are good reasons to assume these estimates are conservative. The IPCC has consist-ently underestimated the real pace of climate change. Its estimates of emissions, temperature increases, the melting of the Arctic, the disintegration of ice-sheets, tundra thaw, rising sea levels and ocean acidification have all been staggeringly outpaced by reality. The first three IPCC reports didn't even mention ocean acidification as a problem, while its earliest reports anticipated no significant changes to Greenland and Antarctic ice sheets. Until relatively recently, it has consistently held that the Arctic ice is safe until beyond 2050, a clearly untenable position.

One reason for the IPCC's disastrous conservatism is its preference for linear models of change, which fail to take adequate account of feedback mechanisms and tipping points. By now, for example, it is well known that the loss of polar ice reduces the 'albedo effect', wherein solar radiation is reflected back into outer space, thereby warming the waters and melting more ice. The heating of the oceans is likely to kill much of the marine life that acts as a carbon sink, thereby increasing the amount of carbon in the atmosphere and heating the oceans further still.

The extended reproduction of capitalism, in its allegedly 'green' phase, is the extended reproduction of apocalypse.

The language of 'sustainable development', Gareth Dale points out, has become the language of sustained capitalist growth. It has become the language of implicatory denial. Capitalist states proclaiming the objective of 'zero net emissions', while their means entail the massive expansion of emissions. 'Green' economies expanding airports and extending motorways. The unsinkable rubber duck of 'green capitalism'.

> What the bourgeoisie ... produces, above all, are its own
> grave-diggers.
>
> Karl Marx and Friedrich Engels,
> *The Communist Manifesto*

The tragedy of the worker is that, as long as she works for capitalism, she must be her own grave-digger. Capital never extracts energy from the earth, but it makes a taxing withdrawal from the worker's body.

If the entire problem facing humanity was how to source a fixed quantity of energy without destroying the planet, the problem might have been solved by now. For example, solar energy could in principle meet our needs many times over. Yet energy as such, like value, is an abstraction. No physicist is able to say what it is. It is not, as Vaclav Smil writes, a 'single, easily-identifiable entity'. Calories, biomass, electro-magnetism, light-waves, heat and motion all have the property of being energy, and for human societies it matters greatly what sort of energy is available, electricity not being edible. The sun, indeed, is already our main source of energy. As Vernadsky put it, 'the biosphere is at least as much a *creation of the sun* as a result of terrestrial processes'. What we consume as caloric energy has been captured by photosynthesis. That depends on life-processes whose degradation through overfishing, deforestation and intensive agriculture would not be remedied by technofix, even if capturing high-entropy solar radiation were simple and adaptable enough to power such crucial industries as aviation.

It is, to repeat, a signal error to think that the ideological secretions of fossil capital begin and end with the climate denialist industry, currently abandoned even by the majority of fossil capitalists. Rather, ideology is sedimented into its scientific knowledge. Capital must, of course, attend to physical realities, in a way that the Heritage Foundation need not. However, it tends to read these realities through its own screen of commodity production. Knowledge of energy as an abstract entity, subject to laws of conversion, conservation, and quantification is one such secretion. As Thomas Kuhn argued, it is no coincidence that the major contributions to energy science from Carnot, Kelvin, Helmholtz and Clausius, emerged just as industry was converting energy from wind, wood, water and coal. It was the steam engine that sparked interest, not so much in 'the *nature* of heat', Ilya Progigone and Isabelle Stengers point out, as in 'heat's *possibilities* for producing "mechanical energy"'. If thermodynamics, whose discovery was borne of this interest, treated energy as though it were indestructible and substitutable, this was also exactly how fossil capital treated it. The industrial revolution was also the moment, as Anson Rabinbach has shown, when the Enlightenment-begot productivist view of human energy and its deployment was consolidated. Work became linked, not to 'Christian dignity', nor to medieval artisanship, but to flows of energy deemed to be limitless in principle: labour-power.

Capital's inexhaustible demand for exhaustible energy entails a distinctive form of what Dominic Boyer terms 'energopolitics'. Capital isn't hungry for energy in the way that a machine or a living body is. It grows on the value added to that energy by human labour. It doesn't just rip open stocks of purified carbon deposited by ancient life, with utter disregard for the 'externalities'. Its relationship to non-human energy is structured by its dependence on human energy, its extraction of fossil energy a byproduct of its extraction of caloric energy, purchased as labour-power and converted into economic value. The role of non-human energy in the production process might best be captured by Marx's term 'dead labour'. Dead labour is infrastructure, where an infrastructure is whatever allows new work to take place. It is the mixing of human caloric energy extracted from the labouring body, with fossil energy and resources to produce stockpiles, machinery, buildings, railways, the grid, all to intensify the work of living labour.

The labour theory of value is a theory of our apocalypse.

Energy by itself, though abundant in the natural world, does not produce economic value. An aggregate expansion in the use of energy both enables and, from the point of view of capital, requires an aggregate expansion of the labour force. From that point of view, whatever its impact on particular groups of workers, fears of automation destroying work *tout court* are misplaced as long as capitalism is around.

The capitalist 'work/energy regime', as George Caffentzis and Jason W Moore dub it, entails a relentless raid on human energy in a production process whose product is extinction. The only ultimate limits to this process are revolt, and/or physical exhaustion. Resistance to fossil capital is class self-defence. The tragedy of the worker is that the workers' movement has only episodically been able to embrace this understanding. The worker's hopes have been tied to the energetic foundations of capitalism and its apparent proffer of liberation from back-breaking labour.

Scant years ago, the hopes of much of the Left were pinned to the stability of 'pink tide' regimes in Latin America, such as Venezuela, dependent on the resource base of extractivism. Crucial left debates about these regimes' strategies bracketed, immediate questions of political survival thereof and the amelioration of working-class conditions therein were urgent, and, in that context, the resources of the extractive industries irresistible, even for many quite clear-eyed about the ecological ramifications. This is the tragedy of the worker. It does not imply that no alternatives at all could have been developed: but it abjures moralism, and acknowledges the constraints of space for manoeuvre.

Such empathy ebbs in less embattled contexts. Even as the catastrophe strikes ever more visibly, parts of the labour movement are willing to put themselves in the offensive vanguard of fossil capitalist expansion, as with the 'left' leadership of Unite the Union lobbying for the expansion of the aviation industry for the holy grail of 'jobs'. As if they should never challenge capital's priorities. As if, even absent liberation from the wage-form, if jobs must exist, only those granted by capital, performing what tasks for what ends it demands, can exist, and must be defended. As if no alternatives can be demanded.

This was far from inevitable. The shopworn cliché according to which environmental consciousness is incorrigibly bourgeois, a 'post-materialist' concern that eludes workers, is yet another secretion of fossil capital, a putatively left variant of the right-populism-versus-greenery deployed by Trump 'in support' of the gilets jaunes. Such claims originate in the publicity strategies of industries threatened by regulation, seeking to draw workers to their side. And they ignore, as they must, that it is workers in the first instance who bear the environmental costs of capitalist production – something that the German-American economist William Kapp noticed as early as 1950. Whatever else they have been, struggles over waste in Naples, or toxic dumping in Love Canal, or the Bhopal disaster, have been class struggles waged by the poor.

The bourgeois myth does not even hold in the United States where the labour movement has been weak, the Left even weaker, and the ideological power of petromodernity and its offer of capitalist freedom at its strongest. As Chad Montrie's labour histories suggest, modern ecological consciousness (as distinct from indigenous cosmovisions) initially sprang from the direct conflict between capital and labour, as agrarian workers were drawn into dirty towns and cities to work in factories that befouled the rivers and besmogged the air: the same 'filth and horrors' that Engels discerned in the living conditions of the English working-class. From working-class sporting clubs to labour unions, conservationist pressure long preceded the cultural impact of Rachel Carson's breakthrough work, *Silent Spring*. In the Appalachians, it was workers – in often violent struggle with energy capitalists – who defended the natural environment. The existence of clean-air and -water legislation owes itself to a coalition between oil, chemical, atomic, steel and farm workers' unions with environmental groups.

Still less does the bourgeois myth hold outside of the United States. In Italy, the modern environmental movement was born in class struggle against the industrial degradation of living conditions and occupational health. It found programmatic expression in the experience of 'working-class ecology' that arose in the Communist Party and the organisations of the radical left in the Sixties and Seventies. As Stefania Barca points out, left ecologists in this era such as Laura Conti and Giovanni Berlinguer not only made important theoretical contributions to a working-class ecology, which respected the existence of physical limitations, but also helped build class alliances between unions and professionals that formed the basis for Italian labour environmentalism. For the Brazilian working-class movement, strongly influenced by the Italian experience, rural workers brought an added dimension of struggles against deforestation and for land rights. For the landless workers' movement, currently menaced by Bolsonaro, class livelihoods and environmental justice have never been self-evidently opposed.

The very power of the discourse that pits jobs against climate, is a contingent outcome of class struggle, above all of the successful neoliberal offensives against working-class self-organisation and the defensive narrowing of horizons it has produced. How many workers in rustbelts and mining communities would have voted for Donald Trump, for example, had the 'new economy' championed by centre-right Democrats as their main solution to climate change offered anything but joblessness, low-paid service work, de-union-isation, a savaged public sector and an opioid epidemic?

Yet these horizons are not only formed by the immediate context of weakness and failure. The spectre of a much larger defeat haunts the worker. Here, the Left must register its own illusions, its own hubris, its own defeats.

> The Smoke of the Factory is Better than the Smoke of Incense.
>
> Pioneer Slogan, Russia 1924

Fossil capitalism was seriously threatened only once in its history, before the worst damage had already been done. The October revolution took place amid the annihilatory clatter and hammer and thunder of World War I, a war whose shattering impact on flora and fauna is overshadowed by its incomparable bloodletting, with forty million working-class men and women killed for imperialism. And yet, imperialism in its most violent mobilisation could not but produce an ecological death-storm. In the conquest of the Americas and Australasia, indigenous genocide was part of a cascading cataclysm of extinction, with ecosystems brought to ruin for the sake of domains for capitalist agriculture, hunting and settlement. These 'neo-Europes', as Alfred Crosby dubbed them, brought with them a 'world-altering avalanche' at gunpoint. So it would necessarily prove when colonial violence returned to the metropole.

Where the bodies fell, complex ecosystems were transformed by industrialised war into 'fields of sterility', the novelist Henri Barbusse wrote. 'Where there are no dead, the earth itself is corpselike'. In the trenches, pervaded with poisonous gases and studded with exploded and unexploded ordnances, the photojournalist Michael St Maur Sheil found zones of death 'where every living thing was killed'. Far beyond the front, the war's demand for resources such as timber, coal and tin meant that deciduous forests were cut down, and the industrialisation of mining was accelerated not only in Europe but across its colonial empires. As in almost every twentieth century war, wild animals were an unremarked on casualty, and the European bison was exterminated in Russia by German hunting parties.

The revolution was not fought for the environment, but to raise almost 125 million people out of war, poverty and despotism: yet it ramified ecologically. 'Land, bread and peace' entailed an end to ecocidal war and, to the great relief of Russian conservationists, social ownership and rational management of the land and its energy and mineral resources. The Soviet government, attempting to overcome the irrationality of Tsarist traditions and prevent capitalist plunder, implemented strict limits on hunting, logging, and the exploitation of resources, and created dozens of protected natural reserves. These efforts, though imperilled by civil war and famine, were perpetuated well into the 1920s. The Soviet government was the first in the world, as historian Douglas Wiener points out, to set aside protected territories for the scientific study of nature. This was also the era of scientific breakthroughs, from phytosociology (the study of plant communities) to trophic dynamics (the study of energy flows in food chains). Bolshevism not only strove to be rational and scientific in its husbandry of a devastated ecosystem, but also undertook what Weiner calls a 'singular experiment in scientific conservation'. It was even open, in some quarters, as Kunal Chattopadhyay has shown, to strains of early, more radical materialist ecological thought such as that associated with Kozhevnikov, which broke from 'growth'-oriented and reductive utilitarianism – Kozhevnikov, for example, was behind early proposals for those *zapovedniki*, nature reserves, not to be used for harvest or hunting, but to guard against monocultures and to protect fragile species. Even during the civil war, in 1919, the agronomist Nikolai Podyapolski met Lenin to argue for a new *zapovednik* in Astrakhan. He recalls being as fearful 'as before an exam in high school' – but '[h]aving asked me some questions about the military and political situation in the ... region, Vladimir Ilich expressed his approval ... He stated that the cause of conservation was important not only for the Astrakhan krai, but for the whole republic'.

Yet ultimately, of course, one strand within Bolshevism, in circumstances very much not of its own choosing, proved decisive.

It is a form of crude anticommunism to claim, as Jairus Victor Grove does, that Marxism is 'committed to a project of homogenization at the expense of human and nonhuman animal forms of life'. What is unarguably the case, however, is that the Marxist commitment to red plenty, a superabundance, a life beyond scarcity, was fused in the Bolshevik era, particularly in the context of unrelenting existential threat, to an urgent race toward industrialisation. 'Communism,' Lenin's famous speech in 1920 ran, 'is Soviet power plus the electrification of the whole country'. Hundreds of engineers and scientists, millions of workers, and the giant coal basins of Siberia and eastern Russia, were recruited to this end. Without a 'huge industrial machine' at its disposal, the besieged, famine-struck revolutionary state would not survive. The situation was, as Trotsky lamented in the same year, 'in the highest degree tragic'.

Transport, industry and food production had been driven to the point of collapse by imperialist war, and civil war. Disastrous harvests, famine, typhus, cholera and dysentery, all bespoke a generalised ecological collapse. The demographic basis for soviet power, let alone the political basis, had been shredded. Russia, so far from realising socialism, was 'a blockaded fortress with a disorganised economy and exhausted resources'. Socialism, for the Bolsheviks, had to be at least as productive as capitalism in order to survive – yet the Russian economy would not recover to pre-war levels until 1930. Hence the calls, in the midnight of civil war, to militarise the labour force. Hence the heroically productivist exhortations, the invocation of a distinctly socialist form of labour productivity, in language that pre-empted *haute* Stakhanovism.

The stabilisation of the Bolshevik regime was purchased at the cost, ultimately, of destroying what remained of Soviet democracy, and increasing the power of party managers and the state apparatus over the Russian working class. Moreover, in the panic years of War Communism, Bolsheviks had seeded the rationales for heedless industrialisation and intensive labour exploitation that would return in the Stalin years. Gosplan, the bureau created by Lenin to

electrify the Soviet Union, was one of the main supporters of a return to centralised planning, and later became the ministry responsible for five-year plans. The formal interment of Soviet power in
1928, with the first Five Year Plan, prompted a hypertrophic return
of the culture of War Communism. In which era, any incipient socialist ecology was permanently crushed. The always-jostling balance of power of various streams within the party and the ecological sciences shifted dramatically, as Chattopadhyay shows. In the
context of international economically and militarily competitive
state struggle, the vulgarly utilitarian model veered to victory, in-
strumentalised by Stalinism. 'The *zapovedniki*', Foster says, 'were
converted more and more from reserves for the scientific study of
pristine nature into a new role as transformation-of-nature cent-
ers', and dissenting ecologists were purged. The subordination of
science and nature itself to crudely productivist economics was
overt: under torture, the ecologist Stanchinskii 'confessed' that
'the theoretical problems of ecology and biocenology that I posited
were completely removed from economic exigencies'.

From that point on, the Russian state was a fossil state.
Dedicated to competing with Western economies in conditions
of autarky, it required breakneck industrialisation. That in turn
required the most efficient and relentless exploitation of the natural resources and labour forces available to a vast overland empire.
From the 1960s to the 1980s, against the resistance of Sami locals,
the Arctic Ocean was used as a nuclear dump. In 1990, forty per
cent of Soviet people lived in areas of three to four times higher air
pollution than was supposedly permissible, and half of all waste
water in the capital went untreated. Nothing, of course, was solved
by the transition to the most feral iteration of 'free-market capitalism'. By 1996 fifty per cent of Russian water was polluted. In 2010,
two hundred cities in Russia exceeded their own air pollution
limits. A 2018 Russian environmental ministry document reports
an elevenfold increase in deaths due to environmental disasters
between 2016 and 2017, and temperatures increasing at more than
double the average global rate. Russia remains the fourth-highest
greenhouse-gas-emitting country in the world.

The 'metabolic rift', to use John Bellamy Foster's term for Marx's notion of the 'irreparable rift in the interdependent process of social metabolism', that chasmal source of ecological crisis, was, to Soviet planners, a growth strategy.

> They explored and explored
> And travelled back
> With maps of the country
> And descriptions of the lifestyle
> For honour and glory
> For medal and degrees
> For having explored a country
> Where people live and dwell
>
> Aqqaluk Lynge

'The collapse of the Soviet system,' McKenzie Wark argues in *Molecular Red*, 'prefigures the collapse of the American one'. Whether that counts as optimism or not, the implication is that the two systems share a logic, and were and are ailed by a similar problem of exhaustion.

Perhaps nothing better exemplifies this better than the fate of the Arctic, the combined work of European imperialists, Russian modernisers, American colonisers, not to mention fossil capital and its twin, 'green capitalism'. That fate, as Cambridge researcher Peter Wadhams dubs it, is a 'death spiral'.

Between 1980 and 2012, the Arctic lost 40 per cent of its sea ice cover, and 65 per cent of ice thickness. Of the oldest ice, 95 per cent is gone, what remains is increasingly fragile 'first year ice'. The waters will imminently be completely ice free each September. And then, for the whole year.

Narwhals, polar bears, beluga whales, the Pacific walrus, peregrine falcons, ringed seals, spoonbill sandpipers, golden plovers, kittiwakes, black guillemots. Design after exquisite designless design, evolutionary one-offs, anatomical glories, once gone never to be seen again, edging closer to the furnace of global heating. We are proceeding with unprecedented haste toward a new 'hothouse planet'. The last time the Arctic was blue and Antarctica was a warm continent was during the age of the dinosaurs. The Anthropocene is the name, not for the most advanced phase of evolved life, but for a sudden derailing: a spin-off reality, a meltdown.

Jauntily reporting on Canadian and Russian preparations for the big melt, the BBC asks whether the Arctic is 'set to become a main shipping route?' In the summer of 2018 (as discussed in China Miéville's essay in this issue), as the region burned, heat-waves and droughts across the world resulted in thousands dying like insects under a magnifying glass. Little noticed at the time, a Danish cargo ship successfully completed a trial voyage through the Russian Arctic. While the British state has historically invested more in the Antarctic than the Arctic, the government's Office for Science has recently released a report looking at the 'climatic potential for Arctic shipping'. The Arctic, being 'extremely sensitive to climate change', is melting faster than climate-model simulations predict, it says, which could result in 'investment worth $100bn or more' in such profitable domains as mineral resources, fisheries, logistics and Arctic tourism. Of course, the government insists that such development must be 'sustainable'. The US Geological Survey, meanwhile, estimates that 30 per cent of the world's undiscovered gas, and 13 per cent of its oil, may be in the Arctic.

Here is a climate feedback mechanism that is purely intrinsic to capitalism, wherein accumulation-by-extinction is a means to further accumulation-by-extinction.

The disappearance of the Arctic is a commercial boon for which the major Arctic powers are prepared to fight. The United States has a clear military lead in this struggle, demonstrated in a grandstanding US-led NATO exercise in the Arctic last November. The largest since the Cold War, the exercise involved 50,000 troops, and tens of thousands of vehicles, vessels and air crafts, ostensibly simulating their response to an attack on an ally. Russia, however, has the largest Arctic land mass, is immediately adjacent to the planned transpolar sea route, has re-opened military bases in its north, and possesses the world's largest fleet of icebreakers: a legacy of the Stalinist dictatorship. It was also the first to, theatrically, plant its flag in the north pole. The United States and Canada are investing rapidly in upgrading their own icebreakers, while the UK, responding to Russia's military exercises in the Arctic, despatched 800 commandos to, pathetically, 'demonstrate we're there'. In light of this, the theatrical astonishment at Trump's Secretary of State Mike Pompeo for making all this explicit, calling the melting sea ice a source of 'opportunity and abundance', is cant.

A key danger now is that climate-management will be absorbed into defence budgets, 'natural security' made an aspect of 'national security'. For the last two decades, the Pentagon has positioned itself as an opponent of climate change, which it depicts – not incorrectly – as a threat-multiplier, catalyst of social instability and source of future wars. Here is a potential militarised despotism of climate-change management, the germinal climate leviathan of which Geoff Mann and Joel Wainwright have warned. A sovereign 'decider' that takes it upon itself to impose 'natural security' on the basis of an ersatz universalism: protecting life. The natural security state is *faire pattes de velours*. It is, after all, the military and its supply industries which supply much of our knowledge about climate. Cold War spy satellites provide decades of evidence of glacier melt in the Himalayas. US submarines in the Arctic measure the thinning of ice, while Army and Navy vessels police US access to oil and gas resources, which become more accessible as the ice disappears. Intel, a major military supplier, boasts of the use of its drones for tracking patterns of Arctic ocean wildlife. The CIA funds scientific research into geoengineering, which has a long military pedigree, resulting in predictable mutterings from some quarters (of deflected, degraded resistance, or worse) about chemtrails and equally predictable rebuttals. This is the god's-eye-view of military and state bureaucracies that, as Christophe Bonneuil and Jean-Baptiste Fressoz argue, has infiltrated the Anthropocene imaginary. A totalising technovision, which enables the planet to be secured for the fraction of the Anthropos that has brought us to this impasse.

Most of the techno-fixes proposed for the Arctic involve geoengineering schemes. One team plans to sprinkle silicate dust over the ice to deflect solar radiation. Another proposes to use wind-powered pumps to bring sea-water to the surface in the hope that it will freeze. Another suggests orchestrating glaciers to firm up ice shelves against accelerated disintegration. Few of these schemes are as yet viable, certainly economically, often scientifically. Far worse, like most such geoengineering proposals, their possible and possibly irreversible effects on regional life and remote weather systems are poorly understood, yet they are vaunted with aston-ishingly little cognisance of what that means. Climate crisis is, after all, precisely a case of colossal rebound: the fruit of massive scien-tific-technical intervention into planetary processes. In furthering capitalist mastery over the earth's energy resources, it has already bolstered systemic longevity at the expense of species longevity, and is set to wreak worse hecatombs.

This is not to slip into aestheticized moralism, to mutter of the dangers of Meddling with Powers One Cannot Possibly Understand. It *is*, however, a severe crisis for the authority of scientific knowl-edge, particularly insofar as it is subordinated the imperatives of military bureaucracy and capitalist enterprise. And while some of the consequences of fossil capitalism could have been anticipated, nothing like the specific scale and gravity of the crisis was. It is not irrationalism but rational, rigorous and due humility to suggest that 'knowledge' itself, in the abstract, indispensable as it us, must have a reduced status after the catastrophe. Yet, almost as if none of this had happened, there is now a drive to pile on new, untested and potentially disastrous interventions where it would be effec-tive and ecologically simpler to stop *emitting* carbon.

But even in a best-case scenario, we will be unable to avoid the question of geoengineering entirely. It would – will – require huge and co-ordinated efforts to lower carbon levels and attempt to cool the planet. As Holly Buck makes vividly clear in her vital new work, *After Geoengineering*, we have come to the appalling pass that we must investigate scientific geoengineering as a mitigatory strategy for human and other survival even in a post-capitalist world.

This is a world away from what is generally meant by geo-engineering, which is the orchestration of planetary processes toward continued – eternal – perpetual accumulation.

This points to the real problem with geoengineering as presently conceived. Capitalism *is* geoengineering. To be anything other than capitalist would be another form of geoengineering. There is no human metabolic relationship with nature that does not engineer planetary processes – potentially this might proceed in considered and commensurate fashion, but overwhelmingly it has been reckless and benighted.

The confluence of capitalist imperialism and ecological disaster is not a recent innovation. The polar regions have long been the object of military designs, their life-processes subsumed under the web of capital. They have also been the object of a complicated imperialist imaginary that both justifies and questions, celebrates and maunders anxiously about, this absorption. Explorers, from Peary to Scott, leading expedition teams of biologists, geologists, botanists and zoologists, marched under the flags of empire, with the intention of transforming what appeared to be a terrifyingly unconquered zone into a mapped, topographically manipulable, space. A space for resources, military outposts, whaling and commercial routes, littered with the names of explorers and imperial sponsors. Swerving wildly between mystique, even mysticism, and desublimation, they were most consistent in finding the polar regions *empty*, yet also pregnant with possibility. Much as, in the Lockean tradition, every potential colonisable land was found empty-yet-fecund, however populated. Even where the endangerment of Inuit, mammal and marine life by whalers, trappers and oil-developers operating in the Arctic was acknowledged, it was a pretext for heightened paternalistic control: Britain in Arctic seas, Denmark in Greenland and Iceland, Canada in the north-west territories, and the United States in Alaska. Colonialism itself was, in this sense, styled as a precocious, noble form of green capitalism.

The colonial poetics of the polar regions is marked by such ambivalence. Consider Isaac Hayes, the Yankee doctor and explorer of Greenland, who found nothing in that long-populated land but a 'vast plane of desolate whiteness', a 'land of desolation' – one, nonetheless, ripe for commercial profit. Consider Robert Falcon Scott and Apsley Cherry-Garrard, explorers of Antarctica. Faces scalded by snow, blistered fingers filled with tiny icicles, feet marching through permadark, constantly failing and falling into crevasses, they were still entranced by the 'ghostly illumination', the 'cold immensity'. Through their encounters with this 'Monstrous-Feminine', as Barbara Creed terms it, they defined an imperial masculinity at odds with the softening effects of urban civilisation. These tropes, of enchanting and ethereal bleakness, have worked their way into contemporary travel writing, even where it is sensible of the non-emptiness of the polar regions. Thus, Sara Wheeler, the British writer, can't resist describing the frozen north as a 'white Mars', as though it were lifeless. (One reason Lovecraft's *At the Mountains of Madness* remains such a key text of reactionary anxiety is its political-unconscious perspicacity that the seeming blankness of the ice is undergirded by brutal exploitation of a raced underclass – to which insight is added the right-ecstatic terror of triumphant revolution.)

The kernel of truth in such poetics is that, however ambivalently, and with whatever disregard for the life they white out, they acknowledge that the polar spaces are incomparable, irreplaceable.

Is a Red Arctic still possible? What would it even look like?

The rubble of the Left's defeats reaches to the retreating ice. Russia's current subjugation of the Arctic has its roots in a period of Stalinist industrialisation that was markedly unsentimental about the natural environment. The Russian state built on the ruins of revolution was ambitiously gigantist in its plans for the north. Faulting the fallen Tsarist regime for its irrational neglect of the tundra, and its sale of Alaska to the United States, Stalin set grandiose development targets in each Five Year Plan. Primitive accumulation in the Arctic was managed by the secret police, and manned by gulag slaves. Coal, gold and spar, extracted from the camps at Kolyma and the Arctic north-east, were the loot from an absolute increase in the rate of exploitation of prison labour, and a brusque overriding of indigenous interests.

Arctic Stalinism was about more than breakneck industrialisation, however. Though a counter-revolutionary dictatorship, the USSR still grounded its legitimacy on a mutilated version of the Bolshevik idiom. Red Plenty, built on a rational, scientifically-guided, industrial order. From the White Sea Canal project, to early Cold war efforts led by climatologist Petr Mikhailovich Borisov to geoengineer *Arctic warming*, the glamour of Stalinism rested in part on this quasi-mythical Arctic modernism. Stalin's favourite writer, Vladimir Zazubrin, rang in the conquest of the Arctic with gusto. 'Let the fragile green beast of Siberia be dressed in the cement armour of cities,' he declared. 'Let the taiga be burned and felled, let the steppes be trampled'. The 'iron brotherhood' of humanity would be moulded in 'cement and iron'. An authentically Bolshevik note. This story of human uplift, of a gigantic elevation of one-sixth of humanity out of centuries of poverty and ignorance, was tremendously appealing, even to non-communists. Even Fridtjof Nansen, the Norwegian internationalist, sympathised with Russia's attempt to modernise the 'Ice Temple of the polar regions': from a White Mars to a Red Arctic.

There is, was, no Red Arctic. Behind the red ensign of fossil communism, there lay a ruinous reality. Fossil autarky? Fossil state-capitalism? Fossil bureaucratic-collectivism? Whichever it was, however we interpret its system, the dispersal of that dream saw the dwindling in the public imaginary of all non-capitalist roads. Now we meet the death-spiral of the ice-caps without even knowing what a Red Arctic could look like. Instead, once again, science fuses with capitalist imperialism under a 'green' patina. Military bureaucracies, with their panoptic gaze, extend their grip over the framing of solutions. And in this way, secure the terrain for relentless capital accumulation.

> Pity would be no more,
> If we did not make somebody Poor
> > William Blake, The Human Abstract

The accumulating evidence suggests that we are doomed. But who, exactly, is 'we'? The possibility of political response to the Anthropocene turns upon how we answer this question. In the same way that the responses to the twin revolutions, industrial and political, of the late eighteenth and early nineteenth centuries formed the contours of the intellectual traditions of modernity – conservative to counterrevolutionary, and reformist to revolutionary – so the lineaments of late carbon politics are taking shape in answer to the meaning of 'Anthropos'.

One possibility is to agree with Dipesh Chakrabarty that 'left unmitigated, climate change affects us all, rich and poor.' The hell-world likely to be born on present projections of warming 'cannot be beneficial to the rich who live today or to their grandchildren', even if they can afford to synthesise their own oxygen. Chakrabarty takes seriously the 'anthropos' of the anthropocene: it is the expanding footprint of humanity in general that bears responsibility for the coming storm. Bearers of a common, if unevenly distributed, guilt, we face a shared if unequal fate.

The politics that follow from this position have been pursued most prominently by Extinction Rebellion (XR), a campaign that seeks to use civil disobedience to achieve decarbonisation of the UK economy by 2025. The utopian character of this target admirably reflects the urgency of the task: yet rather than forcing XR into making the fundamental necessary political choice between friends and enemies, the campaign seeks to make capital and the state its – if occasionally truculent – collaborators. 'If you believe', says XR's agitprop video *Act Now*, 'in people's right to property and if you believe that the state should keep order and safety for people, then you also now have to be against the impacts of catastrophic climate change': thus, deftly, is avoided any reckoning with the connection between those phenomena. Melding the horizontalism of 1990s roads protests with the epistocracy of people who Fucking Love Science, XR actually relies upon the exercise of state violence in its strategy. If enough people get arrested, goes the claim, the state will have to concede the demands to 'tell the truth'and 'act now.'

The courage and sincerity of XR, as well as the shift its activists have achieved in public consciousness of the immanency of climate collapse, are not in doubt. Their strategic perspective and the tactics that flow from it nonetheless, as the Out of the Woods collective point out, display a startling and dangerous naivete. To rely on moral suasion alone – indeed to treat capital and the state allies in a programme 'beyond politics' that nonetheless amounts to a complete rupture with the present – is to try and make a social revolution without enemies. Such a thing is impossible. As the radical periodical *Science for the People* put it forty-five years ago in response to the aspiration: 'Ecologists should not waste their time telling the rich to share.'

What of attempts to politicise the Anthropos in a more egalitarian, even anti-capitalist, direction? The most straightforward critique points out a simple truth – the Anthropos presents too thin a category to capture now, in the time of guilt, those who were cast out in the time of plenty. Hence the multiplication of the 'cenes', each delineating a particular privileged subject now enthroned in the geological record: the Eurocene, the Manthropocene, the Anthrobscene. The false universalism of the Anthropocene, writes Kathryn Yusoff in *A Billion Black Anthropocenes or None* 'erases histories of racism … incubated through the regulatory structure of geologic relations.' What the inscription of human activity in the geological record really represents is an exclusion from the category of human of the colonised and enslaved: 'racialization belongs to a material categorization of the division of matter (corporeal and mineralogical) into active and inert.'

If there is hope, it lies with the victims.

There is clear truth to this when we consider, for example, the heroic and groundbreaking activism of the Indigenous Environmental Network. Beyond that? Some indigenous cosmologies – what Jairus Grove calls 'forms of life' threatened equally by the homogenising aspirations of (some, we might riposte) Marxists as by those of settler-colonialism – reject the separation of natural and human, object and subject that has precipitated the fossil catastrophe. Traditional environmental knowledges, religions, monotheisms, polytheisms, a-theisms, indigenous cosmovisions uprooted and fragmented by colonial capitalism are summoned in resistance movements. Deep Ecology finds intuitive partnerships with versions of Buddhism, Daoism, and Confucianism. In Bolivia, the Pachamama law, which ascribes rights to the natural world, is partly rooted in an indigenous cosmology in which the earth is a living deity. African rural religious traditions are called on in self-defence by those populations who are routinely described by the IPCC as the most vulnerable to climate change and the least responsible for it. Now they offer instruction on how to be resilient in the face of, or at least necessarily reconciled to, that catastrophe.

Would that it were so. The promise of decolonizing the Anthropocene offers us redeemers: those who are not fallen, for whose sake the Earth is not cursed. Yet even here we find the *memento mori* of the real abstraction of capital. Contrary to Yussof's Afro-pessimist claim (cleaving with the theoretical tendency criticised by Okoth in this issue) that 'Blackness, by its very negation in the category of nonbeing within economies of Whiteness, lives differently in the Earth', plantation slavery was interested not in the purported inertness of its victims but precisely in their human species-being: their capacity for labour. European settler colonists first desired the land and, as Yusoff notes, the precious metals of the Americas. The land was inhabited. They solved this problem by genocide, political, physical and cultural of the inhabitants – producing a new problem of the lack of labour. This problem they solved by enslaving Africans. As Barbara and Karen Fields remind us, the point of slavery was to make profits from 'cotton, sugar, rice and tobacco', not White supremacy. Race, and all the categories and cultures that go to make it up, does not belong to a different way of being on the Earth. It is and always has been a part of the cosmology of capital, the value-form-of-life.

The Marxist critique of the Anthropocene is often misunderstood because of the commonsense conception of class as a characteristic held by particular human beings – how people dress, how their accents sound, what their parents did for a living. In this conception, groups defined by such characteristics are assigned either the guilt of climate collapse or the potential to prevent or mitigate it. Much as the rich certainly deserve to go extinct first, this is not the Marxist conception of class. Humans act as *traeger*, bearers of a position in the circuit of M-C-M'. Class is a relation, not a characteristic. To conceive of the Anthropocene as Capitalocene means not to restrict the responsibility for it to a particular group of people, the capitalists, but rather to expand it to a process, the accumulation of capital, of which settler-colonialism formed a part. Capital already forms a more-than-human assemblage, one regulated by its own productive and reproductive logics and consuming its various forms of prey – abstract labour, cheap nature – in the process. One might even extend Anna Tsing's insight that the Sueharto regime in Indonesia 'made capital into a predator': is the value form now the apex species on the planet?

Seeing accumulation as the pulse of the Anthropocene implies a further step, too, one at odds with the notion of different forms of Worlding: that of acknowledging the astonishing achievements, fossil-fuelled and carbon-dreamt as they perforce have been, of national bourgeoisies of colour.

In a previous phase of capitalism, the 'long boom' of roughly 1945–75, 'development' formed the watchword of those fighting for sovereignty against colonialism. Witness the twenty-point programme issued by the American Indian Movement in the early 1970s: a terse and militant document, reflecting the shared assumptions of anti-colonial revolutionaries of the time, it invoked not an indigenous cosmology but the right to 'health, housing, employment, economic development and education for all Indian people.' Nor was such development predicated on catch-up. The Indians of All Tribes, during their year-long liberation of the island of Alcatraz in 1971, offered to the European settlers to 'help them achieve our level of civilization' and 'raise them and all their white brothers up from their savage and unhappy state.'

This enterprise, unfortunately, was unsuccessful. Nonetheless, globally, after protracted and heroic struggle, most anti-colonial movements ultimately achieved independence and constructed new centres of accumulation. Context – not least the ruthless predations of imperialism in new 'postcolonial' forms – has meant such concentrations have varied enormously in their natures and levels of efficiency. They have exploded in spectacular fashion in such states as China, India and Brazil. There of course, and, too, in the most compromised and weaker iterations, we see the accumulation of fossil capital at one pole, and proletarian labour embedded in the fossil form of life at the other.

It is no accident, as Hegelians once said, that the vast increase in carbon emissions since 1990, and the fall of the Soviet Union, was accompanied by a world-historic expansion of the global proletariat. According to the International Labor Organisation report *The Great Employment Transformation in China*, even with declining employment participation, China added 150 million people to its labour force between 1990 and 2015. Similar trends could be observed, and continue, in Pakistan, India, Indonesia and Nigeria. The revolutions of the latter twentieth century, concentrated in the colonial and semi-colonial world, were essentially peasant wars in which the (sometimes settler, sometimes indigenous) landlords lost but the peasants did not win. These revolutions provided the basis for the separation of rural labour from the means of production and its agglomeration into cities predicated on carbon infrastructures, even in places where the 'formal' economy provided little secure employment. As noted by the Chuang collective, Chinese growth and industrialisation reversed the Maoist-era 'balkanisation' of the cities, hatching new mega-centres tied to fossil-fuelled logistics, whatever the efforts of the CCP to establish what Wainwright and Mann call 'climate Mao.'

Leaving agrarian life enforces the real abstraction of the separation of nature and culture: one must attach oneself to machines of various kinds in order to gain the subsistence once produced by interaction with the land. For the first time in human history, a majority of our species must live in this way, as proletarians. Capitalism has, one hundred and fifty years after Marx predicted, finally produced enough diggers to complete the grave, but in doing so it ensured all that was left to inherit was the graveyard. A *welt-klasse* has at last come into being but at the price, unchosen, of the world it was promised. This is the tragedy of the worker.

You're not entitled to a pain-free execution.
Ohio Assistant Attorney General Thomas Madden

And should the climate leviathan fall into the hands of twenty-first century fascism?

Throughout Europe and the Americas, the resurgent far Right and the most reactionary Right in power is overwhelmingly associated with climate denial, the latter's conspiracist predicates finding a convivial home alongside fantasies about Eurabia and 'cultural Marxism', channelling resentment at the revelation of climate collapse into the death drive: Bolsonaro opening the rainforest to profitable destruction, Trump tearing up even the feeble commitments of the Paris accords. Yet as populations move from the Global South, fleeing conditions that will never be purely and solely recognisable as climate collapse but are already clearly inextricable from and imbricated with it, the reactionary Right stakes its popularity on dreams of walls, of pulling up drawbridges and manning gunboats, of insisting that the desperate will not be saved – from which, of course, it should follow that there is a crisis from which escape is needed. Thus out of its very sadism and racist predicates some in the denialist Right may become either gloaters invested in the change that hurts others more than them or 'conservationist' ecofascists themselves – or, given the power of disavowal, both.

The denialism of the far Right differs in several respects from that of the class self-defence of fossil capital. Since Kyoto, the fossil giants, with salient exceptions, have abandoned open affiliation with the denialist industry in favour of greenwashed capitalism. Where once a well-funded global denial operation linked the defence of fossil fuels to the fading dreams of petromodernity – fast cars and free markets – now BP segues smoothly into claiming to be 'Beyond Petroleum', and even ExxonMobil is a supporter of the Paris Accords. It is left to the hard-right Trump administration to rebrand fossil fuels 'molecules of freedom'. Where once it was the extraction firms themselves declaiming that carbon dioxide was a precious, life-giving gas that had been unfairly demonised, now it is the far-right Alternative für Deutschland that denounces Greta

Thunberg as part of a public-relations hoax that seeks to 'bedevil the plant-nutrient carbon dioxide'.

The firms specialising in extraction had known for some decades of the damage they were doing. Since their profit model depended on the most up-to-date scientific knowledge, they were unable to live in delusion. Frank Ikard, president of the American Petroleum Institute, had explained as early as 1965 the 'catastrophic consequences of pollution'. The carbon dioxide 'being added to the earth's atmosphere by the burning of coal, oil, and natural gas' would caused 'marked changes in climate beyond local or even national efforts' by the turn of the Millennium.

To the aggressively pro-capitalist politics of the traditionalist denialist industry, moreover, the new far-right has added a Spenglerian metaphysics of race and civilization. To Fear of a Red Planet, they have added Fear of a Black Planet. The denial industry always warned that climate change is a Marxist Trojan horse; now, as Trump reiterates in tweeted block capitals, the claim is that it is a Chinese Trojan horse, an attempt to undermine Western economies. Pamela Geller, using the language of Ayn Rand, denounces climate change as a scam to loot the wealth of the 'producers' in favour of the 'moochers'. Breivik's manifesto warns of 'Enviro-Communism', claiming that the 'global warming scam' is a means to pillage the resources of the West and redistribute them to the Third World. In some cases, this dread of the world's poor and raced is fused with loathing for (tacitly raced) speculators, as when UKIP's Gerard Batten denounces the 'hoax' as a 'scam to milk the masses!'. From Donald Trump to Andrzej Duda, moreover, the new far right is consistent in linking fossil extraction to national revival, as though such territorially aloof energy sources as water, wind and sun are not to be trusted with national-popular rebirth. Trump is, after all, surprisingly open to certain renewals, such as ethanol: 'the rich harvest of American soil,' he enthused, 'is turned into fuel that powers American cars and industries.'

Old-school paleo-denialism is always just one step away from outright nihilistic affirmation. The Trump administration lets slip, as an attempt to justify abandoning fuel-efficiency standards, that it expects a catastrophic four degrees global warming by 2100. And yet, as ideologically committed as most of the far Right is to its denialism, there is a tendency for it to slip into outright affirmation. What does it mean, for example, that that Trump administration cites catastrophic climate change as a justification for abandoning fuel-efficiency, and openly gloats over the economic opportunities presented by the disappearance of Arctic ice? Part of the implicit logic is, party now while there's time. The Bolsonaro administration, if not always Bolsonaro himself, is quite explicit in these underpinnings. Its appointed boss of the national oil company, Petrobras, openly affirms that fossil fuels must be extracted 'while there is time. In some decades, oil will lose the relevance it has today'. As Naomi Klein points out, the siren song of capitalist nowhilism was already audible in denial propaganda and among its supporters in the state and Evangelical churches. Yet, it is too generous to read affirmation as indifference toward future generations. There is a tendency, which Klein calls the 'meaner side of denial', for it to manifest as an open embrace of the rigors of apocalypse.

Faced with concrete, real-world evidence of climate change, they become crude pseudo-Darwinians, citing the virtues of adaptation. Populations 'can acclimatize to warmer climates', the US Chamber of Commerce insisted. 'When it rains, we find shelter. When it's hot, we find shade,' Texas congressman Joe Barton asserted. Disaster capitalism offers its services to the rich in the form of Xanadu-like climate-secure residences, an ecological variation on nuclear-age survivalism. If some can't adapt, that's their problem. Tory columnist Andrew Lilico accepts that climate change is happening, but argues that it's too costly to capitalism to stop it, so we must adapt. How would the tropics adapt to four degrees of warming? By 'being wastelands with few folk living in them. Why's that not an option?' The rightwing columnist, Jim Geraghty, looks forward to climate change destroying 'threatening states' and 'ensuring a second consecutive American century'. Here, then, is a darker telos of the new far Right. In practice, the effects of ecological despoliation have always, as a matter of deliberate and calculated strategy, been offloaded onto the working class, especially raced workers. Now, climate change can become a weapon of open race war, and of eco-eugenic class war.

And yet the far Right does not live only in denial.

It is also manifestly not the case, as Rebecca Solnit contends, that environmentalism is intrinsically antithetical to white-supremacy. That this claim appeared mere days after the Christchurch massacre, carried out by a declared ecofascist, is evidence of a sort of cruel optimism: the faith that ecological consciousness on its own, and the holistic appreciation of the 'web of life' that it engenders, is sufficient to dissolve the libidinal ties of race and nation and clear the path for liberal cosmopolitanism. The earliest manifestations of ecological consciousness, of the connectedness of all matter, biotic and abiotic, were fused with romantic nationalism.

Long before the Pachamama law enshrined the rights of nature in Bolivia, the German nationalist Ernst Moritz Arndt hymned 'the rights of wilderness', urged fellow citizens to 'save the forest', as much as to save the spirit of the German people and stave off industrial modernity as anything else. In this purview, every 'shrub, worm, plant, human, stone' belonged to a 'single unity': but some humans, such as Jews and Slavs, were least in this unity. The Volkish movement that emerged to protect this set of natural relations, and what they viewed as man's natural habitat, blamed Jews for foisting industrial capitalism on the German people. Ernst Haeckel's invention of the term 'ecology' was founded in his combination of eco-holism, racist social Darwinism, and volkishness. Historically, the far-right treated racist murder as biological conservation, segregation as good husbandry.

The predicates of a future eco-fascism are well-conserved, and propagated by authoritative and more mainstream – if, increasingly, unease-generating – figures in the green movement, from Garret Hardin's crypto-fascistic fables to Paul Kingsnorth's 'Dark Mountain' lamentations for an England submerged by globalisation and immigration.

Among those strains of the European far Right which are not militantly denialist, the consensus is overwhelmingly that immigration, and the growth of poor populations, is the problem. In France,

Marine Le Pen's Rassemblement National derides and despises 'nomads'. This is a category that, like classical anti-Semitic imagery, or indeed like May's 'citizens of nowhere', binds the global poor and the mobile rich in a single phantasmagoria of national treason. 'Nomadism' is to blame, according to Le Pen's ally Hervé Juvin, for environmental degradation, by turning 'the most fertile and diverse ecosystems' into 'unsustainable territories under demographic pressure'. In Germany, the AfD's Björn Höcke espouses 'population ecology', in which violent borders prevent Europe from absorbing surplus population and contributing to galloping overpopulation. Christchurch murderer Brenton Tarrant's maudlin, greened-up Breivikism mined a similar ideological vein.

It is, unfortunately, not impossible for distinctly fascist solutions to climate change to be imposed, along despotic and ultimately genocidal lines. The *mise-anthropo-scène* presents ample opportunities for various lines of racist, patriarchal and militarist policy to be represented as mitigatory, or adaptive – and, from within the predicates of fascism, such policies would in fact be mitigations and adaptations. The very aspects of ecological disaster which throw capitalism into crisis, and which indicate the need for a social mobilisation tantamount to war, are exactly those which could give rise to a far-right climate leviathan, with the military organising what the bourgeoisie cannot.

The drive to protect fundamentally capitalist social relations while reducing global energy use and overcoming polluting industrial methods is exactly what could spawn a new eugenics, a new extractive imperialism (as lithium, and perhaps uranium, are obtained by force), and renewed forms of patriarchy. The scarcities and market failures produced by heated, acidic seas and unfertile soil, the increased rate of natural disasters consequent on global heating, lend themselves to every form of apocalyptic reaction, whether theocratic or secular. Above all, they would tend to intensify the libidinal bonds tying subjects to the apparent securities and consolations of the nation.

> To learn which questions are unanswerable, and not to
> answer them: this skill is most needful in times of stress
> and darkness.
> Ursula K. Le Guin, *The Left Hand of Darkness*

The new far Right has yet to mature into anything displaying the organised and armed force of historical fascism. However, this only buys the Left breathing room. Out of the business of history-making for so long, we must swiftly revise our classical visions and strategic preconceptions. We must formulate a version of plenty, of abundance, that does not brazenly override ecological limitations.

The Left is particularly sensitive to anything smacking of Malthusian arguments about 'overpopulation': given the historic resonance of such arguments with racism and eugenicism, this is not surprising. Thus, for example, the understandable and widespread criticisms levelled at Donna Haraway for her recent urgent insistence on reducing population to around two billion as part of left strategy, which Sophie Lewis in a sympathetic, almost anguished critique, calls 'primitivism-tinged, misanthropic populationism'.

Such justified criticism, however, can elide with less persuasive contrarianism on the axis of productivism. This underlies the wide-ranging arguments on the Left over issues of economic 'degrowth', its necessity or otherwise. The so-called 'ecomodernist' position, advocating climate intervention by radical redistribution plus tech-nofix, has recently been (notoriously, for many) examplified in the *Jacobin* issue, *Earth, Wind and Fire*, and in Leigh Phillips' *Austerity Ecology and the Collapse-Porn Addicts*, with its provocatarian, Marxist-*épatering* chapter titles such as 'There Is No "Metabolic Rift"' and 'In Defense of Stuff'.

Unlike many ecosocialists, *Salvage* is not, in principle, opposed to Promethean aspiration and speculation – the opposite, in fact. Quite apart from the literally epoch-shaking nature of the revolutionary social change we espouse, we dissent from the view of those many socialists for whom any talk of geoengineering, for example, is anti-socialist – 'science-fiction fantasy bankrolled by the ruling class', as Keith Brunner puts it. Contrary, with comradely respect, to John Bellamy Foster, we do not see it as self-evidently ecologically questionable that 'smart parking meters, robo-bees, and new potentialities for geoengineering' are 'perfectly compatible with "socialist ecology"'. The hermeneutics of ecomodernist suspicion are not without traction: dystopias can be politically polyvalent, but misanthropic, even symptomatically sadistic, collapse-porn is certainly a culturally prevalent current thereof. And, too, it is undoubtedly the case that some left opponents of ecomodernism indulge in the kind of 'green moralizing' of which Peter Frase complains.

But such moralising is a political failure, not definitional to a left ecology. And there are, moreover, major problems and lacunae in left ecomodernism. It is predicated on a faith position that 'we can' overcome ecological problems, on the basis of the most tendentious scientific and/or sociological extrapolation, if any, as when Phillips blithely insists that 'you can actually have infinite growth on a finite world'. It validates that particular narrow conception of the polysemic word 'growth' – 'growth', for Phillips, 'is freedom' – without anything approaching adequate interrogation of the history and ideology of the concept, as extensively outlined by Gareth Dale, for whom '[t]he growth paradigm ... is a form of fetishistic consciousness' that 'functions as commodity fetishism at one remove'. It performs a relentless elision of analysis with a kind of cruel-optimistic hectoring: when Connor Kilpatrick criticises 'a politics of fearmongering', or Phillips 'catastrophism', they ignore the possibility that ecological fear, far from being mongered, is entirely appropriate, if not too little and too late, that catastrophe is indeed almost here. Let alone the crucial point that after decades of exhausting boosterism, left and right, that such earned fear can be politically inspiring – that, as Gerard Passannante puts it, 'as we face the frightening effects of climate change, catastrophizing may be something we can't do without'.

The most robust and inadequately fearful ecomodernist extropianism, the Elon Muskrattery of the Left, feels predicated on a category error: it has mistaken a kind of ludic meme culture around the aesthetics of post-scarcity and 'Luxury Communism' for a research programme, or even, at its worst, for a conclusion. This is not to denigrate the memes. Provocations and utopianism are play, relief, and can be goads to thought and action and *Sehnsucht*. They are valuable – if vanishingly rarely worth much as blueprints. But it does not take much for provocation to become swagger to become mannerism, and a new kind of rote thinking.

The instant one starts to get into granular details about possible ecological limits, problems arise – as, indeed, often do anger. But limits haunt ecomodernist writing too. Phillips cheerfully cites various studies suggesting – depending on various ecological and technological variables – that the world could potentially support more people than are alive today by factors of twelve and more – 96 billion, 150 billion, 282 billion, a hundred quintillion people. Crucial, though, is not only that the desirability of those various possibilities is questionable (the last involving a cramped planet of cannibals): what is also key is that even for a writer so committed to limitlessness, there *are* conceptual upper limits.

Where Phillips is clearly right is that the question of what this number is has no meaning absent a wide range of other variables and aspirations. We can go further. It is precisely due to the Promethean scale of the project to utterly reconfigure of the world and *thus the humans who will remake it* that we can know neither their capabilities nor their drives and desiderata in advance. This is not an evasion but rigour.

The obvious problem with Haraway's proposal is that she proposes a drop in population, one dramatic enough to provoke alarm: an underlying problem is that she proposes a specific number at all, because she – anyone – can only do so with a pre-revolutionary consciousness, stained by the muck of history. Not only do we not claim that speculation about a post-capitalist future is *verboten*, we hold it to be necessary. But we must be clear about the categoric nature of those ruminations, the veil between us and prediction. *Eco*socialists, we take the existence of limits seriously; eco*socialists*, we take seriously the fact that we cannot yet know them. Indeed, it is an urgent task to usher in a society in which we might. No more than we can write the cookbooks of the future can we plan its population limits. To think otherwise is unseemly prefiguration – the bad Prometheanism of the quotidian. Which, too, afflicts the ecomodernist. Who is, on the axis of the human soul, not Promethean enough.

The repeated evocations of left 'austerity' in the bestiary of the ecomodernists is rhetorically effective in the rubble of the neoliberal project of that name. Against which are deployed defences of the *having of stuff* that are pitifully uncurious about the possibility of the emancipated human of the future wanting anything other than yet more stuff. 'What exactly is wrong with gaming consoles, OhMiBod dildos that plug into an iPhone, or Hello Kitty Fortieth Anniversary plastic toys in Happy Meals anyway?' asks Phillips. To which the radical answers should not be histrionic anticonsumerist moralism, but the counter-question 'What exactly is right about them?' Indeed, what exactly is right about there *being* anything right about them at all? What is right or inevitable about object-oriented cathexis? Is its relationship to commodity fetishism of so little interest to the radical?

As with population limits, so with trinkets: we cannot ultimately know what the tchotchkes of a liberated people will be, nor how many they will have, nor if they will have any at all. But that aporia does not preclude critique of such hankering or scepticism about its immortality, and the acknowledgement that we cannot be certain goes for the ecomodernists no less than for those they chastise. 'Why shouldn't people have these things that bring them pleasure?' Phillips insists. As if what la-las bring us pleasure is immutable, apolitical, unconflicted. As if, under capitalism, those things and our pleasure itself cannot be sources of despair.

Production is not productivism. Intervening in and acting on nature is not ruining it, nor humanity. There is not, in Lenin's urgent aspiration for nationwide electrification, any necessary and intrinsic subordination of radical ecological politics to narrowly defined productivism. Nor even is there – quite – in Trotsky's sternly ecstatic utopian dreams of geological reconfiguration – terramorphing – at the close of *Literature and Revolution*, his assertions that the literal movement of mountains will, after capitalism, 'be done onan immeasurably larger scale [than hitherto], according to a general industrial and artistic plan', that 'man', in the end, 'will have rebuilt the earth, if not in his own image, at least according to his own taste'. But it would be disingenuous to deny a strong tendential logic towards it therein, and it is hardly a surprise that it was used as epigraph for *Earth, Wind, and Fire*, nor that Trotsky's own record of support for projects such as, for example, the construction of the Dnieper Dam was characterised by unedifying attacks on critics, like the Bolshevik engineer Peter Palchinsky, of the ecological and social effects of its ill-conceived gigantism: Trotsky's 1928 smear about 'the collusion of the Shakhty specialists [Palchinsky's circle] with capitalists' saw him side with Stalin against the accused in the first major show trial in Russia. Victor Serge, famously, argued against the facile equation of Bolshevism and Stalinism not on the grounds that the former did not contain a germ of the latter, but that it 'also contained many other germs, a mass of other germs'. So, too, for what Foster calls 'reckless productivism'.

Literal 'conservation' – a dream of stasis – is not in and of itself necessarily a good. And indeed, there must be, for any dream of the future, of emancipation, a place for truly epochal and transformative aspirations. But if this is Prometheanism, Prometheus here must be, not bound by, perhaps, but *sublated with* a rigorous humility. Otherwise it will be at best a kitsch performance, at worst dangerous.

> Amidst the ruins, within the terrible opening of the interruption, pitched against the conditions that produce and seek to capitalize upon that interruption, we are close to complete change
> Out of the Woods, 'The Uses of Disaster'

All politics must become disaster politics. The 'disaster capitalism' of which Naomi Klein has written, in learning ways to instrumentalise and profit from disaster, will be less disinclined to avert disaster in future. In and of a warming world, politics must perforce adapt. This does not mean only the incorporation into traditional political currents of newly pressing themes, to have 'a line' on such issues: it means the reconfiguring under pressure of those currents, new ways of having and acting on any lines. This the nature of political adaptation to contexts of catastrophe.

Now, as the evidence for catastrophe piles up, we are even seeing the development of an instrumentalist Bad Hope-inflected thin pessimism, an inadequate catastrophism in the service of liberal status quo. Nowhere is this more clear than in the recent remarks of Democratic Presidential candidate Andrew Yang.

> Even if we were to curb our emissions dramatically, the Earth is going to get warmer. ... We are too late. We are ten years too late. We need to do everything we can to start moving the climate in the right direction, but we also need to start moving our people to higher ground – and the best way to do that is to put economic resources into your hands so you can protect yourself and your families.

Yang, feted as a futurist, is indeed here a vanguardist in the construction of an extraordinary Disaster Centrism, of which we can expect to see much more. Still a little strange in the liberal mouth, in some form or other it is likely rapidly to become the most era-appropriate iteration of the ideology of Betterness-than-nothing among liberal elites. What exactly is deemed 'better than nothing' (BTN) of course, is a matter of ideology. As outlined here, the dominant BTN ideology, in variants of green capitalism, has not, in fact, been amelioratory at all, and holds great responsibility for the continued development of the worst.

Particularly where catastrophe bites hardest, more radical politics, too, will increasingly take on such a colouration. After the terrible 2018 Kerala floods, the Communist-ruled local government was allotted a quarter of the funds it requested for reconstruction. When foreign states offered financial help, Modi's government instructed Indian embassies that it was not to be accepted. Trolls and right-wingers spread claims that the floods were somehow a result of Kerala being too communist, containing too many eaters of beef, and so forth. The government's plan, writes Binu Mathew, is that '[w]hen Kerala is crushed the right wing will step in with charity to help people ... to prepare the ground in the "fortress" Kerala to be receptive of the fascist Hindutva ideology ... And that is called "Disaster Fascism"'.

It is a small hope that some communisms, too, adapt. As the Out of the Woods collective has eloquently argued, it must become a disaster communism that 'emphasizes the revolutionary process of developing our collective capacity to endure and flourish'.

What forms of intervention, what nature of activism that might mean we are still learning. Salvage-Marxism is a disaster communism conditioned by and pining for a party form that it knows did not deserve to survive, and did not: learning to walk again, pain in that phantom limb and all.

The whole landscape flushes on a sudden at a sound.
Gerard Manley Hopkins

The climate crisis is so comprehensive in its reach, so thorough in its unsettling effects, that it has called into question not only the foundations of a certain kind of socialism, but also the Enlightened verities upon which both capitalism and its opposition have sought their foundation.

The crisis is totalising, destabilising the epistemological atomism of capital, provoking a search for holisms, spiritual and theological alternatives to the death cult. After all, as Catherine Keller puts it in *The Political Theology of the Earth*, the appointed time is running short: a kairotic contraction akin to Walter Benjamin's 'messianic time'. All realistic solutions, defined by capitalist realism, are inadequate. All adequate solutions, defined by the exigency of the crisis, are unrealistic. Recent debates in the *New Left Review* bring this into stark relief. The economist Robert Pollin strives for political efficacy in calling for a green techno-solution that allows all global populations to continue to consume as much energy as they presently do, albeit within a New Deal framework. That this appears to be realism, is an indication of how captive we are to capitalist theology, so that our very mental operations, our conception of what is feasible, is governed by its rituals. On the other hand, our *Towards the Proletarocene* contributor Troy Vettese calls for E. O. Wilson's 'half-earth' approach to the use of the planet and a transition to vegan communism. That this, though obviously equal to the crisis, appears to be wildly, desperately *unrealistic*, is an indication of how much would have to be achieved, and how quickly consent gained for radical new ideas, coalitions assembled, tactics innovated, the unthinkable realised.

The striving toward a new totality, a new cosmic apperception, is ubiquitous. From Roy Rappaport to Ursula Goodenough, those apprehensive of the role of capitalist science in climate change have often sought religious answers. Traditional environmental knowledges, religions, monotheisms, polytheisms, a-theisms, indigenous cosmovisions uprooted and fragmented by colonial capitalism, are summoned in resistance movements. Deep Ecology finds intuitive partnerships with versions of Buddhism, Daoism, and Confucianism. In Bolivia, the Pachamama law, and its ascription of rights to the natural world, is rooted in an indigenous cosmology in which the earth is a living deity, the Pachamama. African rural religious traditions are called on in self-defence by those populations who are routinely described by the IPCC as the most vulnerable to climate change and the least responsible for it.

The striving toward new holisms thus recognises the scale of the crisis afflicting life. To truly address it would necessitate a transformation of a scale scarcely imaginable from this low vantage-point. A revolution in how we metabolise the planet, how we relate to all matter, what we eat, how we travel, what we think is good, what we think is pleasurable. A complete and irreversible transvaluation of values. Not for nothing, both new materialisms and new theologies strive for a re-enchantment of the earth, a hope shared by Jewish mystic Arthur Green and philosopher Jane Bennett. Though it changes nothing physical about matter to describe it as miraculous or inhabited by deities or ancestors, to enchant it and be enchanted by it, it changes the human relationship to matter. But such moves, however appealing, are hardly risk-free. The danger here is that, as with the polar enchantments of nineteenth century explorers, it becomes part of the means of natural annihilation.

The poetics of eco-theology evokes, in its totalising, the prospect of restored 'balance'. Of a mending of what Marxists have called the 'metabolic rift' with nature. Of a restoration of the 'sacred balance', hymned by the Rabbinic Letter. Of a stewardship of God's original 'perfect equilibrium' rhymed by the Islamic Declaration from Istanbul in 2016. Of the brotherly treatment of our 'sister earth' carolled by Pope Francis in his second encyclical 'Laudato Si': a lamentation which, in the tradition of the 'environmentalism of the poor', registers the 'cry of the earth' as the 'cry of the poor'. 'Balance' is the cri de coeur of Eco Dharma, the Māori cosmos and the Green Bahá'i.

Etymologically, 'balance' contains a root word for 'two', suggesting a coupling, a conjugation of two distinct yet related and roughly equivalent quantities. Taken too literally, this ranks humanity too highly in the scale of cosmic history. Insofar as it faults human stewardship for not keeping with perfect equilibrium, which according to the law of entropy is equivalent to the heat death of the universe, it also asks too much. Insofar as it faults human meddling, it misrepresents our dilemma. The universe is observably not the sort of place that would be just dandy without human meddling. We were always just a stray asteroid, or a chance shift of the earth's tectonic plates or a volcanic explosion, away from extinction. To these prospects, of course, we have added new and lethal dangers. Yet never in the history of the planet, through its eons of snowball earth, hothouse earth, and regular, ruthless mass extinctions, has it been in anything but the most chance and temporary of equilibria. And to the baleful prospects, of course, we have added new and lethal likelihoods.

The danger here is that the ideologeme of 'balance', even when raised in self-defence by the exploited, colonised and racially oppressed, could perform in roughly the same way as 'sustainability'. That, we may end up calling for an appropriate 'balance' between the needs of a society covertly defined as always-already capitalist or becoming-capitalist, and the needs of the earth defined so as to trump certain capitalist rituals of investment while remaining permanently captive to and in danger of being encircled by the cult. Capitalism in perpetuity, even if it were conceivable outside its cultic now-hilism, would not be commensurate with any plausible scenario of human survival. Worse still, it can be retconned as that some variant of that slowly growing ecofascism, wherein the raced populace and cosmopolitan modernity are blamed for unbalancing the earth, making the homely unhomely, the *oikos unoikos*.

Nor can theology be restored as a story of divine creativity, in the style of the 'geologian' Thomas Berry, for whom 'each of the events in the natural world is a poem, a painting, a drama, a celebration,' the great evolutionary transformation of the Cenozoic era was 'a wildly creative period of inspired fantasy and extravagant play' leading to a 'supremely lyrical moment when humans emerged on the scene'. Idealise 'Mother Nature', she – it – sneezes some pandemic in your face. All such creative acts, if such they can be considered to have been, were maniacally indifferent to suffering and need. This kind of god's-eye-view must perforce be far too callous, far too inappropriate to the intense reality of a lived experience on the everyday scale, for humans to be happy with it.

If, as Keller puts it, theology is the study of that which matters unconditionally, we must have a better theology. A materialist theology, respectful of the texture of matter, disrespectful of capitalist anti-matter. We call, not for a Deep Ecology, but for a Deep-Historical Materialism: the extension of materialist theology into the realm of geologic 'Deep Time', of paleo-ontology, paleo-oceanography, and paleo-climatology. We call for an aleatory materialism, a materialism of the encounter, which recognises life as a fluke worth preserving, and human existence as a lucky 'spandrel', a contingent byproduct of the cycle of earthly extinctions that Stephen Jay Gould called 'Siva's dance of death'. We call for a Darwinian ecology, which recognises as Darwin did the irrevocable human dependence on the most humble creatures: not least the worms and microbes which consume us when we die. We call for a mass outbreak of red geoengineering, collective work farther reaching and deeper in its action, than the Renaissance, or the Enlightenment, or the bourgeois-democratic revolutions, or the colonial freedom movement. We call, as Berry does, in all the necessary humility imposed by the climate crisis, for a 'Great Work'.

In the era of Marx and Engels, and in the long century after, communists dreamed of liberating humanity and enjoying a world of plenty, sharing in abundance. Had October inaugurated a new era of revolutions, had barbarism's reign ended a century sooner, perhaps that is the world we would have. If Luxury Communism – automated or otherwise – was possible at that moment, our hypothesis is that now, as we race past tipping point after tipping point, it is no longer – at least not before a long and difficult age of repair. From our benighted vantage point, the birth, growth and exploitation of the working class has been inextricable from biocide and catastrophe. That is to say, global proletarianisation and ecological disaster have been products of the *same process*. The earth the wretched would – will – inherit, will be in need of an assiduous programme of restoration. While we may yearn for luxury, what will be necessary first is Salvage Communism.

We yearn for the commencement of human history, after an irrevocable decision against barbarism. Such an epoch of classless ecology and society would – will – be of and for a humanity that neither denies its unique nature among Terran life, nor retreats into blinkered exceptionalism – that articulates, that is, an *aufhebung* of Prometheanism and humility that does not yet have a name. But to have the slightest chance of reaching such a moment, we must strive precisely for a class unbalancing of the Earth. Against all dreams of compromise, against geo-Fabianism, the only path to an Anthropocene of a liberated and self-transformed Anthropos runs through the destruction of the Capitalocene, the Proletarocene dawn.

Full pre-Raphaelite

for DH

in Brighton, pissing like a racehorse. here's a tender slope
for softness fidgeting against your body with no-one in it,
fighting off nimbleness with valid instant. soft salt fuzz,
comfy rocks. so all that kissing repeats as co-presence.
like a dark pool anyway, and fling orbit tiny balls in solid
gold or just pearls, at a petalled rate from red. sequins:
this spinning already awaiting separate. clarify water now
with sheer so out of myself, hydrated, ungathered and
visibly glowing. ermine; magpie; hound: where curtains
impatience wed Nereids to Pleiades it's only phonemes,
or clothes. in tobacco leaf worn lightly there's a spray
of branched relief adjacent to strength. *whichever sea it was*
never there for more than a day, replaced by another which
at times resembled it. the law of mimicry requires apart,
press all our anxiousness to love, and jet it skywards and
beyond the pier, fishing hungrily for cockles possible
or only a single second book of revelation

KATYA TEPPER

Hysteric Signs
and
Wall Bowl
Constellations

Image 1-2: Gaping Candle Tripod
2018
106" H X 81" X 10" D
INDUSTRIAL FELT, CAULK, EPOXY, BEESWAX, SOY WAX,
LAVENDER PETALS, CANDLE WICKS, FOUND BRICKS, PLASTIC
BAGS, EGGSHELLS, POLYESTER FILM, CLOTH AND DYED CLOTH,
DYED FELT, PLASTER, FOAM, NYLON FROM AN INFLATABLE POOL,
NITRILE MEDICAL GLOVES, WOOD, HARDWARE

Image 3: Hysteric Sign (Distended J Bean)
2018
88" H X 123" W X 18" D
INDUSTRIAL FELT, CAULK, LATEX RUBBER, EPOXY, THREAD,
PLASTIC THREAD SPOOLS, QUILTING PINS, CLOTH AND DYED
CLOTH, EGGSHELLS, FOAM, WOOD, HARDWARE, PAINT

Image 4: Horizon Slice
2017
113" X 121.5" X 7"
WATER + OIL BASED PAINTS, CERAMIC, UNDERGLAZE,
HARDWARE

*Image 5-6: Wall Bowl Constellation
(1,2,3; Penetration with Rays; Olive Garden
Restaurant; Sign)*
2017
96" X 311.75" X 9"
WATER + OIL BASED PAINTS, CERAMIC, UNDERGLAZE,
HARDWARE

Image 6: Wall Bowl Constellations [installation view]
2017

KEVIN OCHIENG OKOTH

The Flatness of Blackness: Afro-Pessimism and the Erasure of Anti-Colonial Thought

I. Pop-Hegelianism

When the term Afro-pessimism began appearing in books, journal articles and, curiously, on activist social media, I was (presumably along with others familiar with the scholarship on African history and politics) slightly perplexed. For decades, 'Afro-pessimism' had referred to the unrelentingly negative coverage of Africa in Western news media, especially in terms of its tendency toward arrested development. This discourse, loosely united by an emphasis on the hopelessness of the African continent – and exemplified by the scandalous 2000 *Economist* headline describing Africa as 'The Hopeless Continent' – provided the rationale for the imperialist economic policies of the 1970s' and 80s' structural adjustment programmes. Today, it bolsters neo-colonial relations between the Global North and Africa, and is often conjured up as the go-to argument to justify the entirely unnecessary and counterproductive presence of the development industry and its practitioners on the continent.

If we wish to examine a given news headline or academic article for traces of Afro-pessimism, there is a pretty clear set of criteria that can be applied. Afro-pessimist discourses impose a Eurocentric developmental model on the continent, and assess its progress in relation to a set of arbitrary criteria – i.e. Western liberal democracies as the final stage in the progress of world history, epitomised in the ideas of 'pop-Hegelians' Samuel Huntington and Francis Fukuyama. Within the discourse there is a tendency to view Africa as one big, tragic mess: corruption, cronyism and ethnic conflict are thought to provide the governing logics of politics and other daily experiences. Afro-pessimist representations never actually refer to the continent as a geographical territory; when the term 'African' is used, it denotes only those who are (visibly) Black and live in Africa. Unsurprisingly, all non-Black inhabitants of the continent are intuitively treated as non-African.

A recent report on 'Africa in the Media' shows just how tenacious the logic of Afro-pessimism really is. Compiled by The Africa Narrative – a research project working out of the University of Southern California – the report suggests that representations of Africa and Africans in US media and entertainment are still 'overwhelmingly focused on negative stories such as Boko Haram, corruption, poverty, electoral crises, migrants and terrorism'. Of course, little attention is paid to the complex histories and experiences of actual African subjects. In scripted US television, for instance, five countries – Egypt, South Africa, Kenya, the Seychelles and Congo (without reference to which Congo) – accounted for almost half of all mentions of African countries. Six out of ten references to Africa in TV dramas were about crime, terrorism and corruption, while the unspecified use of 'Africa' as a country received 27 per cent of all mentions. Clearly, little progress has been made in our collective understanding of Africa. Especially in the US media and entertainment industries, attitudes towards the continent continue to show a lack of engagement or interest, and a predilection for sensationalism and simplistic narratives.

Many scholars, including Emmanuel Chukwudi Eze and V. Y. Mudimbe have argued that the genealogy of this particular mode of thinking about Africa stretches all the way back to Hegel's philosophy of history, although this is by no means the first instance of exoticised portrayals of Africa as a 'dark continent', that exists entirely outside of the world-historical trajectory of Geist. In the appendix to his *Lectures on the Philosophy of World History*, Hegel briefly discusses the role of Africa in the world-historical progress of the consciousness of freedom; since history moves from East to West (with increasing degrees of consciousness of freedom), Africa plays no real part in this process. For Hegel 'man as we find him in Africa has not progressed beyond his immediate existence' and Africans are 'animal men', who have no conception of freedom, God or Spirit (or any absolute Being, higher than the individual self). Moreover, Hegel argues that there is no geographical entity that we can call 'Africa'. A not very subtle theoretical move enables him to divide the continent into three parts that are culturally and historically distinct: Africa proper (Black Africa or Sub-Saharan Africa), European Africa (North Africa), and the River Region of the Nile (Egypt). While Hegel acknowledges that the River Region of the Nile has contributed to the progress of world history, he claims that it is distinct from the rest of the continent, and that it had few historical or cultural ties to the Black 'animal men' south of the Sahara.

This division has been contested by historians and theorists such as Cheikh Anta Diop, Théophile Obenga, and George M. James, whose alternative histories of Africa posit a cultural and historical continuity between Egypt and 'Black Africa'. They argued that the roots of modern European philosophy can be found not in Greece, but in Egypt, and that the legacy of the origins of philosophy has been wrongfully 'stolen' from African people. While such Afrocentric theories can restore pride in Black people whose histories have been erased or denied by Eurocentric scholarship, we must be careful about uncritically embracing these narratives of African grandeur. It is indeed possible to favourably compare the achievements of African civilisations – like Ife/Benin sculpture, the churches of Lalibela, or the pilgrimages of Mansa Musa – to those of Europe in the same period. But this would still leave us measuring the value of African history and life in terms of arbitrary Eurocentric standards. As Walter Rodney argues in *The Groundings with my Brothers*, we must focus our historical efforts on fostering an 'understanding of ordinary African life' to show that it had 'meaning and value'.

Despite the controversies surrounding the Afrocentric histories of Diop, Obenga and James, it is becoming increasingly unfeasible to deny the historical realities of cultural, philosophical and trade links between Egypt and 'Sub-Saharan Africa' or 'Africa proper' in the face of a growing body of historical scholarship on the subject. As Senegalese philosopher Souleymane Bachir Diagne has convincingly argued, one cannot understand the history of philosophy in Africa without reference to Islamic scholarship (including Black Islamic scholarship!) in North and West Africa. His work on the intellectual history of Timbuktu is instructive here: the Timbuktu manuscripts show that Islam and Arabic script were adopted in the region prior to colonialism, and that intellectuals wrote didactic poetry, prose on jurisprudence and theological texts in both Arabic and native dialects (using Arabic script). The intellectual history of Africa, as a geographical entity, is thus not a history of isolation but rather a history of cultural, political and economic interconnection.

Unfortunately, such evidence has only led to superficial changes in the ways in which Africa is perceived in the Global North. The 'failure to accommodate Africa [...] in the concert of humanity' – to borrow a phrase from Nigerian philosopher Olúfemi Táíwò – 'illustrates the continuing impact of the reach of Hegel's ghost'. To theorists as diverse as Afro-pessimists and Western Marxists (or Euro Marxists, or whatever one prefers calling the Eurocentric strand of Marxism) Africans, and particularly Black Africans, remain something essentially 'other' and play no role in the trajectory of world history or the history of philosophy.

II. The Flatness of Blackness

Afro-pessimism in this original sense has reflected a disastrous approach to, and had disastrous consequences for Africa and its inhabitants. So how can we understand the bizarre use of this historically loaded term (complete with its own history of colonial and imperialist exploitation) by numerous African-American intellectuals and activists? The use of the term 'Afro-pessimism' is symptomatic of the historical ignorance of the Afro-pessimist™ (or what Greg James has recently called Afro-pessimism 2.0), whose grasp of African history is about as solid as that of Hegel. In its initial iteration, Afro-pessimism 2.0 (from now on AP™) is a product of middle-class academia; a framework either consciously or subconsciously created to allow relatively well-off academics to view themselves as the most discriminated and oppressed people in the world. Characterised by misinterpretations and clever appropriations of Black radicals like Frantz Fanon and Silvia Wynter, the theories of the AP™ have spilled over into activist circles, contaminating the global political discourse on race.

The central premise of the AP™ is that anti-Black violence is the structuring regime of the modern world. Drawing on Orlando Patterson's concept of 'social death', Frank Wilderson, arguably the most prominent and controversial AP™ intellectual, asserts that the Black condition is not characterised by oppression or exploitation, like that of the Marxist proletariat or the (neo)colonial subject, but rather by the distinction between the Human and the Slave. For Wilderson, the Black is a priori a slave and therefore we cannot speak of Blackness without reference to the Slaveness that constitutes it on an ontological level. In his essay 'Ante-Anti-Blackness: Afterthoughts', fellow University of California professor Jared Sexton argues that the condition of the Black/Slave is a state of total powerlessness, natal alienation ('the loss of ties of birth in both ascending and descending generations') and generalised dishonour. In short, Black existence is an ontological absence of sorts, and the Black/Slave is a living dead (non-entity) in the modern world.

In 'The Black Liberation Army and the Paradox of Political Engagement', Wilderson offers some further meditations on the concept of 'social death', explaining that 'the point of social death is a condition, void, not of land, but of a capacity to secure relational status through transindividual objects – be those objects elaborated by land, labour or love'. Unlike colonial racisms perpetuated by the rational systems of white supremacy, neo-colonialism or imperialism, or women's oppression and exploitation driven by patriarchy and capitalism's need for reproductive labour, anti-Black violence is humanity's irrational desire for violence against Black people. As Wilderson declares in an interview with C. S. Soong, 'violence against Black people is a mechanism for the usurpation of subjectivity, of life of being'. What settlers wanted from Indians is land, so they killed Indians 'in the main' to get it, whereas what non-Blacks want from Blacks is not land but 'being'. Anti-Blackness is thus qualitatively different from the regimes of violence that affect the Marxist proletariat; or the non-Black person of colour; or the non-Black woman; or the non-Black woman of colour; or (as Wilderson has famously claimed) Palestinians. Black suffering is incomparable and unique: to speak of any experience of oppression without reference to the ontological disparities between Black/non-Black people is ultimately an act of 'anti-Blackness'.

But what exactly is it about the makeup of modern society that displaces the Black/Slave from the realm of politics and precludes the articulation of concrete political demands? For Wilderson and Sexton, the very foundations of political discourse are inherently anti-Black. Or, to put it in terms of Giorgio Agamben's political ontology (of which the AP™ are rather fond), the political – i.e. the ontological character of a political situation that separates it from other social actions – or what he calls 'the Symbolic Order', is skewed against the Black/Slave. The Symbolic Order is based on the recognition of the 'other's' humanity, which then enables this 'other' to challenge the order on the grounds of, for instance, political economy. Since the Black is a priori a Slave, and Blackness and Slaveness are coterminous, the Black/Slave cannot participate in the Symbolic Order as her status is not that of the Human. And because the category of humanity is founded and relies on the existence of the slave, there is no way the Black/Slave can ever gain the recognition required to assert political demands and identities in the realm of the Symbolic Order. It is for this reason that, as Sexton points out in his essay 'The Social Life of Social Death: On Afro-Pessimism and Black Optimism', we must posit a 'political ontology dividing the Slave from the world of the Human in a constitutive way' and take this as our analytical starting point.

Wilderson's and Sexton's work contributes to a wider debate on the nature of Black studies in the United States, which is frequently tied into discussions on Black performance art, evidenced by the titles of Wilderson's Red, *White and Black: Cinema and the Structure of US Antagonisms*, Kara Keeling's *The Witch's Flight: The Cinematic, the Black Femme, and the Image of Common Sense* or Fred Moten's essays on Black Operations/Black Optimism in musical performance. Despite various disagreements and differences among these scholars, they are united by the common interest in 'the afterlife of slavery' – first described by Saidiya Hartman in her 2006 memoir *Lose Your Mother*. For Hartman – whose project is not that of AP™ and should not be mistaken for this essay's target – official abolition in the United States did not engender a decisive break with the racialised violence of slavery; in contemporary society, we can see traces of such violence in the 'skewed life chances, limited access to health and education, premature death, incarceration, and impoverishment' of African-Americans. The 'afterlife of slavery' she describes constitutes Black studies' object, and loosely ties a range of scholars together into a coherent discourse.

It is worth briefly considering Fred Moten's work to understand the AP™'s ability to co-opt or usurp other approaches to Black Studies and activism. Moten attempted to counter the AP™ conception of social death by foregrounding Black agency and asserting that it is ontologically prior to the all-encompassing anti-Blackness of the modern world. In the unpublished paper 'Black Optimism/Black Operation', Moten attempts to counter the 'anti-essentialism' of radical discourses that disavow Black studies' own object i.e. Blackness. For Moten, this Blackness exists in what he (along with his frequent collaborator Stefano Harney) has famously called 'the undercommons' – a space outside of official social structures, where Black people can assert their 'right to refuse'.

But as Annie Olaloku-Teriba points out in her excellent critique 'Afro-Pessimism and the (Un)Logic of Anti-Blackness', the AP™ finds a 'comfortable antagonist' in Moten, whose Black Ops can be neatly reintegrated into the concept of social death. It is also telling that Sexton, in 'Ante-Anti-Blackness', rather successfully merges the AP™ conception of social death with Moten's Black Ops by arguing that:

> A living death is as much a death as it is living. Nothing in Afro-pessimism suggests that there is no black (social) life, only that black life is not social life in the universe formed by the codes of state and civil society, of citizen and subject, of nation and culture, of people and place, of history and heritage, of all the things that colonial society has in common with the colonised, of all the things that capital has in common with labour – the modern world system.

Sexton shows that Moten's Black Ops is nothing other than what he instead calls 'the social life of social death'. There is no either/or distinction between social life and social death: we can think both together by positing that Black life is lived in the underground. Moten even acknowledges, in 'Blackness and Nothingness (Mysticism in the Flesh)', that the AP™ and Black Ops are engaged in the same theoretical project:

> In the end, though life and optimism are the terms under which I speak, I agree with Sexton – by way of the slightest most immeasurable reversal of emphasis – that Afro-pessimism and black optimism are not but nothing other than one another. I will continue to prefer the black optimism of his work just as, I am sure, he will continue to prefer the Afro-pessimism of mine.

For both Afro-pessimists and Black Optimists, the afterlife of slavery is characterised by the social death of the Black/Slave and a heavily distorted version of Fanon's concept of the 'fact of blackness'. This assumption, however, precludes the participation of Black Ops in radical politics and confines resistance to spaces of Black performance art.

By confining Black resistance to spaces outside of the anti-Black structures of civil society, and by undercutting the possibility for anti-imperialist solidarity between racialised people across the world, the AP™ theories have opened up a space for the corporate capture of Blackness. We need only recall last year's Nike campaign, prominently featuring the face of former NFL quarterback Colin Kaepernick, who has been blackballed by the league for kneeling during the national anthem. Since the incident, he has taken on the role of radical Black activist, complete with Panther-esque leather jackets, an afro and Afrocentric jewellery. While Kaepernick's struggle against the racist and exploitative NFL owners and executives is, of course, legitimate and necessary, the co-optation of his struggle by a large corporation is certainly a cause for concern. Nike is notorious for its use of sweatshop labour (including both forced and child labour), and its history of exploitative labour practices has been well-documented throughout the years. By detaching the struggles of African-Americans from those of racialised workers in the Global South, Nike can present itself as a progressive vehicle for Black emancipatory politics, while completely sidelining the plight of non-white workers outside of the US. Here we might recall a powerful statement by Fred Hampton to illustrate just how far from revolutionary Black politics we find ourselves:

> We don't think you fight fire with fire best; we think you fight fire with water best. We're going to fight racism not with racism, but we're going to fight with solidarity. We say we're not going to fight capitalism

> with black capitalism, but we're going to fight it with socialism [...] We're going to fight [...] with all of us people getting together and having an international proletarian revolution.

Wilderson and Sexton have been captured by corporate interests in much the same way. In their case, however, it is not a large corporation that co-opts Blackness, but rather the neoliberal university. Is it at all surprising that two professors working within the prestigious University of California system promote a theoretical framework that requires no political action from Black writers and activists other than simply being Black? Not only is AP™ a product of the neoliberal university, it also promotes its authors survival and flourishing within the corporate structures of higher education. When asked about his framework for psychological and physical resistance by the hosts of *iMiXWHATiLiKE*, Wilderson neatly dodges any commitment to radical politics with the excuse that it could cost him his academic job.

> This is so much a part of what it means to be a professor. I feel like cussing people out all the time. But if I do, I violate University of California's civility laws, tenure or not I'm out the door, right? And that tempers my speech. So, I think that what I have to offer is not a way out. What I have to offer is an analysis of the problem. And I don't trust me as much as I trust Black people on the ground.

Wilderson is aware that the AP™ rely on their activist supporters and social media following to maintain their privileged position within the university – without the activists and organisers on the ground, the AP™ could not prove the market value of its work to the neoliberal institution. By creating a framework for the analysis of race that lends itself to co-optation by corporate interests, the AP™ has certainly demonstrated that it can convert Blackness into profit. All the while, these theorists delude themselves that they are spearheading a truly radical Black movement. In the introduction to a collection of essays on AP™, the editors (who presumably include Sexton and Wilderson) even have the audacity to claim that they are 'motivated by a desire to contribute to [...] bringing these writings out of the ivory towers of the academy' and that they wish to 'remove the materials from this sitting place and see them proliferate among those in the streets and prisons'. True, they have succeeded in disseminating a watered-down version of their musings to activists and organisers; but what they have passed on is nothing short of anti-Black, in the sense that it works against the true liberation of Black people of all classes.

Today, such Blackness (and the pseudo-politics that is attached to it) is more useful for academic promotions, Instagram hashtags, and Nike adverts than for any revolutionary or emancipatory politics worthy of the name. The people who truly benefit – or rather profit – from the AP™ brand are the academics and the various university presses and journals who jump at every opportunity to unleash a plethora of AP™ books and articles onto the academic book market. While the AP™ may seem like a niche theoretical discourse, its influence extends far beyond the university: as Olaloku-Teriba argues, the AP™'s theoretical framework provides 'the structuring logic of various political formations in the era of #BlackLivesMatter'. What is at stake in the debate, therefore, is nothing less than the possibility of a revolutionary Black politics. Maybe African-Americans on the streets or in prison would do well to reach for George Jackson's Soledad Brother and steer clear of the AP™ and Black Ops.

III. The Afterlives of Slavery
The retreat of the AP™ and Black Ops from politics poses a problem for activists and scholars looking to engage in struggles that take seriously the political economy of race and the need for cross-racial solidarity. But how have these key themes of radical Black movements from the 1960s and 70s – from the Black Panthers to African

anti-colonial struggles – disappeared in the AP™'s theories? The erasure of radical Black and anti-colonial struggles rests almost entirely on misreading – or in some cases not reading – Marxist contributions to the study of race, colonialism and slavery. And this unfounded dismissal of the entire Marxist tradition allows the AP™ to kill two birds with one stone: on the one hand, it can position itself as a radical critique of Eurocentric left discourses. On the other hand, it allows the AP™ to disregard a vast body of Marxist scholarship that has 'raced' the history of capitalism and developed a nuanced analysis of the relationship between New World Slavery and capitalist accumulation on a global scale. Thus, the AP™ can ignore the specificities of how different Black populations are racialised and displace the study of political economy (and particularly of imperialism) in favour of ontological questions.

In the interview 'We're trying to destroy the world: Anti-Blackness & Police Violence after Ferguson' Wilderson makes the bizarre claim that 'slaveness is something that has consumed Blackness and Africanness, making it impossible to divide slavery from Blackness'. If this assumption sounds familiar, look no further than the Afro-pessimism of old, with its conflation of Africanness and Blackness and its disregard for the African continent and its inhabitants. But how has an approach that attempts to grapple with the complexities of Black being ended up rehashing the same assumptions and prejudices of Eurocentric discourse designed to dehumanise Black people on the African continent in the first place? The AP™'s theoretical position is riddled with contradictions: how can Blackness be separated from white supremacy, neocolonialism or imperialism and women's reproductive labour, when these are the mechanisms that structure the quotidien experience of most people racialised as Black on a global scale? Moreover, if the Black/Slave exists in a state of powerlessness and natal alienation – characterised by the loss of ties of birth in ascending and descending generations – how do we theorise the Blackness of those whose ancestors remained in Africa throughout the translatlantic slave trade?

Skimming the AP™'s bibliographies, one can be forgiven for thinking that the sheer number of references to radical scholarship reflects a close reading and consideration of the texts and arguments in question. Unfortunately, this is not the case. In 'The Avant-Garde of White Supremacy', Steve Martinot and Jared Sexton claim that Marxist approaches treat racism as merely a divide-and-conquer strategy for class struggle and super exploitation, and that Marxists fail to understand that racism – and anti-Blackness in particular – is not an ideology that can be refuted but is rather 'fundamental to class relations themselves'. Wilderson's 'Gramsci's Black Marx: Whither the Slave in Civil Society' advances a similar critique, arguing that the Black/Slave poses an insoluble problem for the Gramscian discourse on race, since it is not wage labour exploitation but 'the despotism of the unwaged relation' that drives anti-Black racism. For Wilderson, this discourse fails to think anything other than capitalism as the 'base' structure, from which other superstructural phenomena such as racism emerge. Marxists have thus failed to recognise that 'Capital was kick-started by the rape of the African continent' and that it is 'as close to capital's primal desire than is exploitation'. The Black/Slave blows apart key assumptions in Marxist thought, which renders it useless to for the analysis of the afterlife of slavery; this is the 'scandal of historical materialism'.

But Wilderson's and Sexton's critique of Marxism is shallow at best. In volume one of *Capital*, Marx clearly states that 'the turning of Africa into a warren for the commercial hunting of black skins' signalled 'the rosy dawn of the era of capitalist production'. In a letter to Russian literary critic Pavel Vasilyyevich Annenkov, Marx also writes that:

> We are not dealing here with indirect slavery, the slavery of the proletariat, we are dealing with direct slavery, the slavery of Blacks in Surinam, in Brazil, in the southern states of North America

Marx makes a clear distinction between slave labour and wage labour, refusing to conflate both in the category of the proletarian. In the specific case of the United States, he believed that the worker's movements had been paralysed by the existence of slave labour and their inability to adequately address it. In *Capital*, he writes, 'labour in a white skin cannot emancipate itself where it is branded in a black skin.' The possibility of a unified proletarian revolution thus relies on the abolition of slavery. While this may sound as if Marx' is theorising race as merely a divide and conquer strategy, as many critics have accused him of doing, there is an entire discourse within Marxism that has taken seriously the role that the racial plays in structuring social formations in the Americas. Instead of going back to what Marx did or didn't say about slavery, however, it may be more constructive to ask in what ways transatlantic slavery forces us to rethink the fundamental categories of Marxist political economy.

Robin Blackburn's historical studies of the transatlantic slave trade offer a more nuanced perspective that is entirely at odds with the strawman Marxism of the AP™. Blackburn acknowledges that New World slavery was more than just a divide and conquer strategy; it represented an intensification and racialisation of prior forms of slavery. Like early African or Roman slavery, chattel slavery was based on the idea that a person could be bought and sold. But unlike previous techniques, the New World version institutionalised slavery and made it hereditary. Once a person had been enslaved, it was highly likely that their descendants would continue to exist in a relation of bondage. Where Blackburn's analysis diverges from the AP™ is in his emphasis on the interrelation between slavery, colonialism and capitalism, and his efforts to understand how the racial structures the mode of production in each instance. For Blackburn, New World slavery was a central product of the rise of capitalism, not of an a priori anti-Blackness, and therefore cannot be neatly be separated from the early stages of capitalist accumulation and the violent expansion of European (early Spanish and Portuguese as well as later British) colonialism in Africa, Asia and the Americas. As Greg Thomas argues in 'Afro-Blue Notes', Walter

Rodney already recognised this, in 'Slavery and Underdevelopment' and 'Plantation Society in Guyana', when he showed that plantation slavery in America is colonial slavery. In short, 'there is no system of slavery in any part of these Americas that is not still settler colonial slavery; no settler colonialism without chattel slavery or racial slavery and their neo-slaveries',

Blackburn and other radical historians of slavery draw on Cedric Robinson's concept of 'racial capitalism', which can be used to refute the claim that slaveness and Africanness are one and the same. In *Black Marxism* Robinson argues that racism was already present in Western civilisation prior to the flourishing of capitalism. Thus, capitalism and racism grew together from the old order to produce the 'racial capitalism' characteristic of the modern world; a new world system relying on slavery, violence, imperialism and genocide for its continued expansion. The value of Robinson's work lies in its ability to uncover the contingent relationship between slavery and Blackness: he argues that early European proletarians were racialised subjects from oppressed groups, such as the Irish, Jews, Roma or Slavs, who were victims of dispossession, colonialism and slavery within Europe. With the dawn of the transatlantic slave trade, new notions of difference emerged, based on more aggressively racialised conceptions, that were used to justify the political economy of slavery. For Robinson, white supremacy masked itself as an economic rationale, which in turn organised racial hierarchies, with the production of cotton at its core. As Chris Chen writes in 'The Limit Points of Capitalist Equality',

> the colonial and racial genealogy of European capitalism' were 'encoded directly into the economic "base" through an ongoing history of racial violence which [...] binds surplus populations to capitalist markets.

There are also several surprising omissions in the AP™ account of slavery that point towards its entrenched African-American exceptionalism, most notably that of the slave trade in the Americas more broadly. Although the African-American experience of chattel slavery is overrepresented in the AP™ narrative, only about 4 per cent of all enslaved Africans, out of over 10 million that were taken to the Americas between the sixteenth and nineteenth centuries, were carried to North America. Close to five million enslaved Africans were taken to Portuguese America (Brazil) alone between 1501 and 1866, and whose labour became the driving force for the sugar economy in the early 1600s, and gold and diamond mining from about 1690 onwards. While the AP™ continue to structure their analysis of Blackness and slaveness around the official abolition of slavery in the United States in 1865, they seem to forget that slavery wasn't abolished in Brazil until 1888. But in the AP™'s 'afterlife of slavery', these histories don't play any role. The legacy of US chattel slavery consumes all Black experience, both historical and contemporary.

If the AP™ were to pay attention to the peculiarities of Brazilian slavery, it would have to adapt its concept of Blackness to develop an account of how race has structured a social formation with the second largest Black population in the world. In Nigeria, the country with the world's largest Black population, the 'afterlife of slavery' takes on a completely different meaning than in the US. While slavery had existed in Igbo society before colonisation, it accelerated with the increasing demand for slaves on the other side of the Atlantic. When slavery was officially abolished in many parts of the West, Adiele Afigbo writes in *The Abolition of the Slave Trade in Southeastern Nigeria, 1885–1950*, Igbo slave markets were flooded with ohu and osu slaves, whose descendants to this day retain the stigma of their ancestors – they cannot intermarry with freeborn and are excluded from important community organisations. In a recent *New Yorker* article Nigerian novelist Adaobi Tricia Nwaubani argues that:

> Igbo discrimination is not based on race, and there are no visual markers to differentiate slave descendants from freeborn. Instead, it trades on cultural beliefs about lineage and spirituality.

Discrimination of slave descendants is thus based on their role as outsiders, since the ohu have never really lost their outsider status in a society where community ties are extremely important. Afigbo's periodisation also points to another important aspect of slavery in Nigeria: it was only officially abolished by the British in the early 1900s but continued informally for at least another forty to fifty years. What this means is that we cannot understand slavery in Nigeria within the Igbo system with reference to an African-American concept of race, conditioned entirely by the experiences of US chattel slavery. For the descendants of ohu slaves, the afterlife of slavery is not characterised by the condition of the Black/Slave but rather by something quite different. In this case, the equation of the Black/Slave with the African does not hold.

So what can we learn from these different histories of slavery and racialisation? Brazilian academic Denise Ferreira da Silva draws the following conclusion in 'Facts of Blackness', her comparative study of race in the US and Brazil,

> I was convinced that our shared blackness has been traversed by the particular effects of specific nation, gender and class conditions. Slavery and colonialism composed the historical ground upon which race, gender and nationess have written the various versions of black subjectivity [...] That instrinsically multiple quality of black subjectivity demands attention to the specific historical and discursive developments informing a society's strategies of racial subordination.

In her more recent book *Toward a Global Idea of Race*, Silva further contends that we cannot comprehend the 'present global configuration' unless we 'unpack how the racial, the cultural and the nation institute the modern subject' and analyse the context in which the modern subject emerged and was produced. For Silva, racial difference is not an ideological or cultural construction but rather a real category and is responsible for structuring the contemporary global configuration. And precisely because race supplies the discursive basis for the subordination of non-white people, even specific studies of Blackness must be placed in the global historical context in which racialised subjects emerged. In this way, we can avoid US-centric ontological (supposedly universal) conceptions of Blackness while simultaneously emphasising the histories of interconnection between Black populations across the world. In short, the object of analysis is not the afterlife of slavery but the multiplicity of afterlives of slavery and colonisation; the aim is to study how these exist within a global system structured by imperialism.

This is not to say that there aren't glimmers of hope in the US literary and academic scene. John Keene's part-historical, part-fictional (and undoubtedly political) retelling of the slave experience in *Counternarratives*, gives equal weight to the specificities of slavery in Brazil under Portuguese rule and in North America in the pre-Civil War era. *Counternarratives* weaves together these diverging but interconnected histories to draw out the underlying logic structuring gender, race and class under different forms of slavery and colonisation. Most importantly, however, Keene plays with the engrained Eurocentric prejudices that colonisers used to belittle and 'other' colonial subjects. Irrationality and spirituality become sources of power: Keene's characters actually possess the magical powers that have been attributed to them by the colonisers – these are in turn transformed into a basis for Black insurgency. While Keene opens the collection with a quote from Fred Moten on the relationship between philosophy and slavery ('The social situation of philosophy is slavery'), his exposition of the lived histories of enslaved peoples in various social formations, moves beyond the realm of simple African-American exceptionalism, and his deconstruction of Eurocentric prejudices more in line with the 'thin' and strategic deployment of essentialism than the 'thick' ontological essentialism of the AP™.

IV. Anti-Anti-Colonialism
Wilderson, Sexton and their activist followers frequently erase or

distort beyond recognition, the various Black liberation movements that fought against racism, colonialism, and imperialism throughout the Global South, particularly the African liberation struggles of the 1960s and 70s. In the 'Avant-Garde of White Supremacy', Martinot and Sexton for instance claim that:

> For anti-colonialist thinking, racism is a social ideology that can be refuted, a structure of privilege to be given up, again at the local or individual level. Where liberalism subordinates the issue of racism to the presumed potentialities of individual development, Marxism subordinates the issue of race to class relations of struggle, and anti-colonial radicalism pretends its mere existence as a 'movement' is the first step toward eradicating racism.

Anti-colonial discourses consequently 'subsume the issue of racism in promises of future transformations of the power relations to which racialisation is deferred' and assume that it will disappear if it is 'no longer useful to the relations of production or the security of territorial boundaries'. Anti-colonial movements' (or postcolonial as they are often referred to by the AP™) misdiagnosis of racism, Wilderson argues in *Red, White and Black*, stems from their fundamentally different positionality in relation to anti-Blackness: while the 'postcolonial' can quite literally throw the settler out of her zone, the Black/Slave must throw the Human out of her zone if she is to overcome the condition of social death that characterises Black life. The postcolonial exists as Human in the symbolic order, whereas the Black/Slave can never. This, for Wilderson, is also the difference between the postcolonial Fanon of *The Wretched of the Earth* and the Black/Slave Fanon of *Black Skin, White Masks*.

The blatant (mis)use of Fanon is a particularly infuriating example of how the AP™ distorts anti-colonial thought. By selectively reading parts of his early work (*Black Skin, White Masks*) and disregarding pretty much everything else, AP™ scholars try to incorporate Fanon into the genealogy of their misguided attempt at creating a radical Black discourse. Since *Black Skin, White Masks* makes for a more comfortable read than *The Wretched of the Earth* or *A Dying Colonialism* – the more important Fanon texts for the liberation movements on the continent – AP™ has reached for the young Fanon, and tried to isolate him from the rest of his oeuvre. As Wilderson himself contends: 'Frantz Fanon's *The Wretched of the Earth* [...] does not build upon Fanon's *Black Skin, White Masks*'. While the AP™ is correct in pointing out that there is a difference in approach between Fanon's early and later work, this does not mean that we should prioritise the former over the latter. Nor does it mean that Fanon's early work is necessarily based on the assumption of an ontologically flat conception of Blackness. In the introduction to *Black Skin, White Masks* Fanon concedes that:

> Since I was born in the Antilles, my observations and my conclusions are valid only for the Antilles – at least concerning the black man at home. Another book could be dedicated to explaining the differences that separate the Negro of the Antilles from the Negro of Africa.

The appropriation of Fanon by some African-American scholars and activists – who reduce his thought to a hashtag, and make proclamations that Fanon himself would have fundamentally disagreed with – also begs the question of why only Fanon, singled out and isolated from all other anti-colonial thought, has been granted a cushy place in the Ivory Tower. Why is there still very little scholarship on Black revolutionaries such as Amílcar Cabral, one of the foremost anti-colonial theorists and revolutionaries of the twentieth century?

Academia's aversion to Cabral stems from its lack of interest in the crucial everyday work of revolutionary struggle and its fetishisation of revolution in the abstract. Cabral insisted that we must not only fight the battle of ideas, but struggle for material benefits and improved conditions of life. The revolution can never be separated from the daily needs of the people. Given the elitist and corporate nature of higher education, particularly in the

Anglo-American world, it is thus no surprise that the academy has chosen Fanon ('the prophet of revolution') over the tireless anti-colonial strategist Cabral. This is, of course, not to dismiss Fanon's crucial contributions to the study of psychiatry and anti-colonial movements. It is only to say that the perspective of one anti-colonial intellectual does not suffice; instead of decontextualizing Fanon, we must read him in conjunction with other anti-colonial intellectuals who offer valuable insights into fields – such as revolutionary strategy – that Fanon rarely engaged with.

Though it is tempting to blame the AP™ for all that is wrong with the political discourse on race, we must remember that it is only a symptom of a much larger problem. The assumption that there is little difference between African and African-American realities permeates much of the writing on Blackness, and we can already find a sustained critique of these approaches in Fanon's later work. In *The Wretched of the Earth*, Fanon argues there is a fundamental difference between the Civil Rights Movement and the anti-colonial (armed) struggle on the continent. The problems confronting the African-American scholar/activist and the anti-colonial revolutionary only share a single commonality: that they are all defined as Black in relation to whiteness. The difference in objective conditions of struggle that these movements face, cannot be overcome by simply asserting the existence of a unifying Black culture and history. But the AP™ version of Fanon is stripped of such remarks, and presented as a diasporic alienated intellectual *par excellence*, whose anti-colonialism is swallowed by slavery and social death.

Achille Mbembe's 2003 essay 'Necropolitics' is frequently highlighted as a foundational text for the AP™'s musings on the afterlife of slavery. But this is not necessarily the entire picture, and contrary to popular belief, Mbembe does not fit neatly into the AP™. For instance, David Marriott, another AP™ associate, has criticised Mbembe for his anti-Black concept of Blackness, whereas Mbembe has in turn dismissed the theoretical apparatus for equating Africanness and Blackness. Although Mbembe is a somewhat uncomfortable interlocutor for the AP™, they do share a common distrust of Marxism and anti-colonial thought. What is most interesting about Mbembe's position, however, is that he somehow manages to conflate three distinct discourses into one, in order to dismiss each approach with the claim that it is inadequate for the study of African subjectivity. Given Mbembe's status as a leading public intellectual, it is worth interrogating the discourses he dismisses to draw out why and to what effect Mbembe aims to push them aside, and how his critique has influenced the AP™.

In 'African Modes of Self-Writing', Mbembe launches an attack on what he refers to as 'Afro-radicalism': an amalgamation of two interrelated discourses that have the same disposition, and emerged from African engagement with Marxism and nationalism. For both the nativist and instrumentalist currents, Mbembe argues, history is split into three major historical events (slavery, colonialism and apartheid) through which the 'African self has become alienated from itself' and degraded to the status of non-being and social death. Only with reference to these three fundamental historical events can Africans unite and recapture their destiny (sovereignty), and to belong to themselves in the world (autonomy). Mbembe, however, warns us that this is not the case: both nativism and Afro-Marxism ('the instrumentalist paradigm') are 'faked philosophies' that are more dogma than methods of interrogation. Afro-radicalism's claim to have created a revolutionary politics that breaks with imperialism and dependence is illusory; all the discourse provides is a 'mechanistic vision of history, a fetishisation of state power, the disqualification of liberal democracy, and the populist and authoritarian dream of mass society'.

Mbembe's main argument is that both discourses share the same episteme: They both 'subscribe to the postulate of difference', despite claiming to distance themselves from Western ideas of alterity. At its core, Mbembe's critique boils down to the claim that 'nationalist and Marxist narratives of the African self and the world' are superficial and unphilosophical; as political weapons and systems of knowledge these paradigms are entirely outdated and must be replaced by some other philosophical discourse that emphasises the importance of the universal and does not fall into the trap of nativism. While critical of the nativist impulse, Mbembe reserves his most polemical gestures for Afro-radicalism. In a (melo)dramatic passage, he claims:

> Expiatory, substitutive, or self-sacrificial, violence was deployed – and death unleashed – in the name of a Marxist telos. Murder itself was commuted and concealed through ascription to a final moral truth, while the proof of virtue and morality lay in pain and suffering.

According to this narrative of anti-colonial struggle, the liberation movements were only concerned with power and the capturing of the state machinery, with other philosophical questions pushed aside. A destructive belief in redemptive violence as a force of cohesion meant these movements could not succeed in creating a social bond in their nations, and failed to 'refashion' the African subject.

If it seems difficult to make sense of this critique, it may be because Mbembe is conflating a range of different movements and discourses under the banner of 'Afro-radicalism', some of which have very little in common with the other. What exactly is Afro-radicalism? Is it Kwame Nkrumah's or Julius Nyerere's African Socialism? Or is it the Afro-Marxist tradition? And what properties does a 'nativist' discourse such as Négritude share with Afro-Marxist movements? Mbembe's politics are often hard to grasp, and his affinity for strawmanning doesn't make it any easier to discern what the actual aim of his critique is. But surely it is absurd to claim that neither Négritude or 'Afro-Marxism' offered any philosophical and political reflections worthy of theoretical scrutiny.

VI. Négritude as Strategic Essentialism
No discourse is without a history or exists in a vacuum, and the

AP™ is certainly not the first tradition of Black thought to advance an ontologically flat conception of Blackness. In the 1930s, a group of young emigres from different parts of the French colonial empire set out to develop an aesthetic framework designed to counter historical and cultural narratives that exclusively ascribed the properties of beauty and goodness to anything white and European. In Paris, the metropolitan centre of the French colonial empire, these intellectuals found themselves united by a common experience: as educated and sophisticated *évoluées* they had not expected to face racial prejudice. For the French, however, they were still colonial subjects, that belonged to a race of people considered uncivilised and in need of guidance. A privileged class position within the colonies could not save these intellectuals from their visible 'otherness' in the metropole, and for the first time, they were made aware of what 'Africanness' and 'Blackness' really meant for the French.

In its initial iteration, Négritude was an artistic expression that sought to re-appropriate the term 'art nègre' and strip it of its racist connotations. By poetically appropriating the French language, these intellectuals and artists were deconstructing Western society from within, turning its own language and concepts (French and Surrealism) against it, with the aim of exposing the contradictions in the same norms and values that justified colonial oppression and slavery. As part of a group of non-white Surrealists including Aimé and Suzanne Césaire, Étienne Léro, Yva Léro, Wifredo Lam, René Menil and many others – all included in the anthology *Black, Brown and Beige* – the Négritude poets asserted the value of a distinctly Black identity that was entirely at odds with the French colonial policy of 'assimilationism'. The aim was to capture the beauty and vitality of African bodies, culture, and history, and to throw these back in the faces of the French. Western rationality was juxtaposed with African emotion, and the Bergsonian *elan vital* of the African held up as the creative force behind Black cultural production.

While the Négritude poets had different interpretations of what the movement meant, it is often read through Sartre's essay 'Black Orpheus', and his characterisation of Négritude as 'anti-racist racism'. Sartre's essays have frequently shaped how African intellectuals are perceived in both academia and popular discourse. However, like his preface to Fanon's *The Wretched of the Earth*, his essay on Négritude should be taken with a pinch of salt. In 'Black Orpheus' Sartre essentially reduces the whole Négritude movement to Senghor and his *Anthologie de la nouvelle poésie nègre et malgache de langue française*. While it is true that Senghor advanced an essentialist ontology that conflated Blackness with Africanness, and posited a unique African worldview that could be read in African cultures and religions, Suzanne and Aimé Césaire, and Léon Damas refused to extend Négritude into the realm of philosophy and instead emphasised the poetic dimension of the struggle.

In a lecture delivered at Florida International University, Césaire denounces metaphysical conflation of Blackness and Africanness, and clarifies his role as a Négritude poet:

> Négritude in my eyes, is not a philosophy. Négritude is not a metaphysics. Négritude is not a pretentious conception of the universe. It is a way of living history within history: the history of a community whose experience appears to be ... unique, with its deportation of old beliefs, its fragments of murdered cultures. How can we not believe that all this which has its own coherence, constitutes a heritage?

But Césaire was hardly alone in positing a 'thin' essentialism designed to combat racism in France and in the Caribbean. In the 1943 essay 'Surrealism and US', Suzanne Césaire writes that:

> Thus, far from contradicting diluting or diverting our revolutionary attitude toward life, surrealism strengthens it. It nourishes an impatient strength within us endlessly reinforcing the massive army of refusals. [Tomorrow] millions of black hands will hoist their terror across the furious skies of world war. Freed from a long benumbing slumber, the most disinherited of peoples will rise up from the plaints of ashes. Our

surrealism will supply this rising people with a punch
from its very depths. Our surrealism will enable us to
finally transcend the sordid antinomies of the present:
whites/Blacks, Europeans/Africans, civilised/savages
– at last rediscovering the magic power of the mahoulis,
drawn directly from living sources. Colonial idiocy
will be purified in the welder's blue flame. We shall
recover our value as metal, our cutting edge of steel,
our unprecedented communions.

Along with Suzanne, Georges Gratiant, Aristide Maugé, René Menil
and Lucie Thesée, Césaire had also founded the journal *Tropique*
in Martinique in 1941. Only two or so years later, the journal was
censored and interdicted by the Vichy regime for its subversive
content and for being 'a revolutionary review that is racial and
sectarian'. The editors responded to this provocation in an infamous
open letter to Martinique's Chief of Information Services with the
following polemic:

Sir, we have received your indictment of Tropiques.
'Racists', 'sectarians', 'revolutionaries', 'ingrates and
traitors to the country', 'poisoners of souls', none of
these epithets really repulses us. 'Poisoners of souls',
like Racine, 'Ingrates and traitors to our good country',
like Zola, … 'Revolutionaries', like the Hugo of 'Châti-
ments'. 'Sectarians', passionately, like Rimbaud and
Lautréamont. Racists, yes. Of the racism of Toussaint
Louverture, of Claude McKay and Langston Hughes
against that of Drumont and Hitler. As to the rest of it,
don't expect for us to plead our case, nor vain recrimi-
nations, nor discussion. We do not speak the same
language.

For Césaire and the other members of the *Tropiques*, Négritude
was a poetic revolt that sought to reclaim a heritage destroyed
by colonialism. A common history of slavery, Césaire argued,

united Black people around the world – hence the need to assert a common identity to overcome this history of oppression and exploitation. In Césaire's hands, Négritude transforms itself, from a frame of mind and philosophical worldview, into a political act directed at decolonisation. 'In other words', as Souleymane Bachir Diagne's puts it, 'there is something about [Césaire's] Négritude that de-essentialises itself', 'something that comes underneath and deconstructs the essentialist language'.

But even if the recovery of lost traditions and idealised conceptions of African culture are a necessary step towards liberation, Fanon warns us, this is by no means the main objective. The recovery of a suppressed history and cultural production fills the native intellectual with a renewed confidence; looking back into African history, the intellectual finds that there is nothing she should be ashamed of, and that in fact, African history and culture are at the very least on par with European civilisations. To counter the narrative of the African savage, Négritude unconditionally affirms African culture, in the same way intellectuals had previously affirmed European culture. But, the frantic search for cultural figureheads that can be compared to those of Western civilisation is, Fanon argues, a futile task. African history can hardly supply the canonical figures that the intellectual is used to, and as Zanzibari Marxist A. M. Babu has similarly stated, it would be a slap in the face to all African workers and peasants, who have fought for a more equitable and classless society, to look for traces of 'genius' in African history. In many ways, 'the past existence of [civilisation] does not change anything very much in the diet of the [...] peasant today'.

While Babu's critique may be a bit harsh, it does raise an issue that has also been a recurring problem for the Western Marxist tradition: the alienation of radical or revolutionary intellectuals from the masses. This is somewhat exacerbated in the case of Black diasporic intellectuals, as there is the additional element of 'diasporic alienation' from a romanticised 'home'. Négritude – by its own admission – owes a huge debt to the Harlem Renaissance, which in principle is no problem at all. But when we consider Damas' claim that Négritude was founded on a 'wind rising from Black America', which expresses 'the African love for life, the African joy in love, [and] the African dream of death', we begin to understand how much our collective view of race in Africa is shaped by a diasporic standpoint. In its early stages, Négritude thinking on Blackness was conditioned by both alienation from the revolutionary struggle (expressed in their emphasis on poetic and artistic revolt), and diasporic alienation (as intellectuals in the colonial metropole). One can easily spot such double alienation in the AP™ and its emphasis on 'natal alienation' as an inherent feature of Blackness. But this doubly alienated perspective has often drowned out and silenced analyses of race that take seriously the realities and material conditions of Black people on the African continent. Following Ali Mazouri, we must 'ask ourselves the question of why this particular diasporic view of blackness [Black Orientalism] is always applied globally and no attention is paid to the particularities of race relations on the continent?'

On the other hand, Aimé Césaire's attack on Roger Callois in *Discourse on Colonialism* illustrates just how ingrained the cultural exceptionalism of Europe was (is) in many intellectuals' minds, and just how necessary it was (is) to counter such exceptionalism with a 'thin' essentialism of one's own – even if this expression is mainly poetic. Whereas the AP™ essentialism retreats from the realm of politics, the essentialism of the Césaire's surrealism takes racism and colonialism head on. This 'strategic essentialism' – a positivist essentialism that is critical of the ontological idea, while making use of it for specific political purposes – represents something quite different than the 'thick' ontological Blackness of the AP™, who have no political strategy whatsoever! Nonetheless, we must remember that the emphasis in strategic essentialism is on political action; while Césaire focused on achieving the deconstruction of essentialism through poetry and art, we must move beyond the realm of artistic expression and posit a concept of Blackness aimed at the revolutionary transformation of existing social relations.

VII. Remembering a Red Africa

For reasons discussed above, the socialist anti-colonial movements of the 1960s and 70s exist either exist outside of the AP™'s historical scope, or are quickly dismissed along with all other Marxist or feminist discourses. But the AP™ dismissal and erasure of anti-colonial thought is even more bizarre when we consider Wilderson's biography. How did someone who was a member of the African National Congress' military wing, Umkhonto we Sizwe (MK), and a fierce left critic of Nelson Mandela create a theoretical apparatus that is incapable of dealing with the realities of imperialism and neocolonialism on the African continent? In the contemporary global configuration, characterised by super-exploitation of racialised workers in the Global South, we should not be so quick to dismiss a discourse that took seriously the need for cross-racial solidarity in the struggle against imperialism and neocolonialism.

The term 'African socialism' first emerged in the wake of the independence struggles of the 1950s and 60s, when the newly independent governments sought to create the basis for a new African future, and once and for all break with the racial, economic and political legacies of colonialism. There is much debate around the definition of African socialism and many still argue – as the editors of the 1979 *Socialism in Sub-Saharan Africa* did in the introduction to their collection – that the 'passage of time has not led to a precise definition' or 'a general consensus of its nature'. However, there is some agreement that African socialism – as a political and intellectual tradition – can be split into two relatively distinct phases: the first wave of humanist African socialism and a second, more radical wave of Afro-Marxism based on the principles of scientific socialism. Although not all socialist anti-colonial movements fit neatly within this categorisation, it can help us develop some broad themes in both waves of African socialism to gain a better understanding of their aims and limitations.

It is somewhat unsurprising that the humanist wave of African socialism dominates both the academic discourse and the popular imaginary. The socialist experiments of Kwame Nkrumah in Ghana, Julius Nyerere in Tanzania, Sékou Touré in Guinea, Kenneth Kauda in Zambia, Léopold Senghor in Senegal, and Madibo Keïta in Mali provide the most prominent examples of an anti-colonial discourse that was ironically devoid of thorough class analysis. While it is impossible to deduce a cohesive doctrine of this first wave of African Socialism, one can see several overlaps between its diverse manifestations. One such overlap is the argument that traditional communal elements of African culture are inherently socialist and can serve as the basis for a larger socialist programme. As Robin D. G. Kelley points out in his introduction to *Discourse on Colonialism*,

> Césaire's insistence that pre-colonial African and Asian cultures were not only ante-capitalist...but also anti-capitalist, anticipated the romantic claims made by African nationalist leaders such as Julius Nyerere, Kenneth Kaunda, and Senghor himself, that modern Africa can establish socialism on the basis of pre-colonial village life.

In his 1962 pamphlet *Ujamaa – the Basis of African Socialism*, Nyerere argued that: 'We, in Africa, have no more need of being "converted" to socialism than we have of being "taught" democracy. Both are rooted in our past – in the traditional society which produced us.'

But the first wave of African socialism fell short of delivering the radical promises of independence. Attempts at creating idealist humanisms – such as Nkrumah's Consciencism and Kaunda's Zambian Humanism – and their appeal to an idealised past culture (or the cultural uniqueness of Africa) only served to mask class relations in their newly independent nations. What the African socialists failed to understand was that this third way was not possible, and that choice between genuine socialism and neocolonialism was then, as it is now, zero-sum. As A. M. Babu argues in *African Socialism or Socialist Africa*, 'it is not enough to peddle socialist rhetoric or simply nationalise the means of production and then sit back, in the belief that we have set in motion a socialist trend'. For Babu, the official African socialism could only reproduce dependency, exploitation and neo-colonial relations. It did not suffice to simply posit the inherently socialist nature of African culture; rather, it may have been more helpful to keep only those parts of traditional culture that were emancipatory so as to forge a new culture based on the principles of revolutionary socialism.

This narrative is somewhat complicated by the contradictory positions that many African socialist leaders held, particularly with regards to non-alignment and the need for class analysis. Let's take Nkrumah as an example. On the one hand, he had advocated a position of non-alignment by claiming that 'we must face neither East nor West; we face forward'. But in *Revolutionary Path*, on the other hand he argues: 'If we are to achieve revolutionary Socialism, then we must avoid any suggestion that will imply there is any separation between the Socialist World and a "Third World"'.

The 1970 *Class Struggle in Africa* also shows a Nkrumah deeply concerned with analysing how 'the close links of class and race developed in Africa alongside capitalist exploitation'. He writes:

> Slavery, the master-servant relationship, and cheap labour were basic to it. The classic example is South Africa, where Africans experience double exploitation – both on the ground of colour and class. Similar conditions exist in the US, the Caribbean, in Latin America, and in other parts of the world where the nature of the development has resulted in a racist class structure. In these areas, even the shades of colour count – the degree of blackness being a yardstick by which social status is measured.

In the colonial situation, a racist social structure cannot be thought separately from class exploitation and a racist-capitalist power structure. For the Nkrumah of *Class Struggle in Africa*, capitalist exploitation and racism are complementary – 'wherever there is a race problem it has become a linked with the class struggle'. Genuine progress in the struggle against imperialism can only be made if intellectuals adopt Marxism and engage with other Communist organisations that encourage a close contact with workers and peasants. African socialists, thus, must align themselves with the oppressed masses and become conscious of class struggle in Africa.

As Beninese philosopher Paulin Hountondji has convincingly shown in his comparison of the 1964 edition and the 1970 edition of Nkrumah's *Consciencism*, his thought developed further towards class analysis after the 1966 US-backed military coup, where his government was overthrown while he was away on a state visit to North Vietnam and China. In the 1964 edition, Nkrumah still emphasised the socialist elements inherent in African traditional culture; in the 1970 edition he is much more cautious with this claim. This shift of emphasis is also strikingly clear in his 1967 paper 'African Socialism Revisited', where he sharply criticises the African socialists who have associated it 'much more with anthropology than with political economy' and fetishised African communal life by deluding themselves that it was devoid of social hierarchy. Following the military coup, Ghana cultivated a closer relationship with the US (and associated 'international' organisations such as the IMF and World Bank), and cut ties with the Soviet Bloc. The coup was, of course, carried out by US-backed neo-colonial forces – and the second wave of African socialism may help us further understand the internal and external forces driving this process.

The second wave of African socialism – or what is frequently called Afro-Marxism – emerged in the mid 1970s, although the period of preparation for the revolutionary struggle began much earlier. This second phase of socialism on the continent was characterised by the adherence to the principles of official Marxist-Leninism with its focus on a vanguard party that leads the way in a socialist revolution, in countries like Burkina-Faso, Somalia, Congo-Brazaville, Madagascar, Libya, Benin and Ethiopia (although the latter was more militaristic in character than revolutionary). The most radical among this wave, however, were the liberation movements in African Portuguese colonies, who were not constitutional nationalist movements – as the previous African socialists had been – but rather revolutionary movements that sought to overthrow the existing social structures and refashion these along socialist lines. Among the most influential proponents of Afro-Marxism are Amílcar Cabral of Guinea-Bissau and Cape Verde, Agostinho Neto of Angola, Samora Machel of Mozambique, and Thomas Sankara of Burkina-Faso. Lusophone Afro-Marxists faced much tougher conditions than those of the previous wave of African socialists: one need only consider the decade long civil war fought by the People's Movement for the Liberation of Angola (MPLA) against National Union for the Total Independence of Angola (UNITA) rebels in Angola, or the Frelimo's armed struggle against Renamo in Mozambique, with both rebel groups having received significant funding and support from the US and apartheid South Africa.

Because the second wave of African socialists had studied the mistakes of the first, its leaders were acutely aware of the dangers of internal opposition and the nature of class relations within their respective countries. In *Unity and Struggle*, Amílcar Cabral sheds some light on the dynamics driving this process of internal opposition. His theory of neocolonialism can help us understand why African socialist experiments, such as that of Nkrumah failed. In the neo-colonial constellation, Cabral argues, imperialist action often takes the form of creating a native bourgeoisie that is loyal to the bourgeoisie of the imperialist nations. This class of native agents emerges from the petty bourgeoisie of bureaucrats and intermediaries in the trading system. Their loyalty to the imperialist bourgeoisie stifles the development of national productive forces, and inevitably leads to underdevelopment. Hence, this class cannot possibly guide the development of productive forces, and cannot be a truly national bourgeoisie. Under neocolonialism, the struggle for the 'independent' state (and political power) is thus between the native working class and imperialist capital. As sharp class distinctions emerge, and demobilise nationalist forces, other ties such as tribal solidarity make their way to the forefront of politics; the only escape from this predicament is the destruction of capitalist and imperialist structures 'implanted in the national soil'.

What Cabral's analysis can help us understand is why anti-colonial movements were more concerned with the relations of production or the security of territorial boundaries than the eradication of some anti-Black racism. Unlike Mbembe or the AP™, these movements realised that national sovereignty was an indispensible aspect of the struggle against racism (not anti-Blackness) on a global scale. Cabral argued that neocolonialism (as one form of imperialist domination) works on two different levels: both in Europe and in the underdeveloped countries. In Europe, the working class had been pacified through the development of a privileged proletariat that could lower the revolutionary level of the working classes (i.e. labour aristocracy). Similarly, the late Egyptian economist Samir Amin argued that the privileges of those in the Global North, upheld by their control of key monopolies like technology, global finance and media, make it more difficult for an internationalist left to emerge. To be non-Eurocentric, Amin argues, we must address how the ruling classes of the Global North exert control over the South.

Unfortunately, this has failed to happen. The decline of an anti-imperialist left, and the increasing susceptibility of scholars and activists to the pipe dream of a social democracy that doesn't rely on racism and the super-exploitation of workers in the Global South i.e. what Sandro Mezzadra and Mario Neuman call 'Wohlfahrsstaat-Populismus' (welfare state populism) in *Jenseits von Interesse und Identität*, points towards such failure. In the days of anti-colonial revolutions, class exploitation and racial or national oppression were fused in the imperialist order. Today, the same applies. Racism still plays a significant role in structuring imperialism – we should take seriously those who attempted to analyse this interconnection and put aside ontological and flat theories of Blackness that preclude any struggle against imperialism by severing all ties between those who are racialised as Black and other non-white workers.

In 'Racial Formation in an Age of Permanent War', Nikhil Pal Singh argues that racialised groups in the US are incorporated into a system of racialised wage differentials and precarious labour; they represent the relative surplus population in the US. The security state manages 'civilisational threats to the nation' (i.e. its surplus population) by deporting immigrant labour, encouraging mass incarceration and militarising the US border, making those who have been racialised more vulnerable to state violence. But in the contemporary imperialist configuration, value created by the super-exploitation of racialised workers still flows from the Global South to the Global North, where this value is appropriated by multinational companies, the nation states they are based in, and the people that reside in these nation states, as Tony Norfield's *The City* and John Smith's *Imperialism in the Twenty-First Century* show. We must therefore think seriously about how the nation state structures the process of racialisation in the core and in the periphery, and how different national forms of racialisation exist within an imperialist world system.

Given these political-economic realities, the study of race (and consequently also of Blackness) is always enmeshed in a political struggle: this forces us to consider the political implications of our theoretical analysis. True, we can acknowledge that racism has been written into the 'base' of capitalism. And, as with the Césaires' strategic essentialism, there is a space for the affirmation of a positive Blackness directed at challenging colonial prejudices still tied into the national fabric of states in the Global North. Nonetheless, we must also recognise that there is a dire need for anti-imperialist South-South cooperation. It is easy to forget that the global left discourse was once shaped by such debates: the examples of the Panthers in Algeria, Cabral's visits to Cuba, Cuban support of the MPLA in Angola, and more, illustrate just how many Black people (including African-American organisations like the Panthers and Amiri Baraka's Congress of Afrikan People) felt the need for a cross-racial push against colonialism, neocolonialism and imperialism.

There exists a political and intellectual tradition that has tried to bring the interconnection between race, neocolonialism and imperialism to the forefront of radical politics. The erasure of this tradition – stretching from Sankara and Cabral to Samir Amin – has only served to embolden ontological theories of Blackness and racialisation that take an African-American diasporic and alienated perspective as a priori truth and have no purpose or meaning for those struggling against the realities of imperialist super-exploitation and national oppression on the ground. As Thomas Sankara forcefully put it in his speech before the UN General Assembly: 'Down with imperialism! Down with neo-colonialism! [...] Eternal victory to the peoples of Africa, Latin America and Asia in their struggle! Fatherland or death: we shall triumph.'

MORGANE MERTEUIL WITH SOPHIE LEWIS

Gestational Decrim

'Liberté, égalité, paternité!' In France, a coalition headed up by the neoreactionary network 'La Manif Pour Tous' (the Demo for Everyone) is calling for a mass demonstration on 6 October 2019 to protest against a proposed law that would extend access to certain Assisted Reproductive Technologies – such as IVF and artificial insemination, known locally as 'PMA' – to single women and to same-sex female couples. The plan is for the activists, many of whom are on loan from the ranks of the far right, to gather together for the purposes of denouncing 'la PMA sans père et la GPA', that is to say, 'medically assisted procreation without dads' ... and surrogacy. (But surrogacy, as it happens, has long been banned under French law, and – given the tenor of contemporary debates around surrogacy, including in queer and feminist circles – there is little to suggest that the proposed law would do anything to change this.)

With the French Parliament now poised to discuss the aforesaid proposal to extend 'PMA' access to previously excluded groups – 'PMA for everyone!' – there will now be plenty of occasion for reactionaries all across France to reiterate their restrictive definitions of terms such as 'family', 'filiation' and 'kinship', for them to downplay the social dimensions of these relations, and for them to brandish anew the supposed primacy of 'the natural' and 'the biological'.

This is why we so urgently need, today, the kind of exciting and inspiring perspectives that Sophie Lewis develops in Full Surrogacy Now: Feminism Against Family. *Her book combines an argument for decriminalising surrogacy with a thoroughgoing stance of solidarity with struggles waged by gestational labourers everywhere, be they mothers or not, paid or unpaid.*

In so doing, Sophie Lewis revives a form of utopianism that, regrettably, had practically disappeared from the scene of contemporary feminism. She joyfully invites us to think and live, otherwise, beyond the matrix of heteronormativity that structures how we imagine our families and our relationships with others.

The following interview with Sophie was originally conducted in French (by me, Morgane Merteuil) for the Paris-based autonomous online platform Acta, and has been translated into English by Sophie.

MORGANE MERTEUIL: *Full Surrogacy Now* **is timely; its publication has taken place at an extremely turbulent juncture for reproductive justice worldwide. Over the last few years, massive pro-choice (or pro-abortion) campaigns have arisen in Argentina, Ireland, Poland, and also in the US, where mobilisations have simultaneously served as cornerstones of the anti-Trump 'resistance.' The immense popularity of a narrative like** *The Handmaid's Tale***, which has been serialised since 2017 for television, has to be understood in this context, namely, the ascendant power of the far Right and the real threat to reproductive rights this poses. However, in the introductory chapter of** *Full Surrogacy Now***, you submit a number of additional – more critical – explanations for the series' appeal, citing the fascistic allure of the 'reproductive dystopia' as a genre. Can you explain why you do not share many feminists' intense enthusiasm for** *The Handmaid's Tale***?**

SOPHIE LEWIS: Hi, Morgane! Well, as you say, I am a utopian of sorts. But so, in a way, are *The Handmaid's Tale* crowd. Their utopianism consists of the fact that they fantasise (kind of kinkily, let's be real) about a tortured, rape-based situation so simple in its logic – and so very, very bad – that class divisions between women would just instantly fall away in the face of the bare necessity of FEMINISM. And my kink, on the other hand, is the belief that we can build a world in which no one at all ever analogises twenty-first-century cis-heteropatriarchal racial capitalism to the race-blind phallocratic-fascism scenario dreamed up by a bioconservative white-feminist sci-fi writer in the 1980s.

Let me explain what I mean. The resurgent, international struggle for access to abortion is, among other things, absolutely a class struggle. Or it should be. And it's actually because of those dynamics, I would say, that the predominantly white-feminist fandom that formed a couple of years ago around #TheHandmaidsTale has – I'm pleased to say – dwindled dramatically. Because it is a class-erasive narrative that cannot actually connect to real-world, anti-capitalist reproductive justice mobilisations. As I say, its star is on the wane, but still, its popularity irritates me. *Wired* just proclaimed that '*Handmaid's Tale* Garb' is still 'the Viral Protest Uniform of 2019'. Kamala Harris is sending fundraising emails declaring the actuality of the Tale. And something called The Handmaid Coalition™ – 'a nonprofit political action group' and 'trademark of Action Together New Hampshire' – appears to be taking donations towards robe-and-bonnet costumes that will be donned by unspecified Resisters to unspecified ends. But this all might seem innocuous enough as liberalism goes, so why do I beef, in particular, with *The Handmaid's Tale*? Surely, amid the slew of 'foetal heartbeat' bills, the fact that a personal encounter with this particular text has been the moment of feminist coming-to-consciousness for thousands of people is not to be sniffed at. Indeed, it should not, but nor should one overrate the political participation the book directly inspires. There's a reason why, as critic Rachel Symes writes, the Hulu version of the protagonist, especially in seasons two and three, 'dives back into abject degradation' every time she comes close to escaping it: 'June keeps being borne backward into captivity, because her captivity tends to be the show's narrative sweet spot.'

On its face, the identity that has coalesced around *The Handmaid's Tale* is deeply opposed to forced gestation, which it misidentifies as an exclusively totalitarian instrument of governance. Underlyingly, though, the franchise paradoxically summons up a masochistic frisson and an oddly quiescent attendant stance vis-à-vis assaults on abortion access: a stance of ecstatic, crypto-religious mortification that plays out almost as prayer, as costumed stasis, as opposed to queer revolt. Downplaying the queerphobic, racial and class dynamics of fascism, Atwood's narrative centres on what is often framed as 'universal' agony: coupled heterosexual infertility and childlessness. The separation of a mother from her daughter, on the one hand, and a human being's coerced use as a breeder, on the other. Two excellent class-wide demands could readily have been extrapolated from this, namely, the first two axioms of the Reproductive Justice movements credo: the right not to be pregnant; and the right to collectively care for children in a safe environment. It is regrettable that the progressive dress-up Handmaids have on the whole been inspired to shout mostly about the former while omitting to campaign around the latter.

The sterility apocalypse is a largely evil but seductive genre. Remember, the premise of the insurgent American fascists in this book – a premise which, bizarrely, I've not really seen anyone question – is that the infertility explosion, the collapse in birth-rates in that fictional universe, is a terrible thing. Of course, seen from a non-natalist point of view, the overriding political crisis in Gilead, as it is in the real world in 2019, is a border crisis. Sometimes misnamed a 'refugee' or 'migrant' crisis or (by white supremacists) a demographic or natality crisis, the crisis, properly viewed, is the border. But the fictional world of Gilead ultimately naturalises the necessity of the border. While it provides opportunities for Handmaids to flee, seeking asylum in Canada and so on, at root, it provides a space in which modern-day eugenic impulses – including xenophobic feminisms – can be covertly indulged according to the logic of a First World national natalist imperative.

Lastly: rather than swallow whole the idea, indulged so luridly in *The Handmaid's Tale*, that 'surrogacy' per se is the apogee of gynophobic violence, I want us to listen to the Black feminists who, at the same time as Atwood's novel was published, were pointing out that these supposedly 'new' reproductive technologies were in fact nothing new. A ghoulish, deformed kind of surrogacy, in the sense of indentured subordination and bodily instrumentalisation in the service of white supremacy, has already been embedded at the core of US life for centuries. The philosopher Shellee Colen calls this structure of slow violence 'reproductive stratification', pointing to the myriad ways racialised and migrant women have parented their own children while simultaneously nursing, suckling and mothering the children of the bourgeoisie.

Black women had already been surrogates on the chattel plantation, and are still excluded from the property-relation of private motherhood in substantial ways even today. It is, as a result, Black communities, queer refugees from the nuclear household, and other communities excluded both from mainstream familiality and from mainstream (white) feminism who have elaborated practices of polymaternalism and alter-familial abundance. As a new wave of feminists including Alexis Pauline Gumbs contend, Black mamahood is always-already, in a sense, 'queer'. So, keeping in mind the myriad models of 'othermothering' around the world (ie, forms of plural multi-gender mothering whereby kids belong to everyone) I want us to ask: can distributed maternity appear only as the effect of oppressive institutions and technologies? Can't we, as communists, instead, imagine distributed procreation as transformative and productive of differences? These are not questions that the majority of those dressing up in white bonnets and red cloaks to declare 'we are all reproductive slaves' [sic] seem interested in posing.

In chapter two, you convincingly establish the similarities and overlaps between anti-surrogacy and anti-prostitution campaigning, insofar as both epitomise 'an institutional feminist-humanitarianism that greases the wheels of imperial wars and justifies a heavy-handed 'rescue industry'. Even as you insist on the terribleness of the working conditions

people frequently experience within the gestational surrogacy industry (as in the sex industry), you condemn the real-world consequences of feminist 'wrong abolitionisms' in both these domains, and accuse the feminists in question of wanting to 'abolish the commodification without abolishing the work'. Can you elaborate on why those who would criminalise surrogacy, in order to protect women, can never accomplish their stated aims via these means?

The most obvious reasons why RadFem and liberal antisurrogacy efforts cannot achieve liberation for all women have to do with all the usual limitations of top-down humanitarian missions and femonationalisms, such as the naïve attempts in carceral anti-trafficking circles to criminalise only 'the buyer', as though this could ever fail to adversely affect the seller of labour-power. For example, several of the nation-states that formerly served as transnational baby hubs implemented bans on commercial surrogacy in 2016. But, just as the cannier commentators predicted, surrogacy bans do not halt but actually fuel the baby trade, rendering gestational workers far more vulnerable than before. As with sex work, the question of being for or against surrogacy is thus largely irrelevant. The question is, why is it assumed that one should be more against surrogacy than against other risky jobs? And how does this charitable stance impact the people actually doing the work?

However, the more fundamental cleavage between anti-surrogacy feminisms and a putative feminism that would centre surrogates themselves in the struggle for reproductive justice, stems from a profound difference of opinion on the question of abolishing the private nuclear household and the propertarian heteronormative mode of procreation it serves – the question, as Shulamith Firestone termed it in the 1970s, of 'children's liberation'. Under present conditions, defining children's liberation is necessarily a utopian project, but it was attempted in broad strokes by the Sisterhood of Black Single Mothers who stated of children that in the future, '[t]hey will not belong to the patriarchy. They will not belong to us either. They will belong only to themselves.'

In contrast, in the anti-queer, anti-revolutionary and tradi-tionalist world of anti-surrogacy militants, the very worst thing that could ever happen to a person is to be a child who becomes conscious of the fact that we belong to our parents in a contingent rather than an automatic way; a child who realises s/he is the prod-uct of a succession of active choices to care, rather than a necessity of nature. (The Italian Marxist-feminist and world-ecologist Daniela Danna, for example, suggests that a surrogate is a victim of 'false consciousness' who has 'enslaved herself ... with her own hands' by creating a baby destined for separation from its 'mother'.) As for me, I have more faith in children than that. And I take classic revolution-ary (feminist, Marxist, afrofuturist) critiques of the private nuclear household very seriously: critiques that, ironically, were sometimes formulated by the same feminists who now feel compelled to defend the 'natural' family from the threat of surrogacy.

Fifty years ago, it was commonly heard said that the liberation of women and of children are inextricable. Viewed in that light, the feminists who seek today, with all their might, to criminalise surrogacy are easily identified as just one more manifestation of 'truncated' anti-capitalism. Even though their condemnations of the workplace conditions faced by paid gestational labourers are well-founded, at the end of the day, what they are doing is carceral bioethics on the old neo-colonial model – not a class struggle with any kind of chance of winning reproductive justice for all. Hating a particular form of work in no way justifies attacks on those workers' self-organisation – quite the opposite. Instead of signing 'Stop Surrogacy Now' petitions, we would do better to listen to the demands of surrogates, placing their perspective at the forefront of our gestational justice movements.

But as ever, when it comes to the unnatural, the whorish, the freakish, the queer, and the brazenly prosthetic, all this will come down to a question of 'which side are you on?' Anti-feminist conservatives everywhere (not just of the Manif Pour Tous variety) sometimes accuse feminists of cooking up communist plots to abolish the nuclear family and, by extension, the nation-state. This, in my view, is entirely correct – or ought to be. The proper object of feminist critique, since its inception, has been and remains the institution of the family and its offshoots. Don't get me wrong: the actually existing commercial surrogacy industry – Surrogacy™ – which caters to the desire for genetic property, does anything but subvert the nuclear private family, as its conservative and frequently homophobic (and feminist) opponents fear that it will. It is just that in any struggle to actually abolish the family, it will be imperative we take the laborers on that industry's shop floor seriously as political actors – rather than naturalising the desirability of 'children of one's own' and shoring up the consumer rights of the 'infertile' (be they rich or poor, married or unmarried, gay or straight). They exist, these workers. It is worse than useless to flap your hands and declare that 'some things should not be for sale' (with the implication that other things should be for sale). The point is that, unfortunately, because we live under capitalism, they already are.

By calling for real surrogacy, or full surrogacy, I am not just trying to troll the antisurrogacy moralists. I mean a world in which the word 'surrogacy' would have no meaning anymore – because no procreative tie would be original, primary, securitised, or authenticated. I mean a maximal distribution of care labor, based on the recognition that we all share substance. In this sense, as one of my friends remarked recently, an alternative title for the book could have been *Full Family Now: Surrogacy Against Feminism*.

One of the key theoretic interventions in your book is your insistence on viewing pregnancy as alienable labour, as work. As a large number of investigative and ethnographic studies of India's infamous 'baby factories' have shown – one of them serves as the core case study for *Full Surrogacy Now* – patriarchal and racial capitalism has lately shown that it is perfectly able to integrate a superficial recognition of this labour qua labour in the pursuit of profitability and productivity. Could you speak a little about the people employed by the Akanksha clinic, in Gujarat, India, their working conditions, their demands, and the wider struggles they might conceivably catalyse?

Currently, there are no working conditions to speak of per se, because trade has been suspended. But, between 2007 and 2016, India was the international hub for discount gestational services – 'the world's back-womb' – and this particular clinic, which is located in Anand, Gujarat, became the photogenic industry figurehead. Employees were not the poorest of the poor, but they frequently chose to perform repeat gestational cycles because the pay they took home (often billed as a life-changing amount of money) was in reality only enough to support them for two to three years.

But ever since a 2016 (far-right BJP) judicial ruling – couched in the language of 'women's rights' but going against the stated wishes of the vast majority of surrogacy labourers, who did not want the industry banned – commercial and homosexual surrogacy has been outlawed in India (although I foresee this changing again in the not-too-distant future). While commercial surrogacy was operating, payment-related abuses – deception, wage-stealing, and money-skimming – were rife at the Akanksha clinic just as they are elsewhere in the industry. The findings of two local grassroots groups, Sama and the Human Rights Law Network, documented the widespread practice of scouts and touts skimming off the (usually illiterate) surrogates' fee.

Surrogacy workers employed by the Akanksha clinic collaborated with a local farm-labourers' union in order to help formulate their responses to these abuses: they should be paid as much for a baby as any surrogate working in California. And why not? The unique selling-point of the clinic, whose founder-CEO is the inimitable bioclinical 'innovator' and industry figurehead Dr Nayna Patel, is that it is a 'feminist' business. Patel has mouthed empty phrases about building a hospital 'for the surrogates, run by the surrogates' and she has promoted herself, on the *Oprah Winfrey Show* and elsewhere, as 'absolutely a feminist' – of the *Lean In* school. At the same time, she reassures consumers of surrogacy services, her clients, the 'intended parents' of the products her employees gestate, that 'these females' can be trusted because they are docile and poor: 'they can never come knocking' to make claims on 'your baby' in years to come. So, in my view, this fake ruling-class 'feminism' is full of blatant contradictions that could be turned, by the workers, against their boss and used as leverage. Anti-rape campaigners, dispossessed women, industrial unionists, and farm laborers have lately begun to step up the intensity of their struggles throughout India. In this climate, 'coming knocking' might be exactly what surrogates organise themselves to do. Leftists, meanwhile, can abet them by 'coming knocking' on the closed doors of neoliberal feminist ontologies.

Your defence of gestating as work is not an end in itself – it is not a means of integrating gestational labour into the formal capitalist economy – rather, it forms the starting-point of your anti-work orientation, in the same way that the Wages for Housework campaign demanded recognition for unwaged housework as a first step towards doing away with such work. You write that 'life is probably the ultimate commodity fetish' and account for your term 'gestational labour' by calling it 'a manoeuvre intended to counteract capital's capacity to disguise itself as progenitor'. What are the political implications of struggles seeking recognition for reproductive labours, especially in a context still shaped by extremely 'masculinist' imaginings of what constitutes productive labour?

One of the main reasons I stand for treating procreative labour as work we have already touched upon: the freedom, one that I hold extremely dear, not to work if one doesn't want to. In this historic moment, it is not just infrastructure and material access to abortion (which was already scant, especially where I currently live), but even the flimsy legal and philosophical principle of a right not to do forced gestational labour, that are under attack. I feel that, as communists and feminists we have little to lose, and that we should fight back without euphemism.

Secondly, as you have mentioned, I stand for the abolition, not only of the family, but of both work and gender, two of the things the private family is best designed to reproduce. What might struggling against work and gender (ie, racial-capitalist binary gender) look

126

like when it comes to reproductive work? For me, it means that we will have to discover ways to minimise it, distribute it, attenuate its harms to the body, share it, and render it creative, joyous and (at minimum) non-lethal. I am in no sense anti-pregnancy. I think I'm one of the most pro-pregnancy people around, because, instead of the carnage it currently is (costing 300,000 lives a year and crippling millions more) I want it to be its best self! As Silvia Federici contends, 'nothing so effectively stifles our lives as the transformation into work of the activities and relations that satisfy our desires'. It is not feminists like me who are responsible for this transformation. All we are doing is naming it.

Unfortunately, people are often very upset when they encounter language like 'gestational labour.' They ask me: when we treat pregnancy, the joy and pain of motherhood, the art of raising children, with this perspective, don't we lose something from view – something vital? My response to this is yes, of course we lose something. There is always more than one thing in play, within any kind of labour. But, as the many-gendered, white and Black, Italian and US autonomists of the struggle against housework so often repeated to their critics, it's not us choosing to be economistic about gestation, it's capitalism. If we must cop to a kind of counter-economism regarding 'what they call love,' it is a needful demystification strategy.

Unlike the Gender Equality policymakers of the UN, we aren't literally totting up a bill when we utter our stick-'em-up, claiming the wages due for centuries of babymaking 'in cash, retroactive and immediately'. We are demanding everything. That – not some pragmatic state-implemented basic income program for families – is the point of 'serving notice' to the expropriators. 'Wages for all gestation-work' is not a petition, and it does not describe an exciting destination. (Who would get that excited about wages anyway?) What it describes is a process of assault on wage society. It is a noir joke, a provocation, an insurgent orientation that is intended to expose the ludicrousness of treating work as the basis for receiving greater or smaller amounts of the means of survival. It points somewhere beyond the horizon.

Part of recognising gestational work as work, that is to say, denaturalising it, involves de-feminising it, ungendering it. This was one of the aspects of your work I personally found most exciting: the care you take to articulate a vision of feminism that might directly challenge the binarity of gender. In fact, you go so far as to state that 'there can be no utopian thought on reproduction that does not involve uncoupling gestation from the gender binary'. You then go on to flesh out your own utopian thought on the matter, imagining a queer gestational communism that might abolish the family. What are the underlying orientations, principles and slogans of the 'counter-social reproduction' you envision? And how does this utopia connect to the concept of 'a communist amniotechnics', the parting words of your book?

Yes, my book concludes with some speculative thoughts – inspired by First Nations midwives, Donna Haraway and xenofeminism – on the amniotic and cyborg politics of water, water protection, water's morbidity, internal and external pipelines, boundaries, and dialectics of 'holding and letting go'. Here I echo my contention, from the introduction, that beyond the centuries-long circular debate about whether our pregnancies are 'natural' or 'pathological,' there is a gestational commune – and I want to live in it.

For Donna Haraway, 'reproduction' does not actually occur in the human species. It's just our name for an individualist fantasy we have: the fantasy of copying and replicating ourselves. Obviously, infants do belong to the people who care for them in a sense, but they aren't property. Nor is the genetic code that goes into designing them as important as many people like to think: in fact, as biologists Richard Lewontin and Richard Levins provocatively summarise the matter, 'DNA is not self-reproducing ... it makes nothing ... and organisms are not determined by it'.

The overarching principles of *Full Surrogacy Now* are, off the top of my head, the following. All reproduction is assisted. Everyone deserves many mothers of any and all genders (or none). Authorship can only be co-authorship. #nodads. Traditional modes of procreation are in no way superior to plural, polymaternal, adoptive and/or so-called 'non-biological' arts of parenting (including 'single' parenting, and the lesbian parenting soon to be recognised in French law). Which is to say, in Helen Hester's terminology, xenofam ≥ biofam. Recognising our inextricably surrogated contamination with and by everybody else (and everybody else's babies) will not so much 'smash' the nuclear family as make it unthinkable.

In a just society, in other words, there could be no 'surrogacy,' because children would not be exclusive goods. We are the makers of one another, and we could learn to act like it. So, surrogates to the front! It is the holders – not the delusional 'authors', self-replicators, and 'patenters' – who truly people the world. By surrogates I mean all those comradely gestators, midwives, and other sundry interveners in the more slippery moments of social reproduction: bridging or creating gaps; refusing to be temporary; insisting on being temporary; swimming across borders; standing in; carrying; miscarrying. I call 'amniotechnics' the art of holding and caring even while being ripped into, at the same time as being held. Amniotechnics is protecting water and protecting people from water in the spirit of 'full surrogacy' – an impossible, necessary lodestar.

IMOGEN CASSELS

One more time with feeling

A t-shirt never did such work. The simple embarrassment
of a body, spare and haughty. Or the plain arch of a bow,
keen to dissolve to laurel or beechwood, finding a berth.
Without a jawline. I recognise the habit; the anglepoise
of the foot. Having woken by the image of a spider
fat with babies then a crow barking. A kestrel stooping
after a fieldmouse; missing; repeat. His master's voice:
if you can afford it. How many things to realise, mother,
you are dead and they don't love me. The count is out,
the-moon-the-clock is down. And every book I turn off
ends the same, with the smiling fact that you have read it,
lost in a dance-hold. The text flung back at the waist
like a Millais, freshly-dead and practiced; you the reader
holding her by the hips, crying, still as the first idiot.

R. H. LOSSIN

Neoliberalism for Polite Company: Bruno Latour's Pseudo-Materialist Coup

If neoliberalism were a Platonic Republic, Bruno Latour would likely be its philosopher-king. The insidiously anti-Marxist sociologist-cum-philosopher has, over several decades, elaborated a grand system of thought that is seductively materialist in appearance, and deeply reactionary in substance. His academic popularity is both understandable and disturbing.

In 1976 Jean Baudrillard wrote that 'Foucault's discourse is a mirror of the powers it describes. It is there that its strength and its seduction lie and not at all in its "truth index," which is only its leitmotif.' Similarly, Latour's popularity is less due to its newness or difference than to its comfortable and comforting relationship to the status quo. As Marx wrote of the work of the business theorist Andrew Ure, it is worth addressing for its 'undisguised cynicism, but also [for] the naivete with which it blurts out the stupid contradictions of the capitalist brain.'

Latour's accomplishments are numerous and varied: he has written ethnographies of scientific laboratories, was an originator of the seemingly ubiquitous Actor Network Theory (ANT), and has recently turned his attention to climate change. Beginning with *Laboratory Life*, co-authored with Steve Woolgar in 1979, Latour has written sixteen books excluding edited volumes, produced over 60 articles and book chapters, curated art shows, written plays and staged performative lectures. Beginning his career in the sociology of science, he has since come to prominence across countless intellectual disciplines. In 2007 he outranked Marx and Heidegger in the *Times Higher Education* list of most cited works in the humanities. His article 'Why Has Critique Run Out of Steam?' has been referenced 1,290 times and *We Have Never Been Modern* 1,790 times since 2013. He was awarded the Holberg Prize in the humanities for his 'reinterpretation of modernity'. The *New York Times* recently borrowed his term 'purification' to lament the specialisation of philosophy. Historians might refer to archival research as 'following their subjects in action', a more than slightly ridiculous claim about people dead for 300 years, but an indication of how thoroughly Latour and his language have saturated the social sciences.

ANT – a methodological approach to social sciences positing that nothing in the social and natural world exists outside of constantly shifting relationships within a network – has become so widely employed it might reasonably be considered separately from Latour himself. The suggestion that inanimate objects, machines, scientific instruments, etcetera, are in some sense causative is not wholly without merit. Indeed, in their most general formulations several of Latour's ideas are compelling: the dismissal of the nature/culture split, a critique of traditional sociological categories and a serious consideration of what technology *does* rather than what we do with it. Unfortunately, so glossed this is to ignore – and thus reproduce – a philosophy and methodology that recapitulates a reification of capitalist social reality. By considering all aspects of social and political life a bemusing, almost enchanted collection of things, Latour's theories are textbook *Verdinglichung*: literally, 'making into a thing'. This is the *thingification* of social relations.

Latour's astounding popularity is due less to his usefulness and originality than to a combination of complacency and desire on the part of intellectuals under neoliberalism. Pitting himself against the 'generals of critique' and their 'neutron bombs of deconstruction', as well as against science, sociologists of all stripes and truth itself, Latour has captured the imagination of intellectual producers whose labour has repeatedly failed to affect sought-after social change. But behind his extravagant experiments in style and repeated claims of originality are the familiar habits of thought produced and reinforced by neoliberal social organisation. The work reiterates aspects of neoliberal ideology – flatness, contingency, distrust of authority – and borrows from this 'ideology of no ideology' an ability to accommodate intolerable contradictions in thought. Within the academy, the depoliticised materialism of the actor-network approach has added appeal as an alternative to the problematic spectre of Marx. The vulgar materialism of ANT satisfies a desire to operate in the realm of the real – to 'ascend from earth to heaven' rather than 'descend from heaven to earth', as Marx put it. But ANT is a rabidly anti-Marxist theory that participates in the obfuscation of class essential to neoliberal ideology by providing an alternative, empty materialism entirely detached from any theory of production or social relations. And the employment of the network as metaphor functions to legitimise and even celebrate a set of quotidian activities, and a way of being in the world that produces vague but persistent misgivings about our current social relations at the most intimate scale. This all amounts to a philosophy that both reinforces some of the worst characteristics of recent social and political life and offers a soothing intellectual placebo.

Latour claims that ANT is a 'powerful way of rephrasing basic issues of social theory, epistemology, and philosophy'. When deployed, it will 'make what is invisible visible.' This is meant to be tongue-in-cheek, but I think we should treat Latour as he purports to treat his actors, and allow his own 'vocabulary ... to be heard loud and clear'. Taken literally, Latour is claiming to be either magician or microscope. Indeed, his project is one of elaborate showmanship and misdirection, shored up by the presence of technological instruments. It is the philosophical enactment of a spectacular society, hiding the same elitist idealism that works overtime to make capitalism seem natural and inevitable – a seamless, non-heirarchical collection of surface effects that, appearing as reality, provides a convenient index of hard truths and accurate descriptions.

From Science to Society

Latour began his career studying science. He was concerned with how scientific facts became facts, a process he refers to as 'black boxing.' When you open a 'black box' and trace the development of a scientific discovery, you discover such a complex web of scientists, technicians, technology, authority, authorisation, and so on, that it becomes impossible to maintain a dichotomy neatly separating scientists from their objects of study. Furthermore, he discovered that these so-called natural objects of study are so thoroughly mediated by scientists (themselves black boxes of knowledge, instruments, authorisation, etcetera), and scientific instruments (black boxes in turn containing scientists, authority, etcetera) that they are by no means natural. For example, to examine bacteria through a microscope with the accumulated knowledge of scientific training changes the bacteria into something other than a natural object. What you look at is simply not there without the instrument for looking – and to the extent that it remains there, strictly empirically, then it is as something else. So there is no nature, pure and simple, upon which the scientific gaze is cast. Culture cannot work on nature, so to speak, because the nature upon which it is working is always-already cultural. It is therefore incumbent on the theorist to begin at the beginning – to jettison not only the distinction between science and the social but the very categories themselves. The co-constitutive nature of such dichotomies is certainly worth consideration, but what Latour suggests is that abandoning an additive formula allows us to begin an inquiry in advance of accomplished discoveries. As he puts it in 1987's *Science in Action*:

> We will not try to analyze the final products, a computer, a nuclear plant, a cosmological theory ... instead

> we will follow scientists and engineers at the times
> and at the places where they plan a nuclear plant, undo
> a cosmological theory... We go from final products to
> production... Instead of black boxing the technical as-
> pects of science and then looking for social influences
> and biases, we [realise]... how much simpler it [is] to
> be there before the box closes and becomes black.

The Latourian imperative to open the black box rather than accepting it as a stable and reliable point of departure recalls Marx's assertion that 'reflection on the forms of human life, hence also scientific analysis of those forms, takes a course directly opposite to their real development. Reflection begins *post festum*, and therefore with the results of the process of development ready to hand.' Indeed, black boxes do not appear so different from Marx's commodities, but for their content; here, the 'dead labor' contained in commodities is transformed into neutral inputs and outputs, and class disappears to reveal an unending web of technical entanglements.

We Have Never Been Subjects

One of the ANTs central propositions is the equality, or 'symmetry', of human and non-human 'actants'. Related to this proposition is that of the misleading nature of spokespersons – humans who obscure what the non-human actants have to say. But certain factors guiding Latour's distribution of agency are unnervingly clear in his examples. Take his comparison, in *Science in Action*, of an imaginary shop steward named 'Bill', who speaks for workers, to a scientist – the very real Raymond Davis – who speaks for neutrinos.

> It is very important ... not to impose any clear distinc-
> tion between 'things' and 'people' in advance. Bill, for
> instance, represents people who could talk, but who,
> in fact, cannot talk all at once. Davis represents neu-
> trinos that cannot talk, in principle, but who are made

to write, scribble and sign thanks to the device set up
by Davis. So in practice, there is not much difference
between people and things: they both need someone
to talk for them. There is thus no distinction to be made
between representing people and representing things.
In each case the spokesperson literally does the talking
for who or what cannot talk.

What is important in this scenario is not the workers or neutrinos
but the assemblage of workers and plate-glass, not what the shop-
steward says but that he says it on the other side of a sound barrier.
The relationship between union representatives and the rank and
file should not be taken for granted, but nor should Latour's ques-
tioning of authority by placing those not speaking for themselves in
the same category as plate glass, or the assumption that the mediation and translation of the desires humans – who can in fact speak
– is in any way similar to the mechanical legibility of neutrinos.

For Latour, a mistake of the 'anti-fetishists' – Marxists, post-
structuralists, anyone engaged in a project of discovering meaning
within or beyond the surface of an object – is this assumption that
'it is us the human makers ... that you see in those machines, those
implements, us under another guise, our own hard work'. In truth,
the argument goes, those machines and implements also make us.
In this instance, seeing sentient, desiring workers in the speech of
the shop steward or 'hard work' in the objects produced by humans
is to misapprehend the distribution of agency and, ultimately,
misunderstand reality. Of course the design of a factory does structure the negotiations that occur therein. But this is not the same
as saying, as Latour does, that an 'asymmetry' of the human-object
relations constitutes a sort of primal misapprehension.

Imaginary Constitutions and Suffocating Birds
It was in the laboratory that Latour launched his campaign to
rescue non-humans from the tyranny of their human counter-

parts and developed ANT. It was in the service of understanding the construction of scientific facts that he introduced the 'actant', a term applicable to animate and inanimate objects, intentional and non-intentional beings alike, in order to underscore the lack of individual human agency. Thus he developed a set of terms for describing human and non-human relations, ridding them of any political contamination. But like an out-of-control experiment in science fiction, ANT escaped from the laboratory and grew into a monstrous theoretical framework for understanding *everything*.

In 1991 Latour leapt from science studies to cultural studies more broadly with *We Have Never Been Modern*, offering an imagined origin of the problematic nature/culture dichotomy – which he locates in the debate between Robert Boyle and Thomas Hobbes – and an argument for a 'symmetrical anthropology' that would not indulge the modernist predilection for dividing the world into categories. He has revisited this project in *An Inquiry into Modes of Existence: An Anthropology of the Moderns*, a nearly five hundred-page semantic *tour de force* without a single footnote and starring a fake female ethnographer who is studying 'the moderns' as they engage in hypothetical activities.

Such anthropology requires us to approach ourselves as we would a foreign culture. Basic categories of thought, like the difference between humans and non-humans, cannot be taken for granted. But while we cannot indulge culturally proscribed abstractions, we *can*, if we follow his example, use the relativist methodology of Latourian science studies to unravel our misguided modern notions of how the world works. We can also, it seems, employ the overly capacious category of 'the moderns' without interrogating what it includes or has been defined against. And we are invited to take the metaphor of a network entirely for granted.

We Have Never Been Modern reiterates many arguments from Latour's earlier work, deploying the same rhetorical style that places shop stewards on a level with microscopes:

> Contextualists start from the principle that a social
> macro-context exists – England, the dynastic quarrel,

Capitalism, Revolution, Merchants, the Church – and that this context in some way influences, forms, reflects, has repercussions for, and exercises pressure on 'ideas about' matter, the air's spring, vacuums, and Torricelli tubes. But they never explain the prior establishment of a link connecting God, the King, Parliament, and some bird suffocating in the transparent closed chamber of a pump whose air is being removed by means of a crank operated by a technician. How can the bird's experience translate, displace, transport, distort all the other controversies, in such a way that those who master the pump also master the King, God, and the entire context?

Let us imagine that 'the contextualists' have, in fact, never tried to explain the relationship between religion, science and the state. Latour is attempting to do two things here: illustrate the complexity of the relations that go into forming ideas and institutions that we often take as given, and do away with inherited hierarchies that would place God or the King or Science above or behind the bird suffocating in the vacuum chamber. That what has become known as 'Science' was built by tinkerers performing cruel, visually effective demonstrations is a fair point to make but Latour's aims are not so modest as such a run-of-the-mill argument. He wants to show that nature and society are categories we employ in order to simplify this complex mélange of actually separable, microcosmic events, objects and institutions. That even when it appears we are establishing or unpacking a relationship between nature and society, we are still dependent on this primary and absolute distinction.

It is from what Latour refers to as the 'purification' of nature and society that all of our critical mistakes issue. For him, the modern 'constitution' established by Boyle (science) and Hobbes (society) enables all sorts of trickery allowing us 'moderns' to play critical god through a suspect reasoning that uses these categories to account for everything: 'They have not made Nature; they make Society; they make Nature; they have not made Society; they have not made either; God has made everything; God has made nothing, they have made everything.' The illusion of pure Nature and pure Society obscures 'the work of mediation that assembles hybrids invisible, unthinkable, unrepresentable.' And it is 'hybrids' with which we should be concerned, for everything in existence is an assembled hybrid of sorts and to say that it is social or natural is to misrecognise its very nature.

But moderns will not think in terms of hybrids and mediation (do they think in terms of a Hobbesian state of nature?): thus Latour must vanquish them. First they turned 'to nature in order to destroy human prejudices', then they moved 'in the other direction, turning to the newly founded social sciences in order to destroy the excesses of naturalization'. Thus 'sorting out the kernels of science from the chaff of ideology became the task for generations of well-meaning modernizers'.

It is 'the moderns' that give Latour away. His employment of this incoherent category exposes a fundamental inconsistency in his own theory of theory-making, and illustrates the degeneration into self-referential nonsense that inevitably results from argumentation that, in paranoid fashion, seeks to avoid the great sin of representation. It is all good and well to imagine a world in which all people and things are allowed to 'speak for themselves', but in unequal societies, avoiding 'representation' is a luxury reserved for those who are represented everywhere. How this fantasy of unmediated, transparent, and equal speech differs from a boilerplate theory of democracy or the public sphere is unclear. Also unclear is whether, even if it were possible, speaking for yourself and only yourself – never being spoken for – is even desirable. But the avoidance of representation is an extremely important extension of Latour's allegedly anti-modern position, as well as the moral justification of the employment of ANT.

In *Reassembling the Social*, Latour will insist that he prefers to use a language that 'remains strictly meaningless' in order to allow 'the vocabulary of the actors to remain loud and clear.' But while the category of 'the moderns' is incoherent, it is also freighted with meaning. The moderns, like modernity, don't need Latour's help to ignore the ways that class, race, and gender, for example, result in coercion and exclusion; but he does a good job showing how highly individualistic, scientifically oriented microcosmic thinking precludes categories crucial to emancipatory politics, and without which women, the poor, non-heterosexuals, and members of marginalised races cannot break into the symbolic and political realm of representation – cannot, in other words, speak for themselves in a meaningful way. If we start with the modern what we get is the modern. And even if you add to the modern the 'real' meaning of the bird in the vacuum pump, you still come away with a privileged and regressive scientism and the 'rational' white male gaze that comes with it. Latour wants everyone to ignore the forest for the trees because he is the forest. Even if we have never been modern, Latour certainly is.

From Macro-Micro to Micro-Micro

The other crucial way in which Latour imports an unexamined and hazy modernity into his critique of the moderns is through a dependence on technological paradigms. There is, despite his insistence to the contrary, only one direction that Latourian analysis can go: unsurprisingly, it follows the same trajectory as the historical development of the scientific instruments that have allowed us to see ever tinier components of things.

Of course Latour insists that doing away with context does not lead one into dead-end particularities. He claims that ANT provides a solution to the sociological problem of scale – the relationship of the macro, structures such as 'the social', to the micro, individual entities and events such as a teacher or lecture. In *Reassembling the Social*, he claims that approaching the social world through ANT would mean that the

> macro no longer describes a *wider* or *larger* site in
> which the micro would be embedded like some Russian
> Matryoshka doll, but another equally local, equally

micro place which is *connected* to many others through some medium transporting specific types of traces. No place can be said to be bigger than any other place, but some can be said to benefit from far safer connections to many *more* places than others. This move has the beneficial effect to keep the landscape flat, since what earlier, in the pre-relativist sociology, was situated 'above' or 'below' remains side by side and firmly on the same plane as the other loci which they were trying to overlook or include.

If there is a school of sociology that could best be described by the metaphor of the Matryoshka doll – a coherent envelope that can be opened to reveal increasingly smaller, identical replicas of itself – I am not aware of it. But more important than the straw soldiers Latour constructs for himself is his assertion that the macro is itself micro: he is attempting to show that he is concerned with something more than the microscopic relations between neutrinos and electron microscopes, that ANT can account for all of the things that the sociology of the social has attempted and failed to explain.

Latour claims ANT is not doing away with the macro, simply redescribing it, lest we all become trapped inside Russian dolls. The macro is allegedly accounted for, but it is 'neither "above" nor "below" the interactions' described by the micro. Rather, it is '*added* to them as another of their *connections*'. The power of what appears to be macro is actually a matter of what he calls 'concentration', a stronger assemblage on the flat plane of the network facilitated by safer connections. Importantly, these would coalesce in complex ways not predetermined by reductive mechanics of, say, class.

The intuitive thinking here is that because they were not *determined*, strictly, by something like class, nor can they be *explained* by reference to class. When considering power, the concept of concentration, as opposed to that of a predetermined and stable structure, is indeed compelling. However, Latour's micromacro *sans* hyphen is actually always micro, and cannot in fact do any of the explanatory work of the pre-relativist macro. Even when claiming that 'no interaction is what could be called isotopic', Latour simply lists ever more isotopic components. If we want to evaluate a classroom lecture, say, we would include 'the forest out of which the desk is coming, the management office in charge of classroom planning, the workshop that printed the schedule that has helped us find the room, the janitor that tends the place and so on'. It is worth posing an obvious rhetorical question: is it really ridiculous to claim that, in assessing a lecture, the teacher and student are of greater import? In folding the macro back into the micro, Latour has evacuated meaning from either perspective. This may be his intention, but what he offers as replacement – neverending associative thought leading from teachers to trees to janitors – is worthless if we want to know anything about teacher, tree or janitor. Indeed, all we can do is fit ever more inside of this Matryoshka doll of a lecture hall.

Even if we take this flat world of connections seriously, we are still left with questions of causes. Why are certain connections safer? What forces make certain loci attractive? How does money, for example, accumulate in certain bank accounts and not others? Could this have something to do with capitalism? Latour's answer is yes but not really. Because capitalism, like any other 'macro', is actually 'micro', and should be evaluated as such.

> Capitalism ... may be an intractable entity endowed with a 'spirit' but a Wall Street trading room does connect to the 'whole world' through the tiny but expeditious conduits of millions of bits of information per second ... Once these conduits are taken into account, we now have a choice between two routes: we can still believe that capitalism acts surreptitiously as the 'infrastructure' of all the world's transactions and, if so, we have to jump from the local assessment of a specific company's worth to its 'context'... flying into stratospheric considerations instead of walking on foot. Or we can continue doing the footwork and study places such as the Wall Street trading room ... just to see where this decision will lead us.

Latour wants us to think that this descriptive approach to capitalism – one that fetishises the actions of individual traders and bits of information – endows us with more 'leeway for action' than class analysis. 'Capitalism', he writes, 'has no plausible enemy since it is "everywhere", but a given trading room in Wall Street' has many vulnerabilities. 'A computer breakdown, a sneaky movement by a competitor ... a neglected variable in a pricing formula, a risky accounting procedure' may shift 'the balance from obscene profit to a dramatic loss'. This might give us some understanding of how capital moves, but it offers no more leeway for action, positing as it does that capitalism – like everything in the Latourian universe – is a series of accidents. Further, this understanding of capitalism is of no use to anyone except capitalists (and perhaps saboteurs). Focusing on microcosmic features of capital flow will only allow for conclusions at the same scale: an individual profit or loss (no matter how dramatic), a misdirected bit of information, a distracted trader, a number in an algorithm. Many things might be revealed to financial analysts by ANT, but the material effects of these flows and interruptions happen on a massive scale and affect large parts of the population, while barely affecting the select few who perpetrate such 'accidents'.

Ask one of the many victims of sub-prime mortgages if capitalism is a fascinating assemblage of bits and bytes and stock traders and news feeds. What will they tell you? Will you listen? How 'loud and clear' does their language need to be? And how exactly is this language to be amplified and clarified without a technical understanding of trading floors?

Furthermore, infrastructure and context are not synonymous, and capitalism is not an infrastructure: it is a class system that distributes the profits and losses described by Latour in predictably uneven ways. If we want to be Latourian about it, capitalism is an assemblage of infrastructures, human, and non-human actants that act in concert – to concentrate wealth in a tiny percentage of the population. Latour might concede that power and capital agglomerates in certain nodes. But the relationship between the human actants cannot be broached. How the non-human actant land, say, confers privilege on the human actant land-owner over time is not a question a Latourian analysis can accommodate. And even if you were to look at the wealth-accumulating 'hybrid' enfranchised-white-man-land, you would not be able to explain anything about it without a theory of class, politics, labour, and so on. You simply cannot talk about capitalism without talking about class, and Latour cannot talk about class because a world structured by economic class is anything but flat.

Neoliberalism for Polite Company

ANT's rejection of all evaluative and social categories, the flatness and flexibility of the network as a model, the impossibly contingent and mutable nature of the 'assemblage', the ontological equivalence of human and non-human 'actants', and the replacement of the social with 'associations' offer little more than a glorified description of neoliberalism. As the reigning economic policy in the United States since the 1970s neoliberalism has reshaped not only the market but also commonsense ideas about the relationship of the individual to society. It has normalised economic precarity and produced a subject that conceives of itself as 'human capital', easily visualised as a node where value may or may not accumulate depending on the strength of associations – human capital's ability to 'network'. ANT is simply a complicated, expanded iteration of neoliberal ideology where everyone is a monad in an unpredictable, contingent, constantly changing world. It is the perfect philosophy for a system in which people, in exchange for the privilege of self-expression, sacrifice solidarity, social security, or political agency.

If Latour saw his project as strictly descriptive it would still be problematic – describing how things 'really are' has never been neutral – but he does not. He insists, rather, on its political importance, presenting ANT as critical and subversive. In the essay 'On Technical Mediation – Philosophy, Sociology, Genealogy', Latour claims that it is not through coherent social categories around which a 'we' might form, but through a myriad of 'detours' through the network that 'finally, the political order is subverted, since I rely on many delegated actions that themselves make me do things on behalf of others who are no longer here and that I have not elected and the course of whose existence I cannot even trace.' Again, the resonance with Marx is remarkable, recalling the assertion that 'men make their own history but they do not make it as they please'. But ANT is a politics of the accident rather than organised action, the individual rather than the group, contingency rather than reason. Where Marx's line in the *Eighteenth Brumaire* was a point of departure for reflection on a revolutionary failure, Latour suggests that *this is how change happens* – spontaneously, inexplicably.

By abjuring evaluative categories, ANT relinquishes any ability to address political and economic realities, and like the neoliberal medium of its cultivation, it does so deliberately, in the name of realism. It takes these weaknesses, in the words of Kirsch and Mitchell, 'as its main strength: it has no way of distinguishing among "things" – things of different powers, and things of different ontological properties – save only as an effect ... [and it] sets up its own, seemingly unbridgeable binary: either a person is an autonomous subject or a person is the "effect" of networks'. Here is the same tension that exists in neoliberal common sense: on the one hand the autonomous, rational individual that this brand of freedom is intended to produce; on the other, social casualties figured as accidental effects of the system.

Latour claims that 'it is possible to trace more sturdy relations and discover more revealing patterns by finding a way to register the links between unstable and shifting frames of reference rather than by trying to keep one frame stable'. ANT claims to have no social vision whatsoever, and it is on the basis of this rejection of context and social investment that it sets itself up as a solution to the intellectual problems of the past few decades. But there is no more coherent social vision than a claim on *reality* – as disaggregated and mutable as this reality may be. Mere description it may be, but description is in no sense prior to or detachable from its normative operations, and ANT conceals an agenda that is not only uncritical but deeply politically conservative.

In fact to suggest that it 'conceals' this agenda might give Latour too much credit. Despite its apparent complexity – or incoherence disguised as such – ANT's politics are obvious. In Latour's tasteless jokes and ironic provocations ('I know I should have added "Her" for affirmative action reasons' ('Sociology of a Door Closer')), his snarky disdain for intellectuals and heavy-handed defence of the 'little guy', his dedication to 'the most general, the most banal, even the most vulgar' vocabulary, (ANT 'prefers to use [language that] remains strictly meaningless ... [As] a better way for the vocabulary of the actors to be heard') is more than a trace of the false populism and anti-intellectualism of right-wing, neoliberal, rhetoric. As Philip Mirowski notes, Freidrich von Hayek 'placed ignorance at the very center of his political theory'. Hayek's suggestion that 'the case for individual freedom rests chiefly on the recognition of the inevitable ignorance of all', resonates well with Latour's repeated assertion that the informant's liberation is a function of meaninglessness.

In the spirit of the Mont Pellerin Society, Latour rejects any reference to a social context as misleading and elitist. He claims instead in *Reassembling the Social* that this new approach to sociology, reliant on tracing 'associations' and 'assemblages'

> that there is nothing specific to social order; that there is no social dimension of any sort, no 'social context', no distinct domain of reality to which the label 'social' or 'society' could be attributed; that no 'social force' is available to 'explain' the residual features that other domains cannot account for; that members know very well what they are doing even if they don't articulate to the satisfaction of the observers; that actors are never embedded in a social context and so are always much more than 'mere informants; that there is thus no meaning in adding some 'social factors' to other scientific specialties.

While there is certainly reason to question a notion of 'the Social', that stands as a regulative and stable entity above or behind individual actions and interactions, we should be deeply suspicious of a philosophy constructed around such a strong rejection of social *context* at a political moment when the social is being attacked in very concrete ways. Political moves that chiefly benefit a ruling class – no fantasy of a few Marxist academics – such as the privatisation of crucial public services, and a generalised antipathy to state institutions of any kind, is promoted through an appeal to 'average' citizens, with language relying heavily on anti-intellectualism cynically presented as anti-elitism, resonating clearly with Latour's defense of 'mere informants' against the elitism of the sociologists.

Latour's defense of 'the mere informant' is a central theme in ANT. A potentially noble cause, for Latour this seems to be inspired by pretty basic anti-intellectualism *and* elitism. Here is Latour's description of the potential effect of the critical sociology he attacks:

> you have become so estranged from your parents by a university degree that you have become ashamed of how dumb they are. Reading critical sociologists, you realize that this is the common experience of a whole generation of 'upwardly mobile' young kids from 'lower class families lacking 'cultural capital'. And this is when you begin to wonder who has estranged you from your very kin, who has molded your voice, your manners, your face so differently from theirs?

Latour provocatively suggests that ANT 'could use as its slogan what Mrs. Thatcher famously exclaimed (but for very different reasons!): "There is no such thing as society"'. But how different are those reasons? Latour would not state that 'there is only the family', because in the ANT universe this is yet another configuration that only appears to have meaning because powerful pre-ANT sociologists put it in a textbook. But why choose, as a point of departure for a critique of sociology, a hypothetical example of a poor kid getting an education, getting uppity – and hating his family? This may be a sly reference to Pierre Bourdieu, but disparaging an intellectual opponent for their upward mobility hardly makes it more palatable.

This contrarian posture is a typical Latourian move, intended to separate his philosophy and himself from the rest of the academy. But the rhetorical assemblage Latour-the-rebel repeatedly betrays a complete lack of empathy towards the regular people he is so bent on protecting. The assumption that education makes one ashamed of poverty is a disgusting upper-class myth that justifies keeping people in their proper place for their own good, and, in Latour's example at least, implies that this good is the integrity of the family unit.

Despite his apparent disdain for the sociologists,, Latour returns obsessively to their supposed silencing of human and non-human actants: 'For [critical sociologists] actors do not see the whole picture but remain only "informants". This is why they have to be taught what is the context in which they are situated ... while the social scientist, floating above, sees the whole thing'. There is hardly anything objectionable in listening to the experience of individuals outside of academia. How the language of these informants is expected to become meaningful without recourse to social organising – necessarily dependent on some level of abstraction – remains a mystery. And, crucially, the assumption that 'mere informants' might not arrive at these categories themselves is simply insulting.

In a Latourian world the experience of an informant is not in fact validated so much as spatially and temporally contracted, and thereby limited to the particular circumstances they are reporting. Contrary to ANT's claim to liberate informants, in the denial of social categories the informant's speech is only meaningful within the context of the sociological exchange. A situation where 'every choice of a departure point will lead to the drawing of a completely different animal, fully incommensurable with the others', is an intellectual cul de sac – not to mention a precise definition of estrangement. Not only do actants have meaning in particular, finite, non-repeatable configurations, this is the *only* meaning they can possibly have. And it is fleeting – whatever connections are drawn will presently shift and need to be retraced. Retraced by whom? The ANT sociologist, of course.

If there are no social forces, no lasting social groups, no power or emancipatory framework, then there is nothing outside of this exchange to which either the informant or the sociologist can attach their conclusions. There is simply the association described by the informant and studiously and accurately recorded by the student of ANT. Underlying Latour's profession of radical democracy is a structural re-installation of the sociologist as unique interpreter and, if not an authority in the traditional sense, the sole interlocutor, and thus the sole means of creating meaning. This is just a new version of the old French trick of disappearing authors. Tyrannical sociologists indeed.

☭

Networks Are Not Just Metaphors

Given the facts of networked communication, Latour's assertion that 'we are no longer sure about what "we" means; we seem to be bound by ties that don't look like regular social ties', may be accurate. But to accept a state of affairs in which 'we have to [constantly] reshuffle our conceptions of what was associated together because the previous definition has been made somewhat irrelevant', is not intellectually productive but dangerous.

That ANT, a philosophy that 'has tried to render the social world as flat as possible', has gained popularity in the age of Facebook, Thomas Friedman and increasing income inequality is no accident. The metaphorical network has gained popularity in direct proportion to the availability and daily use of networked technology. ANT might run contrary to entrenched academic traditions, but it is consonant with the general cultural sensibility of the past few decades. And as Latour's vocabulary of inputs and plug-ins and isotopes indicates, there is more than a tenuous connection between his philosophy and a more generalised technofetishism.

Latour's logic – a conviction that 'in a minute I may mobilize forces locked in motion hundreds or millions of years ago. The relative shapes of actants and their ontological status may be completely reshuffled ... we hourly encounter hundreds, even thousands, of absent makers who are remote in time and space yet simultaneously active and present' – sounds a lot like an advertisement for an internet provider. This type of thinking is not so much a revolutionary insight as an erudite reiteration of a banal cultural obsession with technological connectedness in the face of destabilising economic precarity and dissolving social safety nets.

Jodi Dean has coined the term 'communicative capitalism' to describe this shaky, twittering, post-industrial landscape. In *Blog Theory*, she argues that 'just as industrial capitalism relied on the exploitation of labor, so does communicative capitalism rely on the exploitation of communication.' The network is central to how this form of communication is both imagined and deployed, and for Dean the result is 'the repeated suspension of narratives, patterns, identities, norms, etc'. In other words, the suspension of categories that might foster solidarity. Within the network there is no longer the possibility of breaking 'out of a set of given expectations because such sets no longer persist as coherent enchainments of meaning.'

Dean's observations about language and argumentation within the circuits of communicative capitalism might also indicate one way the figure of the network insulates Latour from criticism. Within the network, language, she writes, agglomerates into 'word-clouds, frequency and proximity displace meaning … [O]ne can't argue with a word cloud. It doesn't take a position. It marks a moment. It registers aspects of the intensity of that moment … but one doesn't know why or whether it's called for or what it's in relation to … It offers representation without understanding: issues are out there'.

High-Heeled-Shoe-Woman and Other Latourian Fantasies
One of Latour's more lucid observations is that the individual person is an assemblage of things, institutions and other people. But even this potentially useful insight of ANT degenerates into absurdity because of Latour's dogmatic rejection of all things evaluative, and his conviction that we must think 'symmetrically' about human

and non-human actants. With the example of a gunman, Latour in 'On Technical Mediation' engages with the 'guns kill people' versus 'people kill people' argument to show how misguided it is to think in terms of person/object dichotomies. Gun-control advocates are 'materialists' insofar as they argue that 'the gun acts by virtue of material components irreducible to the social qualities of the gunman'. At the other end of the debate is the NRA which offers 'a sociological version more often associated with the Left: for the NRA, the gun does nothing in itself or by virtue of its material components'. Both positions, he points out, are 'absurdly contra-dictory. No materialist claims that guns kill by themselves', and the NRA 'cannot maintain that the gun is so neutral an object that it has no part in the act of killing.' Instead we should attempt to think the 'citizen-gun' or a 'gun-citizen', a hybrid being or 'composite agent' that is neither gun nor citizen but both. The gun has affor-dances, the person intentions, the two are subject to any number of detours, and this hybrid either kills someone or not depending on a number of possible factors specific to that particular configuration.

There are of course many important questions to ask about the 'citizen-gun': is the citizen-gun a citizen? Does the citizen-gun have a criminal record? Is the citizen-gun poor or rich? Did the citizen-gun grow up around gun violence? Is the citizen-gun a man or a woman? Is the citizen-gun mentally stable? Receiving proper psychiatric care? Recently unemployed? All such factors might fall into the Latourian categories of 'interruption' or 'detour', in the equation that results either in the killing or not-killing of another human. They are also questions that connect to social prob-lems that cannot not be productively answered on a case-by-case basis without reference to structural problems. But Latour can't allow for structural explanations, so he presents instead a series of hypothetical factors. 'If the agent is human, is angry, wants to take revenge, and if the accomplishment of the agent's goal is inter-rupted, for whatever reason ... then the agent makes a detour, a deviation: as we have already seen, one cannot speak of techniques without speaking of *daedalia*'. The 'reassembly' of a fully rational, decision-making, essentially liberal subject in these lines is striking. It should also be noted that for all of his assiduous avoidance of social categories, Latour apparently feels entirely comfortable with psychological or emotional ones. Don't we need to know what the revenge is for? What citizen-gun is angry *about*? How is anger assembled? How is it defined?

Such recourse to internal states speaks to a particular conception of the assemblage 'human' that privileges individual intentions over socio-economic circumstances. Again, ANT's supposed challenge turns out to be a verbose recapitulation of neoliberal mythology. While it is absolutely crucial to recognise that material objects and access to them act on human bodies and shape their experiences, it is also crucial to recognise that this materiality is socially distributed by political, market and other logics that are, while not deterministic, both traceable and significant. And that these distributions structure internal states and emotional responses.

Consider another possible example of a Latourian hybrid: high-heeled-shoe-woman. Women have health problems specifically related to wearing the non-human actant commonly referred to as high-heeled shoes. Of course, there is no absolute social rule that only women can wear high-heeled shoes, but it would be absurd to claim that heterosexual men are just as likely to suffer injuries related to the wearing thereof. Consider the following hypothetical situation: the hybrid high-heeled-shoe-woman is scared and wants to run away. If the actant's ankle gets twisted, then the actant cannot run as fast and makes a detour, a deviation, or simply limps along in terror. As we have seen, one cannot speak of techniques without speaking of *daedalia*, or the unlimited detours that are added to these hybrids to produce an outcome.

Gender might be constructed – it may even be a perfect example of assemblage – but to allow that something is constructed is very different from claiming that it is not generalisable and only has meaning in its particular construction. Women are far less likely to shoot people than are men. Americans are far more likely to shoot people than are Canadians. Guns don't kill people, people in general don't kill people, American men kill people. And men kill women – frequently. Which raises the question of whether 'anger' or a 'desire for revenge' is an ontologically stable state rather than itself a black box.

Elliot Roger, the 22-year-old man who went on a killing spree in Santa Barbara in the spring of 2014, was angry and seeking revenge. Mark Lepine, the 25-year-old who opened fire in a classroom at L'Ecole Polytechnique in Montreal in 1989, was also angry and seeking revenge. In 2003, according to the Center for Disease Control, 1,300 deaths occurred as a result of intimate partner violence. We can assume that *these* citizen-guns, citizen-knives, citizen-arsonists and citizen-fists, who are overwhelmingly male, are also angry and possibly seeking revenge – and that high-heeled-shoe-woman is at a particular disadvantage for being a node where power failed to accumulate.

If we want to understand why a particular person shot another particular person with a particular gun then ANT might be just adequate. But if we want to understand the phenomenon of gun violence *as a means of mitigating or ending it*, then social categories, such as 'male' or 'American', must be taken into account. These categories are surely composed of complex networks of people, places, objects and institutions, but they are also much more than the sum of their parts. It is the particular failure of ANT as a sociological approach that, for it, everything is always merely that sum.

We Will Always be Liberals

The constitution of personhood within a Latourian framework is a reversion to categories that the dreaded intellectuals were right to deconstruct. Regardless of the initial gesture of hybridisation – which, superficially, appears to undermine traditional notions of liberal personhood by positing a consciousness connected to, expressed through and in part composed of non-human objects – such hypothetical situations in which a human agent does something for whatever reason lead us right back to the notion of a rational individual with fixed attributes existing in general, prior to and outside of social relations. A very particular subject emerges from this formulation: one that is vulnerable to material contingency but always negotiates that contingency as a conscious, rational individual with no social history to interfere with that decision-making process.

Latour's use of the Daedalus myth as an intellectual template in 'On Technical Mediation' is telling: 'Daedalus folds, weaves, plots, contrives, finds solutions where none is visible, using any expedient at hand in the cracks and gaps of ordinary routines, swapping properties among inert and animal and human materials'. In rescuing 'mere informants' from 'the sociologists' Latour has not undermined or even symbolically threatened political power. Rather, he has constructed a philosophy of the social in line with the Thatcherite claim that 'there is no such thing', at the center of which is a 'rational', atomistic individual who makes decisions for 'whatever reason', thus absolving the state and society from any collective responsibility. In Latour's asociological vision of the world, individuals negotiate detours and assemblages in radically particular ways, and it is the very particularity of such movements within a flat network that implies not just equality between people and objects, but between all human actants – who seem to have, in these scenarios, no accumulated past contributing to these decision-making processes, let alone a position in society that might limit them.

There is a sense in which Latour's oeuvre is unclassifiable. Part of his self-positioning as an outsider occurs at the level of style. Many of his books can be described as experimental or genre-bending: a subway system speaks, cartoon frames interrupt text, interlocutors are invented, academic exchanges interrogated in the form of fictional dialogues, atmospheric descriptions of a planner's office stand in for analysis of urban planning, and scenes in busy cafés offer the cash register drawer as protagonist. Of course the intention of such assays is the literary performance of radical critique – a rejection of the grammatical, typographical and citational practices that constitute legitimate knowledge. But in railing against the legitimating mechanisms of knowledge-production, Latour has abandoned meaning in the name of expanding it.

What Latour has accomplished is impressive and perverse. He has simultaneously re-installed the Author at the center of the work, and inoculated him from criticism. As the only coherent entity in an ever-shifting landscape, Latour, despite his protestations, is the only figure capable of speech and meaning-making. This reduces his intellectual contribution to an individual rebellion. The complete absence of reference and quotation in most of his texts means that he is always the one speaking, and indicates, furthermore, that he sees himself as an exception to his theories – as anything *but* a black-box or hybrid of other scholars and their work. The metaphor of the Matroyshka doll might be taken more as a Freudian slip than a way of thinking about sociological meaning-making. Open Latour and you find more Latour – not a mercurial and messy assemblage but a stable and precise replica. Or perhaps this slip is also a model of meaning-making – for all the elaborate, rhetorical showmanship aimed at defeating and destroying the conventions of academia, the whole enterprise is ultimately propped up by the very modern figure of the individual subject. Indeed that must be the case. Without any intellectual allies, an academic tradition, a class, political movement or any social collective to cite, let alone to work with, Latour-the-person is required to be fully independent and responsible. This anti-social, perpetual outsider affect functions to shore up the authority on which it rests by refusing to acknowledge the terms with which it might be critiqued. The rules that apply to academic discourse do not apply to him or his work. Even basic demands for sense-making can be rejected as reductive. If he could, Latour would do away with language altogether, for its misleading abstraction, and claims to 'represent' ideas, thus evacuating the very possibility of dialogue, the very basis for solidarity.

There is something compelling about calls for meaninglessness, for a complete upheaval of the terms that we rightly suspect are not serving us very well. But this imaginary is deeply anti-social, even sociopathic. It places the burden of meaning and meaningful activity wholly on the individual. Which might be ok if you are Bruno Latour – white, male, able-bodied and wealthy. The rest of us, however, could use some help.

JAMIE ALLINSON

Against Summer

The Japanese language, being more dexterous than English, is exceptionally well-endowed with words to describe the seasons and the reaction of humans to them. This may or may not be connected to the ideology of uniqueness that insists on Japan being an island country with four seasons – as if other countries had eight, or three and a half. Nonetheless, non-Japanese languages are surely the poorer for lacking the word *atsugari* and its cognate *samugari*. The *samugari* is a person who dislikes cold and presents as such. An *atsugari* displays the same attitude towards heat.

I am an *atsugari*, in a culture where *samugari* are the norm not merely in the sense of being more common but of being the accepted mode of human experience. I do not welcome, as others do, the first truly hot day of any year: it opens the way to months of discomfort. Exposure to warm sun reddens my skin and coats my body with a mild but unwelcome ooze. Unprotected by hat and sunglasses I soon feel ill. I resent having to protect my body against the world, much as the *samugari* hates wearing a coat and gloves, but without receiving the commensurate sympathy. A continuous dose of the carcinogenic rays could endanger my life. I have never understood why people fantasise about lying in some sand to feel this way. Summer, in short, is horrid.

I accept that this opinion is likely to be taken as the congenital dourness of someone who comes from a summerless place. 'It is never difficult', as P G Wodehouse accurately remarked, 'to distinguish a Scotsman with a grievance from a ray of sunshine.' On 21 August 1995, the temperature in Dundee, the town of my birth and upbringing, reached 28.7 degrees celsius. 28 degrees would, of course, be a pleasantly mild early autumn in Rome or Seoul but I still remember the chafing, and shiver. As with the 'winter' experienced in Sydney or Rio de Janeiro, the Scottish summer has historically worked as chronological rather than a meteorological concept. The word conveniently denotes the period between May and September but no more than that. For the most part I like it this way. My phenotype seems adapted almost perfectly to this niche. Like the body of an aquatic mammal of the sub-Arctic zone, a warming layer of blubber floats beneath my pale and furry skin.

Removed from such an ecology, I soon flounder. In London one finds a society not just accustomed to warmer weather but one that has developed a set of cultural procedures to deal with it. They complain about the absence of hot weather until it comes. They then traipse around the city that the heat has made unbearable, looking tired and talking about how lovely it is. They simply will not stop speaking about either the presence or absence of hot weather. The men wear shorts, and sunglasses that curve around their heads, and polo shirts with collars turned skywards. They talk about the FA cup and eat pieces of grilled chicken in baps. It seems to be enjoyable, if you like that sort of thing.

It is this aspect that leads to the specifically capitalist appeal of summer. All that is shallow, commercial and unreflective seems to have an affinity with summer: yachts, glossiness, roof-parties and so on. Whether 'fresh from the barber shop or fly from the beauty salon' as Will Smith reminds us, summer's affective consumers spend 'every moment frontin' and maxin', chillin' in the car they spent all day waxin'. Summer is the time and place when everyone must have fun, and if there is one commandment of late late capitalism it is to have fun. Is it too much to say that reflection and critique require danker moments?

I do not mean to imply any climactic determinism here. Places where people recognise summer as hot, interminable and unwelcome do just as well as the more temperate. There is no celebration of sunny days to be found in Tayyib Saleh's *Season of Migration to the North* nor in the hard, ochre worlds of Jorge Amado. Rather, I mean that there is almost a compulsory lerotropy in British culture, that can only see the winter-lover as a deviant. To respond to the statement, 'It's going to be sunny next week' with, 'I know, isn't it horrible', is to encounter a level of shock and intolerance unknown in almost any other context. Weather forecasts routinely refer to higher temperatures as simply 'better weather', but never the opposite. No explanation is required. The assumption is that hot and sunny is good and disproportionate amounts of conversational time are expended agreeing with it.

One wonders if the *samugari* have really given winter the benefit of the doubt. The *echt* winters' day – experienced now far less often than the sought-after bank holiday scorcher – offers a fragile beauty. With or without snow, the first step outdoors meets with a crunch, the first breath with a piercing tingle of the nostrils: reminders of the simultaneous separation from and presence in the world. The effect of the cold can be combatted with flattering clothes, in natural fibres pleasing to the skin. Every degree colder is an opportunity to look better. Each increase in temperature, by contrast, takes a step closer to the world of plimsoles and exposed, flaccid flesh. A cold day is an acquired taste, a grown-up pleasure, and difficult to sell. Perhaps that is why all forms of media turn with anticipation to the first day of summer, and never to the first frost.

Institutional samugarism now threatens us all. Winter is done for. Where once one could have expected frost by October and snow by the end of November, it is rare now to find a truly cold day before Christmas. In decades, if not years, the areas of the globe with a reliably cold season will have shrunk to the polar circles or entirely disappeared. The shorts-wearers and barbecuers are not responsible for this – no more than anyone else – but the reaction to tangibly uncanny climate change seems muted precisely because it means the extension and intensification of summer. Halloween represents, in our inherited symbolic storehouse, a time of freez-ing breath, crisp leaves and bonfires to ward off the chill. On 31 October 2014, the temperature reached 23 degrees in London. The predominant reaction was glee. It is difficult to imagine a shift in the other direction, such as a sub-zero August bank holiday, or a snowy July, being met with anything other than horror. The 28 degree days that proved shocking in Scotland two decades ago are now commonplace. Forty-eight hours into his premiership, the UK's most popular newspaper portrayed Boris Johnson as the sun, beaming down on a country experiencing 40 degree heat – hotter than Cairo – for the first time in recorded history. Johnson, the *Sun* informed us, promised us a 'golden age' of more such rays of sunshine. The terrible thing is, they are right.

SAI ENGLERT

Recentring the State: A Response to Barnaby Raine

With ongoing smear campaigns against the Palestine solidarity movement as organised as they are cynical, and with the genuine growth of anti-Semitic violence – alongside growing racist attacks across the board – grappling seriously with anti-Semitism is of great strategic importance.

In the last issue of *Salvage*, Barnaby Raine's raised important questions about the contemporary nature of anti-Semitism in his article 'Jewophobia'. His contribution in this journal and elsewhere has been valuable given that the debate on anti-Semitism has been taken over by the Right and far Right, which attempts to discredit anti-Zionism or solidarity with the struggle for Palestinian liberation, whilst simultaneously masking its own racism – including against Jewish people.

Much discussion of contemporary anti-Semitism accepts a framing that suggests that the problem somehow emanates from Palestine. International solidarity movements with the Palestinian struggle for liberation, and by extension the Palestinian people themselves, are repeatedly identified as the source of growing anti-Semitism in the West – and this despite all reliable data pointing to the far Right as the overwhelmingly dominant source of anti-Semitic acts. This framing obstructs any understanding of the specific place of Jewish communities in our own societies, the centrality of anti-Semitism in the historic construction of Western states, or the connection between the contemporary growth of anti-Semitism and other forms of racism (primarily Islamophobia). At the same time, it allows discussions relating to Zionism to be framed almost exclusively as relating to Jews in the West, rather than to the ongoing settler-colonial dispossession, murder, and displacement of the Palestinian people at the hands of the Israeli state and its supporters. This erasure of Palestinians from discussions relating to Zionism touches, as we shall see, on the very nature of present-day anti-Semitism. This framing is then an assault on effective anti-racist and anti-imperialist struggles and campaigns.

We lack a clear and precise analysis of contemporary anti-Semitism, its origin and social role, particularly with respect to the West. Raine's work opens up such discussion on the Left, standing in trenchant opposition to the ongoing settler-colonial project in Palestine, and focusing on the specific social role of anti-Semitism today. Crucially, Raine investigates processes of identity formation and racialisation, illustrating how contemporary anti-Semitism has morphed under the neoliberal assault, with its foreclosure of alternative horizons, and today reinforces demobilisation of social struggle through conspiracy theories featuring unchallengeable, secret cabals.

Raine also touches on how the conflation of Judaism and Jewish identities with Zionism, as ideology and political movement, contributes to constructing a new Jewish identity in which Jews are cast as defenders of the Western world at home and abroad – a construction that undermines rather than protecting Jewish populations. This is not necessarily a new observation (indeed, it has been central to anti-Zionist Jewish politics from the late nineteenth century) but it is well worth stressing today once more.

Such a focus allows us to make sense of a world in which figures on the (far) right defend Israel, are celebrated by Zionist organisations as friends of the Jewish people, while simultaneously collaborating with, or actively encouraging, anti-Semitic or even fascist political actors at home. Consider, for example, the British Tory government's close relationship with Israel and simultaneous development of close political ties with the openly anti-Semitic government in Hungary, or Donald Trump's courting of both hard-line Zionists and the white-supremacist and anti-Semitic right. It also helps clarify how the historically anti-Semitic far Right across the Western world has, in recent years, reinvented itself as pro-Israel, a change starkly illustrated in the apparent generational divide within the Le Pen clan.

For all the strengths of Raine's essay, there are shortcomings. Most problematically, Raine's analysis of anti-Semitism overemphasises the phenomenon's specificity vis-à-vis other forms of oppression, while failing to identify how contemporary anti-Semitism emerges and is reproduced. His piece gives a broad overview of the ways in which anti-Semitism operates and manifests, but does not identify its structural origins. This failure tends towards a totalising view of contemporary anti-Semitism, and one which leaves little room for action by the same Left he criticises for failing to understand the current conjecture.

In fact, it seems that it is partly this lacuna that leads Raine to admonish the Left for misunderstanding what he sees as its own variation of anti-Semitism: if the construction of racism has no identifiable origin, then perhaps it might be generated by all social actors, the (often small and institutionally marginalised) Left included. His approach fails to situate anti-Semitism in relation to other forms of racism, reproducing the silo-approach of much contemporary identity politics – on both the Left and the Right – which insists on treating every form of oppression as fundamentally distinct and specific.

My analysis certainly does not contradict Raine's in toto – in fact it resonates with a great deal of the latter parts of his piece. However, key to my analysis – and lacking in Raine's – is the state. In keeping the state at the centre, not only can this account rigorously historicise the emergence of contemporary anti-Semitism, it also indicates strategic directions.

ॐ

A new reading of Anti-Semitism?

In his piece, Raine's position is that anti-Semitism – in fact he often uses the word Jewophobia as a broader category, encompassing different historical expressions of hatred of Jews, including anti-Semitism – should not primarily be understood as racism. Instead, he theorises it as a 'conservative fetish' or, more specifically, 'a conservative form of subaltern consciousness, whose danger lies partly in providing a distorted frame through which to see the world, a frame inimical to meaningful human emancipation'. Following from this, he argues that the extent of real anti-Semitic feeling across society is likely much broader than is generally imagined. Anti-Semitism, for Raine, is primarily about its social function in providing an alternative reading of the world's woes, that does not threaten the status quo or real structures of exploitation and oppression, but instead projects onto Jews responsibility for the violence and poverty of the world.

There is much to agree with here. It is undeniable that conspiracy theories about Rothschilds running the world, secret cabals forcing governments to act against their own interests, or the supposed Jewish control over finance, entertainment, and media function as effective ideological tools to detract from real ruling-class power. If the problem is an unseen, 'different' and unaccountable elite, real structures of control and the system as a whole are off the hook.

But Raine does not stop there. He also appears to understand this as qualitatively different from other forms of oppression. Indeed, despite recognising that other ideological constructions play this role – consider current liberal obsessions with Russian hackers or anti-Asian racism parading as principled opposition to China's rise – Raine claims that

> [t]his is a thoroughly different logic of fear from the
> one common to more patronising racisms, and it is
> especially virulent since it entertains little possibility

of acculturating Jews into Christian mores, as is the
preferred strategy of liberal racists in most cases. We
Jews are already too clever – clever enough to outsmart
only-human gentiles, is the fear – and so anti-Semitism
is perpetually paranoid and defensive where modernity's racisms usually self-present with a benevolent,
'civilising' edge'.

Raine's belief of this fundamental difference – that anti-Semitism is
never only racism, unlike most of its 'more patronising' bedfellows
– is never sufficiently explained, nor why the construction of Jews
as 'superior' marks it out. Why is this different from, let's say, the
way South Asian communities within the former British colonies
in the African continent are constructed as intelligent, cunning and
out to destroy local economies? Does this not also echo strongly
with other so-called model minorities*, such as East-Asians in North
America, who are counterposed to other racialised minorities, and
whose supposed industrious character, international networks,
and cunning poses a threat of future domination? It seems that
what these forms of racism have in common are the (real or imagined) minority status, international networks, and localisation in
trade and finance of its victims.

In addition, it seems, that it is always the role of oppression
to construct certain groups of – already structurally weaker –
people as the physical embodiment of specific social ills. In that
sense while East Asian, Jewish, or South Asian communities might
be constructed as the embodiment of financial inequality, other
groups are blamed for other issues: migrants destroy the welfare
state, women push men out of the workplace, black people undermine the quality of education, Muslims spread violence – to name
but a few.

The state constructs populations that become identified as
embodied social problems; it erects them as shields behind which

---

* In fact, the nineteenth century French critic of emerging capitalism and raving
anti-Semite Charles Fourier identified the Chinese people as equally depraved and
dangerous to civilisation as the Jews.

ruling class power can hide. The role of analysis is to understand how these identities are constructed, imposed, and why they are effective enough to gain a life of their own within society. Crucially, these different forms of oppression are also connected and constructed simultaneously by the state. The specific racialisation of East Asian communities in the US for example, plays an important role in justifying the economic deprivation of African American communities as victims not of structural racism or capitalist exploitation, but from the former's cunning economic strategies. In addition, it then also works as a justifying mechanism for state violence to supposedly protect different racialised and oppressed communities from one another.

This leads to the second issue with Raine's analysis. He never makes clear his explanation for where modern anti-Semitism originates, what structures give rise to it, and therefore – by extension – where one should focus energy to challenge it. The very movement between anti-Semitism and Jewophobia throughout the piece captures something of this lacuna. At times, Raine seems to describe a cultural phenomenon that he feels always already exists, and is not in fact constructed and imposed. As such he describes it variously as an 'unconscious phobia of Jews', 'a structure of thinking', a form of 'anti-political pessimism', and as a 'discourse', never rooting these in anything structurally identifiable. This leaves the reader with the impression that anti-Semitism can be explained by means of mere ideas, or via culture, rather than requiring a material explanation and history.

This nebulous and implied analysis of anti-Semitism, as a primarily ideological rather than material relation, also has the curious consequence of giving weight to the Rabbinical view that sees violence directed against the Jewish people as emanating from the jealousy of the gentile world of their success and blessings. Raine writes, for example that '[i]t is true that times of Jewish security and prosperity have often summoned anti-Semitism, which tells us something important about the anti-Semitic worldview'. What that 'something important' is, is not spelled out. And again: '[t]he paranoid theory of history still contains its ounce of truth. Jewish success always was the perfect catalyst for anti-Semitic thinking'. Anti-Semitism, by this account, does not seem to originate in the social contradictions of the society where it emerges from, but, at least in part, in Jewish success. An idea which would be surprising to the European Jewish masses of the nineteenth and early twentieth century to say the least. It over-emphasises anti-Semitism as a spontaneous grassroots form of hatred amongst the people, rather than identify elite and structural processes – much like contemporary discussion of 'white working-class' racism against migrants.

Raine then paints a picture of anti-Semitism as a reactionary form of subaltern consciousness, which is fundamentally distinct from other forms of oppression. In addition, it is not located in clearly identifiable material relations or structural processes. Instead, it appears in Raine's analysis as a modern form of an idealist and a-historical Jewophobia. With this lack of historical perspective, the analysis presented in his piece is not without parallels to Afro-Pessimist understanding of anti-Blackness as universal and fundamentally distinct from other racializing mechanisms.

The post-WWII state and the 'new Jew'
It was the early Zionist movement's claim that by settling Palestine and constructing agrarian communities of European Jews, it would create a so-called 'new Jew'. This 'new Jew' would cast aside what Zionists imagined to be the traits of diasporic life, and would be reborn through labour and productive contact with the land. The imagery of the new Jew as muscular, male, and both a worker and a soldier became ubiquitous in Zionist propaganda. It represented the ethos of the movement. It aimed at casting off the pariah, the weak, the parasitic, and replacing it with the conquering, the productive, and the strong. Aside from highlighting how deeply Zionism had integrated the caricatures of European anti-Semitism, it also tells an important story about its goal: the construction of a settler colonial state in Palestine was aimed at joining the European family of nations and 'normalising' the Jewish people in a way

neither the Haskala's assimilation, or the radicals' revolutionary struggles could. Yet, it was not in Palestine, but in the heart of the Western world, that the identification of Jews would change drastically in the aftermath of the Nazi genocide and the creation of the Israeli state through the expulsion of hundreds of thousands of Palestinians.

Indeed, after WWII a double process took place that fundamentally transformed the way Jewish populations in the West were understood and racialised, as I have argued at greater length in 'Judaism, Zionism, and the Nazi Genocide', in Historical Materialism. If this process led to the outcome that Raine describes, it is essential to inscribe it within a series of specific state-led processes. Indeed, doing so helps making sense of current political developments, while also clarifying where activists should focus their work.

On the one hand, the Nazi genocide came to play a central role in the West's projection of self from the 1960s onwards. A specific, whitewashed version of the Holocaust – in which European anti-Semitism, its continuities with colonial racial ideologies and practices, and western support for Hitler against the threat of Bolshevism, were silenced – became a central way in which Western states narrated their own recent past. In an increasingly decolonised world, where they were forced to reckon with the horrors of colonialism abroad, and where their oppressive and exploitative treatment of the descendants of the formerly colonised at home was increasingly challenged by growing anti-racist movements, the Holocaust and its remembrance became a way for Western nations to present themselves as having changed, having learned the lessons of history, and having graduated to the status of committed anti-racism. The most striking gap between rhetoric and practice in this respect, is the annual marking by Western states of Holocaust remembrance and celebrating German reparations as crucial aspects of accounting for and repairing the crimes of the past, while continuing to refuse to acknowledge (let alone atone for and repair) the full-extend (and contemporary relevance) of human, cultural, and material destruction wrought by their colonial regimes and slave trading economies across the Global South.

Moreover, the fact that this remembrance was, at the very least, unwilling to recognise the depth of active support for the Nazis and the widespread anti-Semitism within European and North American ruling classes is very telling about the limited nature of this process. It also helps make sense of current events, where Macron can celebrate Marshal Petain's role in leading France to victory in WWI or British pundits can react with outrage to the students who occupied a Churchill themed café in London, without either men's racism or anti-Semitism getting in the way of the national narrative of pride and memory. In his excellent The End of Jewish Modernity, Enzo Traverso argues that the commemoration of the Holocaust has become central to Western nation's civic religions. It has become a cornerstone of their image of self – as liberal, egalitarian, and just – conveniently avoiding structural changes and a broader reckoning with the real history of Western power across the world, of which Jews as well as formerly colonised and enslaved people bore the brunt. Aimé Césaire, the father of the Negritude movement, already pointed out in the 1950s that Nazism could not be understood without being re-inscribed in the global history of European colonisation.

This process of re-directed recognition went hand in hand with the increasingly central role played by Israel in Western foreign policy in the Middle East. In fact, recognition of the horrors of the Nazi genocide was mobilised to justify and explain the military, economic, and diplomatic support to Israel and – by extension – Western foreign policy in the region. It continues to play this role today. It is bitterly significant that the German state was allowed to 'repay' the Jewish people through financial and military deals with Israel, helping the young state expand its control over land and intensify its exclusion of its indigenous inhabitants, while Holocaust survivors continued to live in poverty and isolation both in Europe and Israel.

Simultaneously, it became clear to the United States, and by extension the rest of the Western world, that Nasser's Egypt and other Arab nationalist governments would not join Washington in its efforts to contain the USSR. They then turned fully towards supporting Israel against these regimes. The 1967 war sealed this alliance and made Israel central to US strategy in the region, first in order to defeat Arab nationalist states militarily, and then later to impose their political and economic integration into its sphere of influence. This relationship continues to this day through economic deals signed across the Middle East and North Africa, in which normalisation with Israel continues to be a central way for the US to institutionalise the region's regimes' subservience to its rule (see for example Adam Hanieh's excellent discussion of this process in his Lineages of Revolt).

Jewish people, in the process, found themselves increasingly catapulted out of the position of being essentialised as a population living at the margins of the nation state and identified with communist revolution, and essentialised instead as the gatekeepers of Western legitimacy at home and abroad. They were increasingly cast, by Western states, as the defenders of the legitimacy of the Western world when facing the Global South, as well as Black and Asian populations at home. Jews became the shield behind which the Western states hid when faced with demands of anti-racist and anti-imperialist movements.

This change was highly attractive to the leadership of an oppressed community that saw in this new paradigm a route towards integration and acceptance within elite circles, which had remained, until then, closed off to them. It is striking for example that it is in the early to mid-1970s that AIPAC became a major player in US politics – that is after the US has become Israel's key imperial sponsor. Norman Finkelstein, in his Knowing too Much, points out that the official Jewish leadership in the US became attached to Zionism in the post 1967 period, because it was a way to integrate into the American political elite. They therefore become Zionists as loyal American citizens, rather than as separatist Jewish organisations. Simultaneously, a new cultural image of the 'tough Jew' emerged in American life. Echoing the 'new Jew' of the Zionist movement in pre-1948 Palestine, it focussed on Jewish gangsters, occupying soldiers, and the right for the modern Jew, in the words of Rich Cohen, 'to be a bully'.

This logic, which understands liberation as based on closeness to state-power rather than through the transformation of existing power structures, so common amongst the elites of oppressed communities, is strikingly applicable to the official Muslim institutions today. However, much like its Jewish counterpart in the 1920s and 1930s it has little enticing to bring to the table for the vast majority of the community under attack. David Rosenberg's brilliant Battle for the East End shows how the Board of Deputies' response to growing anti-Semitism in pre-War Britain was one focussed on respectability and a desperate attempt to win favour with those (often anti-Semites) in power. As such the militant responses by Jewish activists who (successfully) organised mass resistance against the British Union of Fascists in the streets were seen as a threat to that strategy. This tension continues to have important ramifications today.

While structurally Jewish life has changed considerably – Jews are no longer structurally discriminated against in socio-economic terms – the focus on closeness to state power by community leaders continues to put their base at risk. Indeed, it normalises the narratives that equate Jews and Zionism/Israel, participates in the state-led strategy of pitting Jews against other racialised groups (primarily Muslims), and closes its eyes on ruling class normalisation of anti-Semitism. The refusal of the BoD in Britain for example to challenge the Conservative government's normalisation of fascist leaders in Hungary or Johnson's close ties with Bannon, or the defence by prominent Jewish organisations in the US of Trump are powerful examples of this tendency.

This is important because what this analysis of the changing racialization of Jews in the West does, is avoid limiting itself to a quasi-conspiratorial approach, which obsesses over the behaviour of the leadership of Zionist Jewish organisations (see for example The Israel Lobby by John Mearsheimer and Stephen Walt), nor does it locate anti-Semitism within ill-defined narrative processes. Instead it reflects on the structures of the state that have created the current political logic within which those organisations operate. It is the change in their states' strategy – at home and abroad

– that has led to a change of status of Jewish people in the West, rather than the other way around. Ironically, this makes their newly acquired status precarious and dependent on the continuation of the current political order.

It helps to make sense of why the assault on the Corbyn-led Labour Party or on the Palestine solidarity movement, on the basis of its supposed institutionally anti-Semitic nature (despite continuous failure to evince anything beyond anecdotal evidence for this claim) has been so effective, because it plays into a narrative which has been central to the policies of Western governments for decades. Jewish communities are only extended access to limited assimilation by the state when it identifies them as extensions of Zionism and/or Israel. Therefore, they can also be used as shields behind which the state hides when Zionism and/or Israel are threatened. Similarly, when Jewish groups or individuals reject Zionism, the state can ignore them, as they do not fit the assimilationist mould.

The question is not whether there has been a concerted effort to attack on these fronts, which has involved the Israel lobby. This much is evident and has been documented extensively, including on camera by Al-Jazeera 'The Lobby' documentaries in both the US and the UK. Nor is the question whether some have engaged in good fate in those campaigns. They undoubtedly have. The question instead is about the effectiveness of these campaigns. Its success should not be laid at the door of the lobby itself and its supposed extraordinary power – with all the worrying undertones that come with it – but understood as rooted in the fact that the attack cleaves in the same political direction as the ideology of Western states: mobilise Jewish populations as shields behind which to hide Western crimes and racism at home and abroad. This is the nature of modern anti-Semitism. It is on this basis that it should be fought.

This approach also helps make sense of how governments in France, Britain, or the US – amongst others – simultaneously move to criminalise Palestine solidarity activism (all three states have taken steps to outlaw BDS, and Macron has recently announced his desire to legally equate anti-Semitism and anti-Zionism) under the guise of protecting Jewish communities at home, while simultaneously normalising the anti-Semitic far-right. All three governments entertain, for example, friendly relations with the openly anti-Semitic government of Hungary. In the UK, it is particularly worrying that Boris Johnson has close ties with the anti-Semitic Steve Bannon, specifically in the latter's attempts to unify the European far-right, while presenting himself as a friend and protector of the Jewish people.

The burden of protecting Western states is pushed onto Jewish communities. The 'new Jew' so desired by the early Zionist movement has emerged in the West. He (he is always a he) is constructed as a defender of the state and the West's interests in the Middle East. He is counterpoised to racialised communities at home who fight for their political liberation. In the process, Jewish communities, as well as the racialised groups they are pitted against by state policy – Muslims and Palestinians primarily – are continuously put in danger in the process. It is therefore not surprising that there is such a strong victimising narrative emerging from Zionist circles. This is not only a political strategy by pro-Israeli organisation. It is also a reality. Ironically, by drawing Jewish communities nearer to the state and constructing them as an extension of their policies, Western states are laying down the basis for the victimisation of Jewish communities.

Bringing Back Political Agency

David Feldman and Brendan McGeever of the Pears Institute for the Study of Anti-Semitism have repeatedly observed, in the public 'debates' of recent months, a split between the struggle against anti-Semitism and the wider anti-racist movement. They have not, however, provided a plausible explanation for this crucial observation (though in fact in one article – which they inexplicably chose to publish in the Israeli press – they seem to point the finger of blame for this at the British anti-racist movement).

The foregoing analysis might go some way to addressing this, and point to a possible direction to challenge it.

The contemporary struggle against anti-Semitism cannot be waged without the state in its focus, nor can it be effective without demanding that the fate of Jewish communities be disentangled from Western states, their foreign policy and the continuation of Israeli settler-colonialism. It must be a unitary struggle against the racialisation of all communities, through which the murderous history of the West can be acknowledged, and the ongoing structures of oppression rooted in this past can be dismantled – to the benefit of all oppressed communities. This includes Jews, who still find themselves collectively defined and identified by the state – to their detriment – in the ways laid out above. In this sense, not only is anti-Zionism not in contradiction with the struggle against anti-Semitism, as our rulers would have us believe, but it is inextricable from it. No one is free, as the saying goes, until we all are.

While the 'official' voices of the Jewish community can often make it seem like this strategy is an impossibility, a flurry of Jewish groups – from Jewish Voice for Peace and the more recent 'Never Again is Now' movement in the US, to the Jewish Network for Palestinians and Jewdas in the UK, among many others – have already started making it a reality. Similarly, every major poll within the Jewish population in the West shows a growing disengagement from Israel amongst young Jews. The task of the Left is to intensify its opposition to the colonisation of Palestine, to the violence meted out against black, Muslim, migrant, and all other racialised peoples. It simultaneously needs to understand that the state's attempt to counterpose Jewish people to these struggles is inextricable from the contemporary nature of anti-Semitism. It must be fought relentlessly. To do so effectively however, those struggling must identify the state as their target and mobilise accordingly.

While much of the historical focus in analyses of anti-Semitism is on Eastern and Central Europe – and for good reason given the specific history of European states with Ashkenazi Jewish communities and their diaspora – there is work to be done on the history of Jewish communities' relation with Europe in colonial contexts. It is striking for example that all the while oppressing Jews at home, the French state granted citizenship to Jewish Algerians, who were thereby given access to French education, better employment opportunities, and semi-integration into colonial society. In so doing, it constructed an intermediary community between itself and the 'indigenes' that could be erected as a shield behind which it could hide. The failure of communist and nationalist activists to win over Jewish Algerians to the project of building an independent Algerian state and to abandon their inclusion into the French state led to the effective destruction, through exile, of the Algerian Jewish community. It also contributed to the emergence of a very limited vision of the identity of the newly independent Algerian state, something that remains a major issue today for non-Arabs and non-Muslims in the country. This state of affairs resonates strongly with the present analysis of contemporary anti-Semitism offered in this article. It also serves as a reminder of the strategic importance of identifying state strategies and structures of identification effectively, in order to lead successful, unifying, liberation struggles from below.

JULES JOANNE GLEESON AND J. N. HOAD

Gender Identity Communism: A Gay Utopian Examination of Trans Healthcare in Britain

We are two trans people who have managed not to be defeated by the process of being clinicalised by the Gender Identity Clinic (GIC) system, which oversees trans healthcare in Britain and occupied Ireland[*].

One of us, through a combination of patience and self-medication, faced down a GIC which, despite being among the swiftest in the country, still had an average waiting time of 51 weeks prior to treatment in 2018. For the other, avoiding processing through a GIC was a major factor in deciding to remain a migrant from Britain. Instead she accessed Hormone Replacement Therapy in Europe, where it was more swiftly and humanely available, taking less than four months from initial phone call to estradiol gel prescription.

Both of us are sick of worrying about our friends. Inspired by twentieth-century utopian communist thinkers and the pioneering healthcare practices of today's trans communities, we write

[*] We each thank Rhiannon Walmslay, Joey French, Angie Normandale, Mirah Gary, Elle O'Rourke, Nat Raha, Juliet Jacques, and ACT-UP London.

not only to bring the dire social conditions of trans people to light, but also to explore the autonomous means with which we have achieved survival despite the state.

Part 1: The clinics have failed

> We are not too ill, too disabled, too anxious, too depressed, too psychotic, too Mad, too foreign, too young, too old, too fat, too thin, too poor, or too queer to make decisions about our bodies and our futures. We are all self-medicating. Our agency will be recognised. We each labour far harder for the health of ourselves and those around us than any doctor ever has, and we will continue [to] build supportive communities on principles of mutual aid.
>
> A4TH Edinburgh Manifesto

The clinics have failed. The current British system for trans health-care provision combines unsustainable centralisation with chronic underprovision. Increasing demand for trans healthcare has coincided with the stripping of resources due to austerity. With only fifteen GICs in England, Scotland and Northern Ireland, lags of two to three years before accessing hormones are a new norm.

This leaves trans people facing down years of anxiety, depression and suicidal tendencies in the fact of pervasive transphobia and harassment, unaided. Such postponements are sentences to an unlivable life. To quote the title of Sylvia McCheyne's incisive criticism of British healthcare, itself taken from a banner at an Irish protest: We are sick of losing people to these waiting lists.

This is a fabricated crisis.

The gratuitous inefficiency of the UK system contrasts with the 'informed consent model' of other healthcare systems, including that of the United States, wherein focus is placed on ensuring that a patient is clear on the potential risks and realistic scope of treatment – that testosterone or estrogen treatment, for example, will ultimately render them infertile. They are given realistic expectations for treatment outcomes: that HRT, for example, will not entirely transform their genitals. While mental health is assessed, this is usually a brief process to confirm the patient is of sound mind – for example, to exclude those undergoing a psychotic episode, or in some such way currently impaired from long-term thinking.

Where informed-consent models are oriented towards providing a *treatment*, the GICs are focused on first verifying the status of the *patient* – to establish that the trans person seeking treatment is trans at all. Trans people often approach official medical channels only as a last resort, having spent years in 'exploration', repression, ineffective therapies and circular conversations. The GIC system then *extends this process* – often by years.

Finding a sympathetic GP who will refer to a GIC can be an initial challenge. Once registered, the GIC becomes the primary service responsible for trans healthcare. This does not mean direct access to hormones or surgery, but more assessments by nurses, doctors and endocrinologists – scrutinisers inscrutable in their standards. The process demands trans people live for months and years at the beck and call of this gatekeeping bureaucracy, while straining to prove an identity that society would obviously rather did not exist.

The Clinic system justifies this delay using the spectre of the mentally unstable trans person, who fails to appreciate the ramifications of their decisions. For decades, clinics have sought to distinguish between 'true transsexuals', and those merely confused gender deviants who must be prevented from making a calamitous decision. In this patrician approach, medical professionals are kindly guides to gendered experience, and authoritative arbitrators of its permissible limits without whom trans people's mental health would be gravely endangered.

The reality is the reverse: strain is *caused* by medical gatekeeping's indignities. The Gender Identity Clinic at once alienates us from our treatment, and imposes agonising waiting times between sessions. Postponing surgeries can be devastating for those undergoing 'social transition'. Trans people who need timely treatment and informed support instead face a rigid structure that Action For Trans Health Edinburgh's manifesto calls a 'war of bureaucratic attrition'.

Since the 1966 foundation of the first clinic, in London, conformity to old-fashioned gender norms, or at least the pretence of such, has conditioned access to treatment. There was little place for non-binary identification, or even non-heterosexual orientation, for earlier generations of trans people navigating the GICs of the mid-twentieth century. While now partially reformed after decades of lobbying, the GIC has not abandoned such gatekeeping.

The GICs vary considerably in size, funding, staffing and practice. Like many other NHS bodies, the GICs have been left crumbling after cuts, and advancing privatisation. A new clinic in Cardiff was supposed to start taking referrals from March 2018, but nationwide coverage has not materialised. Most Welsh trans people still rely on the discretion of their GPs for hormone prescriptions, and rely on expensive travel to London for a full assessment (travel funding is nominally available but limited).

The clinic at Sheffield's Porterbrook Medical Care Centre works to develop a shared culture of respect for patients, but is understaffed, underfunded and oversubscribed. Larger institutions such as Charing Cross GIC have suffered particularly badly from rising waiting lists, a situation hardly conducive to the development of shared values and accountability processes throughout assessment and treatment.

Closeted trans youth living at home and far from clinics are obliged to fabricate excuses for regular trips across the country. Often, appointments are at short notice, requiring patients to hurriedly organise logistics and finances. Failure to attend a single appointment can be met with threats to drop patients from the service.

Those who weather waiting lists and travel expenses need a clinical system sensitive to the desires and understanding of trans people ourselves, but treatment is often dire and approaches outdated.

GIC practitioners have much to learn about the options and subtleties of practice when it comes to HRT. For instance, anti-androgens are routinely prescribed to trans women to block the reception and action of testosterone, according to a medical regime based on boosting estrogen levels and suppressing testosterone at all costs. However, trans women prescribed anti-androgens frequently experience depression and other disabling side effects such as brain fogs and fatigue. Anti-androgens also tend to 'over-suppress' testosterone, often reducing it to undetectable levels, which can inhibit desired outcomes in the long term, leaving trans women wishing to get off them risking permanent damage to hormonal regulation. GIC doctors seem resistant to patients use of increasingly popular 'monotherapeutic' hormones regimes, which uses estradiol as the primary medication, waiting for elevated estrogen levels to trigger an automatic drop in testosterone. This reflex, the aromotose reaction, allows for dramatic rebalancing of circulating sex hormones without anti-andorgens. Despite increasing numbers of trans people reporting good results from this protocol, NHS medics still treat higher levels of estradiol as intrinsically dangerous, based on outdated clinical data.

This stubborn attachment to outmoded paradigms characterises GIC clinical practice. There is mounting evidence that hormones delivered transdermally – through the skin via patches and gel – bypass the liver's first-pass metabolism, and are thus more efficient and safer. But NHS endocrinologists still exclusively offer oral medication, while often failing even to give full instructions on its effective administration through sublingual dissolving. Testosterone treatment is typically more efficiently delivered, but masculinising HRT is outmoded in other ways. Patients are rarely offered dihydrotestosterone (DHT), an androgen produced by the metabolization of testosterone, which can promote genital growth to the point where many find the results so satisfying they no longer feel the need for surgeries.

Trans people of whatever gender can rarely access opportunities to freeze their gametes, resulting in an ongoing lawsuit by the Equality and Human Rights Commission after their pre-action letter declaring the NHS clinical standards outdated was ignored. Though the NHS, unlike some other national systems, has never require trans people be sterilised, this remains the *de facto* norm.

Falling outside the familiar paradigms of 'transsexualism', non-binary trans people in particular have been denied access to the full scope of their potential options. Despite formal changes towards inclusivity since 2018, the very notion of non-binary identities is still excluded from the dominant imaginary of today's GICs, which are notorious among non-binary people for retrograde treatment regimes, old fashioned concepts, and sometimes openly hostile attitudes. Non-binary people routinely encounter sceptical attitudes towards their desired outcomes, as reported for example in a number of accounts collated in 2014 by Action For Trans Health. Most NHS specialists display a dismissive attitude towards the possibility of securing non-binary physiological changes at all. These assumptions are not limited to highlighting specific limitations such as that certain levels of particular hormones are required for sustaining bone integrity, but often amount to tacit or explicit invalidation. Ignorant and insensitive comments are widespread: one patient was asked whether they were non-binary or 'a regular female'. The mutual distrust is such that it's common in non-binary circles, where people are not too discouraged to seek medical support altogether, to hear the advice simply not to mention this aspect of gender identity when approaching medical professionals.

Adding insult to all these injuries, we have lost track of the stories of basic bureaucratic errors in the GIC's handling of – often sensitive – information, which often serves to extend waiting times still further. Incorrect names and pronouns are often used in letters and official reports, aggravating the very dysphoria the whole process is supposedly intended to treat, and eroding any remaining trust.

How have the GICs failed this way?

The late Douglas Crimp observed that US government-sanctioned healthcare advice on AIDS failed to stem the crisis by attempting to address queers and drug users solely in 'a "universal" language that no one speaks and many do not understand'. We might find reference to an 'intravenous drug user', but never skin popping, a skag queen, or any other slang relevant to the lives of actual gays. Similarly, the GICs refuse engagement in the terms trans people use to understand ourselves on a daily basis. Interacting with a GIC can mean abandoning the language best-suited to make sense of a transgender life. Distinctions between 'feminine' and 'effeminate', 'man' and 'boi', 'gay' and 'queer', might be highly important to a trans person under scrutiny, but such nuances simply do not appear in the clipped vocabulary of medical professionals. Instead, trans people are expected to achieve fluency in the tongue of the bureaucrat, without reciprocation.

Even within their own terms, the approach taken by the GICs can be inscrutable. A doctor might deliberate as to whether to make a diagnosis of 'transexualism' or 'gender dysphoria', a distinction baffling in the traditional terms of the professional (persistent gender dysphoria is a diagnostic *symptom* of 'transsexualism'), and alien to the lived experience of trans people. Nonetheless, we have seen the distinction used to sort binary-identified 'full transexuals' from dysphoric non-binary *or* gender-non-conforming individuals.

The Race Equality Foundation has found that trans people of colour remain largely invisible within current research and clinical practice, not least because many feel unable to disclose their identity fully in the face of pervasive transphobia and racism. The research also shows that current clinical practice is poorly equipped to address those who identify in non-Western or non-anglophone terms. Considering, for example, the recent election of Jair Bolsonaro in Brazil, this racist lacuna is a failing that will become increasingly apparent and dangerous as the twenty-first century continues, and LGBT and refugee struggles continue to interlock.

Our actual needs are relatively modest. That services and substances that could so easily be universally provided have been winnowed bespeaks structuring principles of the system: to restrict access, govern a minority population, and complicate transition as an experience. Not only does this mean a shortage of treatment that should be easily provisioned, without delay, but the loss of a wealth of clinical data, and a breakdown of language between patients and clinicians. This disconnect will likely be exacerbated as Generation Z comes of age in a context where transition has been culturally normalised, no longer an unusual pathology, nor even a radical political movement, but a mass phenomenon. Far from preparing for the health needs of femboys or NB testosterone micro-dosers, the Clinics are still wrapping their heads around trans women in trousers, or gay trans men who enjoy contouring before a night out.

In the face of this breakdown in provision and communication, an increasing number of trans people are opting for self-medication regimes. Others rely on private services, such as Gender GP (which styles itself the antithesis of the GIC system, with its slogan 'Putting you in charge of your gender journey'). Such services are beyond the means of most trans people, but we've seen approaches ranging from crowdfunding to spending almost the entirety of a student loan to secure access to these swifter and less humiliating private services. The NHS has responded by doing its best to shutter these stopgap solutions.

For the neoliberal state, the case of trans healthcare is practically unique in that even the ideological principle of providing a 'choice' between nationalised and private healthcare is being abandoned. Even private practitioners are being placed under increasing scrutiny that extends to pressuring them out of practice. One private provider reported that NHS doctors issued third-party complaints to the General Medical Council concerning private practices for not conforming to the retrograde NHS policies. Four medics who provided these services have been suspendedL the most recent was a sole provider of hormones for over 1,600 patients. These interventions were clearly intended to drive the practices out of business, with their longer-term prospects left unclear. In an attempt to remain afloat, one practice readied patients with an offensive disclaimer clearly implicitly informed by the same 'trans-trender' paranoia that guides the GIC. Given the intensity of these efforts by the state, it seems inevitable that in future other medics will be discouraged from opening such services.

Internationally, campaigns against the psychopathologisation of trans people are making steady progress. In 2018, the Eleventh edition of the International Classification of Diseases removed the classification of trans-identification as an illness. Despite this momentous progress, the ICD-11 continues to use the 'temporary and imperfect' language 'Gender Incongruence' to describe trans, gender non-conforming, and dysphoric people, in the face of an international campaign, spearheaded by South African groups such as Iranti, to remove this vestige of stigmatising language.

Back in the British backwater, the clinical lens through which the NHS surveys trans culture remains a blinder. The traumatic imposition of 'Real Life Experience', when trans people were expected to live full-time as their true gender without either hormonal or surgical assistance to prove they were 'for real', has largely been formally abandoned. Yet the huge delays in treatment, and the widespread refusal of GPs to provide reprieve, have resulted in its de facto retention. Often, clinicians' questions amount to the same intrusive and stereotyped adjudication of whether we are living openly in our chosen gender. Left waiting for years for treatment, we negotiate whatever opportunities to live as trans that we can, which means – as with Real Life Experience – exposing ourselves to social transphobia without medical or state recognition.

The GICs have proved remarkably resistant to change, even when administrative breakthroughs gave cause for hope, such as when national NHS best practice guidelines in the 2010s mandated that GPs should be expected to provide 'bridging' medication, and services such as epilation. Unfortunately, despite this official mandate such support has not materialised. Some GPs express reluctance to operate as stopgap sovereigns, given their lack of specialist training: one trans person navigating the system reported being refused by three such doctors, before a fourth would offer the (supposedly nationally mandated) bridging medication.

Allowing access to hormonal treatment on the basis of informed consent would alleviate the current crush with near immediate effect.

The GIC system was always a means of state discipline and managed deprivation, and replacing it has become increasingly urgent. After twenty years of determined campaigning by liberal trans activists, the reforming approach is reaching its limit. Breakthroughs by the trans movement in the cultural and legal spheres have come up against intransigence on the part of government, healthcare institutions, and transphobic press. Efforts to 'reform' the GICs have fallen well short of the overhaul that would allow them to weather austerity. Even the most persistent agitation and spirited fundraising seem unable to overcome the callous logic of this system. The salience of the few valuable reforms that *have* occurred seems unclear in the face of the current meltdown of provision.

Some trans people are able to buy their way out of dealing with the GIC; some make it through the ordeal of awaiting treatment with the support by friends and loved ones; others cross borders to escape it; others flout the law in one way or another; and others do not survive the medical neglect and structural incompetence in a transphobic society. The Clinic system can be seen as a ruthless stretching and testing of the social support each trans person who encounters can call upon. Those who suffer worst from it are those who were most vulnerable to begin with. The system has less to do with any universalist's vision of a benevolent welfare state, and more to do with an interrogator's stress position.

The system developed into its current state with no long-term plan for accessible, effective or reliable provision, and it should be replaced on a new foundation. Trans clinics should serve the newly out and empowered UK trans population wherever we are, taking into account the advances in hormonal, psychological and cultural understanding which have often been led by our political struggle.

We cannot rely on the political class. The new Tory government has kicked its long-touted (and already inadequate) plans to reform the Gender Recognition Act into the long grass.

The Clinic system's historical role of verifying 'valid' transitions has become totally dysfunctional in the context of swingeing cuts, but its approach has also been surpassed by the realities of autonomous action by trans communities to provide for ourselves. Trans people facing myriad attempts to undermine our means of living have, out of desperation, developed capacities for collective survival. What's more, our combined medical knowledge and political vision far surpasses that of government bodies on the matter.

Part 2: Beyond The GIC – DIY Liberation

> There will be no clinics, and no authorities. We will conduct our own research, and experiment with our own bodies. We will heal and grow together. We will accumulate knowledge and share it freely and accessibly. We demand nothing less than the total abolition of the clinic, of psychiatry, and of the medical-industrial complex...We do not consider that our work will ever be complete, there will always be greater things on the horizon.
>
> A4TH Edinburgh Manifesto

Our vision of twenty-first-century trans healthcare is not limited to a more 'efficient' version of the existing process of professionally administered transition, or to ameliorating the choked-up state of British trans healthcare. We demand something new, hatched from the emancipatory practices trans people have already developed for ourselves.

Trans healthcare in the twenty-first century provides many stories of hope, although few from conventional sources. Beyond official websites, Westminster lobbies and NGOs, a churn of social activity sustains and expands trans communities. Affinity circles freely share and discuss the latest scientific research into desired clinical outcomes. New explorations of non-binary transitions are attempted and collated. Social media rallying points such as #trans-docfail persistently challenge and reassess the practice of health-care professionals. Unlike the rigid and proceduralist approach of the GICs, this trans culture crosses borders, contexts, the variations of sensibility and sensitivity which define human experience. Sharing healthcare knowledge on our own terms, trans people across the world are securing the gender expression which we see fit, by whatever means are available.

An increasing number of trans people opt to bypass the GICs, and source our own sex hormones. This approach to transition is known as 'self-medication', and it has become commonplace. Restrictions on non-clinicalised access to such hormones vary. Primarily because of how coveted testosterone is by body builders, it's treated as a restricted substance. By contrast, exogenous estrogen and progesterone are relatively easily available, to cis and trans women alike. This distinction is likely to account for the increasing numbers of young trans men and masculine people approaching the NHS for treatment, unlike the unknown number of trans teenagers relying on estrogen who can bypass the medical system through internet ordering. In turn, trans-masculine people often share NHS prescribed testosterone as an act of mutual aid.

In the face of the current media moral panic around youth transitions, it seems likely that the next stage of widespread medicalisation will be the government restricting access to estrogen. This would not only impact trans teens, and could greatly complicate existing self-medication practices. Any expansion of these legal prohibitions must be resisted. As activist group Action 4 Trans Health Edinburgh put it: 'We are all self-medicating. Our agency will be recognised.' It hardly falls to us to sketch the entirety of a new order: our community has been moving ahead of the state for some time.

Hormones issued by prescription still reach the hands of trans people who can ingest them at our own discretion. We can ignore the advice and chastisement of our doctors. Nonetheless, we still rely heavily on the state and market for their resources. We have to buy our hormones from somewhere. (At least for now – the 'Open Source Gender Codes' project is providing hope for 'home-grown hormones' and a new generation of DIY practices.) But 'DIY' practices exist everywhere. Resources include sizable online communities, but often the skills and encouragement needed to start medical transition are found in more intimate encounters. It may be a matter of knowing one or two fellow travellers in your own town and developing friendships for survival. Those medically qualified might offer vital information and encouragement. Reliable websites are shared. Such collaboration are often provisional: one elaborate operation ran in Austria saw a trans woman leave a stash of medications in an abandoned building, to be collected by a self-medder still awaiting full authorisation.

Much of the work done is exploration of options for hormonal treatments, and verification of the safety and efficacy of those formally prescribed. We educate ourselves through long hours on online medical databases such as PubMed. Many of those most immersed have professional medical or research training (although the nature of medical school makes it rare for trans people to attain full MDs). Others are autodidacts by necessity.

DIY trans healthcare practices are developments in the struggle for trans liberation that must be understood when considering a replacement for the Clinic. Such practices and communities have already achieved a direct impact on those facing otherwise substandard care. The ambition of DIYers is growing, openly challenging the typical hierarchical division of labour characterising medical treatment. Beverly Cosgrove of Modern Trans Hormones has described the approach formulated by her group as a 'new best practice for trans healthcare'. Cosgrove oversees the MTF

Trans HRT Hormone Forum, in which trans people undergoing HRT and medical care in various contexts have both pooled their own experiences, and collected empirical studies, and offer guidelines on HRT. The conclusions the group has developed have proven invaluable for many, and even those who disagree with the particular approach can reapply principles developed there.

In a Reddit DIY forum, one trans woman with apparently exhaustive knowledge of the literature, compiled a fully referenced guide for non-binary transitions for male-assigned trans people. Another thread flagged previously obscure research studying cis men with prostate cancer in Argentina, and extrapolated a new approach to using transdermal gels, immediately drawing responses from trans women sharing their blood levels, demonstrating its efficacy. Another forum runs its own wiki to collect advice and sources. These queer amateur practices often diverge from prescribed knowledge within British and American clinics, but seem to achieve many trans people's desired outcomes.

There is a concrete utopianism at work in DIY trans healthcare, enabling survival in the present, and pushing forward our future understanding through new forms of knowledge and social relations. Such autonomy is typical for LGBT healthcare, at least when conditions are at their most dire. In the 1980s–90s, groups like ACT-UP and its predecessors pioneered efforts to understand and face down the transmission of the virus. More recently, the community-led campaign I Want PrEP Now led to a remarkable collapse in the HIV transmission rate. Founded by Greg Owen, a gay man who had seroconverted while attempting to access treatment, I Want PrEP Now provided an off-brand version of Truvada, making the drug affordable for most gay men. Owens ran the website out of his bedroom, supported by a number of LGBT people sharing his commitment. The website became a focal point for revitalised AIDS activism in the UK, at a time when the NHS still refused to provide the drug on a mass level, only sanctioning small-scale tests. Through community campaigning from groups such as the UK's newly refounded ACT-UP, provision of PrEP was achieved on a much broader scale than the NHS authorised, through non-state means. Between 2015 and 2016, the Dean Street sexual health clinic reported a 42 per cent fall in seroconversions. Nationally between 2015 and 2017, transmission rates fell by 31 per cent: the PrEP provision campaign appears decisive in one of the largest declines in the virus's spread since the start of the crisis. After these results, mass distribution of PrEP was finally permitted under the NHS.

It is in a similar fashion that trans people have bypassed the state, offering informal processes of skill-sharing to distribute technologies, information about trustworthy medics, and the means of navigating gatekeeping as swiftly as possible.

These practices may discomfort those more used to 'professional standards' regulating the most important features of life. Predictably, the British establishment has responded with scaremongering media stories characterising online pharmacies as 'cowboy chemists'. But a certain queer amateurism – related though not identical to the 'radical amateurism' referred to in Helen Hester's *Xenofeminist Manifesto* – has often prevailed in the face of systemic neglect, in Britain and elsewhere.

We do not see these communities as acting in pristine detachment from the established medical institutions. Rather, these 'homebrew' approaches to treatment practices are acts of resistance to a system that under-provides skilled treatment as a matter of course – drawing knowledge from that system through medical databases and medically qualified comrades.

DIY practices are not widely respected within the GICs. Most doctors display a combination of concern about and open hostility towards self-medication. One trans woman, for example had come to her own view of how to dose her estradiol subcutaneously. When she raised the fact she was DIYing at an early GIC meeting, her psychiatrist refused to prescribe bridging medication, and discouraged her continuing DIY treatment. When she subsequently asked how she could safely 'taper off' her current hormone regime, he refused advice, denying her choice altogether, and leaving her without the support to either continue or end treatment safely.

Certain medical professionals have come to respect the urgent need for access and autonomy in our healthcare, which in rare cases has led to a more collaborative approach. Dr. William Powers, for example, has produced documents written in dialogue with, rather than imposed on, us.' I didn't get all this knowledge because I'm a genius,' he has said. 'I got it because transgender women and men are experimenting on themselves ... and it worked, better than anything else did.'

To avoid irrelevance, and to overcome its ignorance, the medical establishment must respect DIY practices and knowledge. Our capacity to make judgements with respect to our bodies, medication, psyche and lifestyle will be expressed with our without medics – who should now justify themselves to us. Today's Gender Identity Clinics are framed around sorting the 'authentic' from 'trans-trenders' or 'fakers', and providing a single pathway to treatment. Their abolition could replace a meatgrinder of surveillance and pathologising, with the development of centres of shared experience and genuine expertise, to be led by trans people ourselves, with expert advice offered as part of a responsive dialogue. Breakthroughs would be produced continuously by transition as an emerging mass phenomenon.

At present, DIY resources exist in unreliably updated blogs, furtive subreddits, and local networks. While indispensable, these channels are ad hoc, and often challenging to those most in need (for instance due to learning disabilities, inability to access the web, or read and speak English fluently). For all their strengths, we should not mistake informal distribution channels for the finished article in utopian healthcare. As Helen Hester has it, 'the "Y" in "DIY" never operates in isolation, but is enmeshed in a web of structural oppressions, networks of power, and technomaterial relationships'. The new trans clinic would make this ever-expanding body of practical wisdom truly accessible to the swelling number of trans people who require these resources for truly informed consent. We envision a synthesis between the vital knowledge produced by trans people through our practice, and the scale, accountability and resources of established medical institutions. In particular, a fixed centre to collect and compare clinical data, on a consensual, anonymised basis, would improve on the thriving informal hubs.

Encounters between clinics and GPs should be premised on the unconditional provision of desired medications and services. But we can go further, to consider what a trans healthcare system that is meaningfully integrated into society would look like, as part of a liberated healthcare for all people in our society – including at its margins, and across borders.

Different aspects of trans healthcare provide distinct challenges. Hair removal can be performed at any number of salons. Voice training could clearly be practiced more flexibly and widely than in the current system, which often restricts us to an affected, 'standard' British vocal register. By contrast, surgeries require trained surgeons in fitted operating theatres: in such a case, we call for more sympathetic professionals, including trained trans surgeons, as well as proper information on the full range of options, unquestioning access, full aftercare and paid leave for recovery. Due to the nature of the developing knowledge base, surgical expertise could be best expanded by transnational collaboration, and platforms for the rigorous discussion, comparison and improvement of the available procedures.

Trans-specific healthcare saturates our everyday life. An inadequate regime can expose us not only to symptoms such as cognitive impairment, spikes of dysphoria, continual hot flushes, but violence on the streets. Therapy and counselling can be valuable throughout transition, not as a means to assess our authenticity, but as a space in which we can articulate ourselves, in expectation of sympathy and insight. Vocal control, hair management, even fashion advice, can be important means of navigating our genders, or refusal thereof, every day. Our needs cannot be summarised in terms of a single, specialised procedure ('the surgery'). Transition is a varying and continually navigated process.

An immediate mandate to make medication and relevant services available on a local level would alleviate the worst strain on the system. But beyond this, a Clinic system which only recognises our experiences within fixed geographic and diagnostic bounds can only oppressively restrict where and how we can live.

The degree to which individual trans people take our healthcare under personal control will vary, based on required treatments and material circumstances. Not all of us will be able to design and prescribe our own hormone regime. Not all of us are interested in growing testosterone in a herb garden. Our decisions will always be shaped to some extent by the care of professionals, family and others in times of medical need. We insist on deep sympathy and understanding from those who claim to care for us.

The pedagogic theory of Ivan Illich helps capture the efficacy of DIY practices, and how they could be extended. Illich was a dissident Catholic priest whose political work with poor Puerto Rican communities influenced the New Left. In *Deschooling Society*, Illich provides a vision for a liberated education system:

A good educational system should have three purposes: it should provide all who want it to learn with access to available resources at any time in their lives; empower all who want to share what they know to find those who want to learn it from them; and, finally, furnish all who want to present any issue to the public with an opportunity to make their knowledge known.

Illich envisioned the development of 'learning webs' using networked computers to make information on any topic available to all, valuing critical refinement but never held back by gatekeeping. These principles of accessibility and free discussion are being developed by DIY communities today.

Illich's futurism preempted widespread internet usage which would cast his arguments in a new light. At the margins of society today, trans communities are doing such work. Online spaces are, for many, the first encounters with trans and queer culture. They facilitate community-building, self-exploration and a sense of subcultural belonging. Through expanding and struggling for such community webs, the forbidden knowledge of queer life has become pervasively available, against the injunctions of a cis- and heterosexist society.

We should begin with and expand the work of DIY communities. These minoritarian practices are incubating a radically new form of healthcare, and we believe a new emancipatory vision can be hatched through their work.

The movement which makes possible the trans clinic as we have described it here has yet to come. It will rely on further struggle, experimentation and democratic participation. Utopian visions are often dismissed as whimsical, impossible to realise. Our argument is that another form of trans healthcare *already exists*: the makeshift social reproduction that keeps trans life continuing in the present tense.

A new queer futurity could open still further the mutual partic-ipation that we already see across Britain and the world. Locally creative marginal politics could be expanded through trusted and democratic channels. The potential exists in the unsung labour of trans people today to reclaim transsexuality itself: from a divisive means of state categorisation, to a mutual field of personal self-fulfillment informed by a collaborative working.

What is called for is not piecemeal institutional reform, but a wholly new science of trans and queer life. In making this call, we echo the words of Mario Mieli in *Towards a Homosexual Communism*:

The movement of communists struggles for the determination of a free future, for that garden of intersubjective existence in which each plucks at will according to their needs the fruits of the tree of pleasure, of knowledge, and of that 'science' that will be a gay science.

We, too, yearn to seize the fruits of contemporary medical prac-tice, and assign them according to our varied needs and desires. The seeds of this emancipated practice are already being cultivated in our own communities, sharing freely from collective knowledge and experience to survive and flourish. We call, now, for a garden fit for these emerging gay sciences.

Faun

I woke up like Nijinsky. You do. I mean, we've all
been there, it happens to the best of us. Now clarity
of gesture, now the hand's rehearsed articulation
over chopsticks, conjuring up rice. There is nothing
immutable about anyone; the barre of the brow's ledge
keeping a soiled metaphor. Anyway there I am, green
faun-eyed and muscles incandescent with quiet,
suspended in a type of rage, clearing out an afternoon.
You put out four dumb suitors with the bins again
as if before, with some bust in jade, and the concept
of ekphrasis, fearing sequins and a line's drowning gravity.
Taking a rite straight from the split air, one-handed,
to mark a torso wholly signatured against time.
Well, shadow of the earth, my arms with bruises
after pondwater. Yes I am beautiful / for noticing.
And leaving *en pointe*, there's happiness following solo,
at a distance, skinning itself into heaven like a snake.

CHINA MIÉVILLE

Death Cults of East Anglia

Church ruins beyond a brutally hot field of dust. You took your pilgrimage route past exhausted pigs, a hollow way to the North Sea.

Once there were chambers hidden underground. As the shoreline erodes they are uncovered to jut from the cliffs. Whenever you come here there are changes to the seaside rubble, concrete rooms tumbled wrong-way-up onto the beach. This time a brick wall lay slanting down in the surf. You sat on it in the sun.

A version of this photo-essay is forthcoming in *Between Catastrophe and Revolution: Essays in Honor of Mike Davis* (2020). I'm grateful to the editors Daniel Bertrand Monk and Michael Sorkin.

You drank the last of your water between desiccated tracts. The map was clear but the world so flat and arid, woodland so distant, your progress so slow you grew confused. You were specks in a stretched-out agribusiness sublime. There were no wrong turnings to take but you rechecked anyway. You grew thirstier and uneasy and wherever you were, it was a long walk back to where you'd started. Something was wrong with the landscape.

July 2018. It's as hot in Britain as anyone remembers. The temperatures peak in Suffolk.

Heat unmoors. You are vivid and smeared like a smudge of ink. Tethers deliquesce between things and their thingness: '[i]n the heat,' L.P. Hartley had it of another remorseless East Anglian summer, 'the commonest objects changed their nature.' The air vibrates on the thresholds of horse exits in the Roman walls at Burgh. In these parts they said horses could see ghosts.

The rags of other heatwaves cling: you're in 2018 and 2006, too, 2003. And 1976, of course. Keeling and his colleagues put out their minatory and seminal piece, 'Atmospheric carbon dioxide variation at Mauna Loa observatory', and you're almost four years old and waiting for the water truck in the midst of a plague of ladybirds. Bishybarnybees, as they are called in local dialect, named for a heretic-hunting priest.

Now Malibu burns again. In Algeria, in Canada, in Japan, in South Korea, the heat kills. The jet stream is drifting north, and weak. There are all-time highs all across the world. The arctic is in flames. According to Hans Joachim Schellnhuber, one of the authors of 'Trajectories of the Earth System in the Anthropocene', '[t]his is the moment when people start to realise that global warming is not a problem for future generations, but for us now'. Nearly half of all Americans feel that they have personal experience of climate change, according to a Yale study. Seventy-five per cent that it will harm future generations.

It's too hot to sleep. So the new nostrum is that this is the year when we wake up. The phrase reverberates in the reports of forest fires, mass extinctions, tipping points and climate cascade, of ice-melt, warming seas, frost no-longer perma.

A lifetime ago, Aldo Leopold wrote that '[o]ne of the penalties of an ecological education is that one lives alone in a world of wounds'. Now millions of us labour towards such education, to live among those wounds. And still we're lonely.

The question is not whether temperatures will rise, but by how much they will. (A year from now in 2019 will come the hottest July ever recorded on this planet.) From which follow the questions of what, if anything, 'we' – that feint again – can do about it, and for how long that window is ajar. The questions come with a toll. According to one survey, more than 70 per cent of Americans are worried, uncertain of their agency, more than half are 'disgusted' or 'helpless' or both. There can, notoriously, be *jouissance*, complex compensation and investment in apocalypse thinking, but that does not countervail forthright and growing angst. In 2017, the American Psychological Association warned not only of '*acute* consequences of psychological well-being' given inevitable weather-pattern disasters, but a longer-term existential impact, that the *longue durée* of climate change 'will cause some of the most resounding *chronic* psychological consequences': depression, trauma, identity-loss, violence, helplessness, suicide.

Cautious data-crunching becomes a strange poetry of necessary imprecision: in the new Yale/George Mason University study, 'Climate Change in the American Mind', one chart is entitled 'A Majority of Americans Who Think Global Warming is Happening Feel A Range of Emotions'.

Global warming is the paradigmatic exemplar of what Timothy Morton has called a hyperobject, a diffuse thing of such enormous temporo-spatial scale that it evades traditional thingness. It can be studied and it can be considered but it is, he writes, 'something you cannot see or touch'. It is 'something on the tips of our tongues'.

Indeed. Language in and of this heat is quite evasive.

'[T]here are hardly any intimate words' for what is happening, writes Zadie Smith, in her 'Elegy for a Country's Seasons'. This epoch is of the groping for utterance. What terms we coin for the sense of lamentation can only gesture at it – 'ecoanxiety', Glenn Albrecht's 'solastalgia', Renee Lertzmann's 'environmental melancholia', Ashlee Cunsolo and Neville Ellis's 'ecological grief', Deborah Bird Rose's 'Anthropocene Noir'. In December 2018, *Le Monde* reports that climatologists have 'le blues'.

(It is not long since you travelled a long way to the north, stood under the borealis, in polar night, and what you remember is that it was not cold enough. You think of it often. It seems the wrong verb for coldness but what cold there was *ebbed*. And with that memory always comes another, of the ebbing of the heat from your mother's skin, under her head, when you held her, when she died.)

Whatever we call them, however much of them we cannot articulate, these blues are real and growing and they are unfinished. 'There is', as Cunsolo and Ellis put it, 'much grief work to be done, and much of it will be hard.'

Too hard for some. In the pages of the British tabloid the *Sun* – *nomen est omen* – Rod Liddle, thuggish jester-bully of the British commentariat, works anxiously to undermine such intuition and perspicacious grief.

'I remember the last few summers we've had — rainy and cool — and the climate change monkeys saying THAT was a consequence of global warming, too. You can't have it both ways.' It's impossible to say how much of this is performance, whether Liddle is genuinely a fool. Weather systems are ultra-complex and overdetermined. No scientist thinks of them in monocausal or certain terms. The point, rather, as in the work of Friederike Otto, is to discern trends and the vastly increasing *likelihoods* of extreme events. On which basis one can, of course, indeed have it both ways, the same systemic cascades being key determinants of contrasting phenomena.

'[T]his summer — a proper summer, at last — is something to be enjoyed, cherished and remembered', Liddle bangs on. His insistence is a cruel optimism of the Right. It exists not despite but because of those growing blues. Hence his deployment, alongside negation blatant enough to embarrass the most vulgar Freudian, of that standard reactionary trope, the demand for complicity. '[T]his hasn't been bad, has it?'

Has it? Has it?

Liddle, *en passant*, claims not to be a climate-change denier. Insofar as any coherent position beyond a baseline spite can be imputed to him, this is likely true, and it is symptomatic. Outright denial, denialism itself, remains and will remain a force. But for all the blare and bluster of its faithful, their numbers now diminish as such denial's season – its usefulness to the ruling class – starts drawing languidly to a close. Now, in the words of the *Financial Times*, somewhere between reportage and decree, 'residual doubts over global warming evaporate'. A Monmouth University poll tracks an increase in the number of Americans who 'believe in' climate change of almost 10 per cent in three years, up to nearly eight in ten – including, even, close to two thirds of Republicans. And according to the Yale numbers, 62 per cent of respondents see warming as mostly caused by human activity.

Here, the Met Office *UK Climate Projections 2018* is wargaming longer-term temperature rises of between one and five degrees for this place. It is already the driest part of the country. East Anglian summers will soon see more droughts. This region, says a representative of the Environmental Agency, is on the 'front line of managing the impacts of climate change in the UK'.

'Managing', here, is a verb with a lot of work to do.

Now as the ideological efficacy of denial decreases, climate hustlers try out various other options. Adequate for some, simple Bad Hope can provide clickbait lists of Reasons For Optimism, soothing lullabies according to which sense will prevail, it will all work out, the adults in the room are bound soon enough to take charge. But there are those for whom more steely-eyed motivational management-think is necessary, and available.

'Like any disruptive force,' writes Dimitris Tsitsiragos breathlessly for the World Bank, as if of an exciting fintech startup, 'climate change is creating opportunities for companies willing to innovate.' In this imaginary, such opportunities might range from, at their most grandiose, geo-dreamwork of some lucrative Promethean technofix or other, all the way down to more quotidian band-aid opportunism, a slavering at exciting markets of carbon capture, and so on.

'Sustainability' is a 'popular field that emerged to teach business how to become a force for ecological preservation', write Alan Bradshaw and Detlev Zwick, in 'The Field of Business Sustainability and the Death Drive: A Radical Intervention'. And it is, they blithely and acutely add, 'a project that *comes with its own guarantee of failure*'.

As that discourse chunters on, so guaranteed, an accompanying whisper is still for the most part subtextual in polite society – but decreasingly so. This is what Naomi Klein calls the 'monstrousness' of a certain supremacist anti-denialism, an outright gloating that climate change *is* real, and growing – and that it will disproportionately affect the wretched of the earth. What is already quite openly celebrated, after all, is the sheer sociopathy of 'entrepreneurialism' and its profiteering, not only from supposed solutions to catastrophe, but from such solutions' absence. From catastrophe itself.

'Take advantage of climate change business opportunities. Climate change may increase demand for certain goods and services, such as water management products and equipment and clothing for extreme weather conditions.' The observation is true, and it is depraved. With disaster does indeed come terrible need. These eager words are not the sub-Ayn Randian enthusiasms of some marginal and disavowed libertarian sadist, but advice from the website nibusinessinfo.co.uk, the official business-guidance channel for Northern Ireland. This remorseless year 2018 'is likely to rank among the top 10 for the amount of sea ice melting in the Arctic Ocean', notes the trade outlet *Insurance Journal*. 'While that's alarming to environmentalists concerned about global warming, ship owners carrying liquefied natural gas and other goods see it as an opportunity.' The sun is shining. Make hay.

Such unflustered opportunism is not a new phenomenon, some excrescence of the moment and a shift in consciousness. Back in 2013, Bloomberg breezily reported that 'working under the assumption that climate change is inevitable, Wall Street firms are investing in businesses that will profit as the planet gets hotter'. In 2011, floods in Thailand killed hundreds outright, and affected over 13 million. The country scrambled to develop flood-management systems – which the British Government's 'national adaptation plan' two years later described as 'a high-value business opportunity', preening that it 'promotes and supports UK companies to access these opportunities'.

'Your whole society', wrote Mike Davis in the voice of Plague, a decade and a half ago, 'is suffering from acute apocalypse denial'. Now both denial and its denial are commodified.

The stark heat seems magnified in this crumbling-edged selcouth of clay and Pleistocene sand. A few cirrus do their best, as do dead trees and the eyelessly gazing watertowers, but there's a drought of shadows too. The sunlight picks out roadside signs and rubble.

With effort and luck you might make anywhere do and mean anything, but there are prevailing semiotic tides to discern and navigate. And there are always undertows thereto, of which we should make sense – this fen chic, this Anglian moment, Caitlín Doherty observes, is hardly uncorrelated with the places of Cambridge, UEA and the Norwich Centre for Writing in the profitable business of BritLit.

Such diagnosis, however, need not vitiate the artefacts of any such moment, of figures in a landscape. And this windblown place is and has long been dense with artistic glowerings, of Ruth Rendell, the Jameses P.D. and M.R., Sarah Perry, all the others in all the many lists. The big sky looms baleful here above a certain existential crime noir, the recondite mooching of edgeland psychogeography, over spectral culture above all, ghosts, and the newly-fashionable bucolic uncanny of 'Folk Horror'.

Quis este site qui venit. Who is this who is coming?

These days *eerieness* is fast catching up with its co-constitutive other, the weird, as an aesthetic to be noted and parsed. Robert MacFarlane has been a crucial skald, and the deeply mourned Mark Fisher its seminal theorist. His book *The Weird and the Eerie* is a fecund entry-point.

For Fisher, the eerie 'is constituted by a *failure of absence* or by a *failure of presence*'. Where the weird is a function of 'the presence of *that which does not belong*', the eerie arises where, and insofar as, 'something [is] present where there should be nothing' – his example is of a bird's cry behind which is a sense of something beyond the animal – 'or there is nothing present where there should be something' – a ruin, say, a place made strange by time, emptied of people. Which means 'the central enigma' of the eerie 'is the problem of agency': for the failure of absence, whether there is agency at all; for the failure of presence, what the nature is of that missing agency of which we feel a trace?

Should it ever come to pass that the conundrum of agency be solved, 'when knowledge is achieved', Fisher writes, 'the eerie disappears'. Unlike the radically unknowable of the Weird, the eerie is, one might say, 'merely' unknown – but constitutively so.

To the Norfolk Broads, 'which lie in the midst of wide level marshes and tracts of sedgy fen', William Dutt writes in his 1906 book on the waterways, there is a 'primeval, isolate beauty'. Like the eco-anguish around us, that beauty evades expression: 'I had almost', Dutt offers, 'written sublimity'. Almost but not quite. It is mountains and oceans that are, traditionally, sublime. Where the 'sublimity of a moor' was, for Thomas Hardy, 'chastened', in the flatland specificity of the broad is sublimity not chastened but *withheld*. The weird is a bad sublime: the eerie is sublime-proximate.

Mark Fisher loved this eerie East Anglian landscape, this haunting land-and-sky. His walks therein were generative of his theories, political phenomenology. His strange heuristics of strangeness itself read aesthetics and the politics thereof and the world that extrudes them. 'Since the eerie turns crucially on the problem of agency, it is about the forces that govern our lives and the world', Fisher wrote. 'It should be especially clear to those of us in a globally tele-connected capitalist world that those forces are not fully available to our sensory apprehension.' No wonder, then, that for him, 'Capital is at every level an eerie entity'.

Thus analysis, radical understanding. And what of the strategic resources, the lessons that might follow? To quote the writer and photographer Matt Colquhoun, aka Xenogoth, in his exemplary articulation of the question oft-repeated by those of us caught up by such eldritchiana, what are the 'emancipatory potentials found within the *other-wordly*'?

For Colquhoun, considering the 'latent act of exit' from putative normality that Fisher terms 'egress', the weird and eerie 'resemble aesthetic tools for the creation of passageways between capitalism and its outside'. Crucially, however, he also uneasily notes of Fisher's text that 'the political implications of egress, the weird and the eerie are not made as explicit as one might expect'.

What if these implications are not so much occult as absent, and not even eerily so? What if such absence is not a political problem, but our own hankering for their presence very much is?

The Left's fervid eagerness to derive politics and techniques from various fleeting and fleetingly succulent cultural morsels, from *the stuff that we like*, is symptomatic of our terrible weakness.

We must allow that not everything that we enjoy or in which we find affective resonance can be effectively, politically, strategically, tactically, *applied*. Enjoin ourselves: test everything that gets you up in the morning, certainly, for whatever contingent inspiration you might find. But know that it comes from you, and that whatever traction there might be therein for you is not traction *tout court*, still less some political Real. We are predisposed to such Procrustean activity, and, but, we are not alone in that. In capitalism all signs are reversible. There are gothic fascisms as well as gothic Marxisms, and there are weird fascisms too, a great number of them, and if the Left decides that it will 'learn the lessons' of the Eerie, so too can and will our enemies. And it is not more or better eeriness that will defeat them, nor any placeness of the places in which we find it.

The admirable hate of #folkloreagainstfascism, of those invested in certain music and landscape, in particular fables and hedge-magic – Yallery Brown, say, the Woolpit Green Children, Black Shuck, *Your preferred folktale here* – and who are aghast that they are snaffled by the far Right for its murderous national kitsch, is righteous. Fascists should not, indeed, be allowed to own what they claim to own. What cannot follow from that, however, for such contested scobs as these traditions, is any Red essentialism – *something something subversive spirits of the land something something radical Albion.*

Yes, let us complicate and enrich what David Southwell calls the 'ghost soil' with counterhistory, with creative reading and unreading. Unwhite it: learn, for example, from Wedaeli Chibelushi's 'A Brief History of Blackness in East Anglia', the stories of Thomas Parker, the 'certayne dark mayne' of sixteenth-century Essex, of Maria Sambo two centuries after that, of Allan Glaisyer Minns of Thetford, in 1904 the first Black mayor in Britain. Commemorate and celebrate all the local histories of insurrection – Bury St Edmunds risings in 1264 and in 1381, Kett's Rebellion of 1549, the riots of 1822, the Burston Rebellion of 1914. Keep all of them in mind, because such insurgencies matter wherever they take place, and because like Fisher you love *this* place, but don't seek to find in them some ineffable intransigence intrinsic to this local earth. Because there is none. Except to the extent that it is everywhere. In her celebration of these environs, 'this uncanny land', Sarah Perry has it that '[t]he character of the East Anglian woman is radical, literate, rebellious, courageous, mystic and astute'. Yes, but only to the extent that also No. This is, of course, no more *au fond* the nature of 'the' East Anglian woman than is the nature of Aldeburgh locals, per George Crabbe's 1783 *The Village*, that of 'a wild amphibious race, / With sullen wo display'd in every face'. There are and there were thoroughly mammalian and cheerful Aldeburghians, and among actually-existing East Anglian women, and men, are the reactionary, the unread, the conformist and the cowardly, the earthbound and dim in usual proportions.

Is this too ungenerous? Too reductionist? Perry herself describe East Anglia as 'ripe with myth'. (As where is not?) Perhaps what such ruminations could call up, create, sustain is precisely a kind of myth. It will be a political myth, as all myths are.

Even so, that literalist caution remains necessary. Too many such invocations fail to distinguish essentialist truth claims – a political ontology of place – and mythopoeitic intervention. Adequately or at all. And such elision as that, whatever the intention and however conscious or not, ultimately always serves reaction.

Myth itself may be inevitable, but it is always ambiguous and polyvalent, and never more so than when naturalised. The far Right knows this very well, as it does that myth is political. A key danger of any mythopoeisis of place is precisely that it cleaves so smoothly with that ugly agenda.

This is clear and appropriately troublesome to practitioners of art and thought within the melancholy field of 'landscape punk' (Gary Budden), of 're-enchantment as resistance' (David Southwell). John Harrigan of the FoolishPeople collective, for example, insists that 'it's vital we don't permit racists/fascists to pervert the landscape of Britain'. But even here is the sign of essentialism, of a *genius loci*, of a 'truth' of place available to be 'perverted'. The danger is not merely of 'technicised' in place of 'genuine myth', in Károly Kerényi's terms, glossed by Andrea Cavaletti as the 'instrumental distortion of ancient mythologemes for the purposes of political propaganda'. The problem is of myth *tout court*, of the edifice that the great radical mythologist Furio Jesi, in his break with Kerényi, came bleakly to see as 'the mythological machine'.

The artist Paul Watson, in his heartfelt straining to salvage landscape from the Right, deems 'the oldest past version of a myth ... the kernel, the most primal incarnation' 'Deep Myth'. He is honest that he finds '[t]he desire to glimpse the deep myth ... a strong one', and for him 'in that glimpse of the primal comes a re-enchantment' – resistance. But he is also clear of such deep myth that '[i]n realistic terms it's unknowable' – and, we should emphatically add, untrustworthy, if there was ever any such kernel at all. No matter how antique or otherwise are the lovingly deployed stories and tropes of locale, this is precisely *poiesis*, political myth-*making*, on one side or another. It is not spiritual archaeology of some ur-truth, not a 'revealed religion', as Jesi once put it, but 'a way to participate in reality, an opening to learning about reality'.

We may feel that 'deep myth' can, as Watson avers, be 'glimpsed as a partial reflection in the contemporary version'. But we cannot know what, if anything, it is that we actually glimpse, nor whence it comes. And, crucially, what capacities we have for enchantment, radical and otherwise, inhere not in *what* we glimpse but in *that we yearn to glimpse it*, and in our sense that glimpse it we can.

These cautions must be explicit.

There is, for all this, a distinct and perhaps more productive conception of myth implicit in Watson's image of uncovering, in his mode of access to the putatively ancient. 'Somewhere in the metaphorically dense language of the contemporary myth', he writes, 'are echoes of the primal deep one'. But the point is that any such echoes are not only relatively but absolutely autonomous of any originary sound. These echoes are not 'within' but *are* those very metaphors of which he speaks, drawing on Adrienne Rich on the 'metaphoric density' of language, and, we can add, of any system of signs. There is no lonely hour of the last instance, no grundnorm of meaning at the metaphors' base.

This matters. Because to contest a machine is not to escape it. Haunting the debates about whether a left mythology is feasible, let alone desirable, is an uneasy awareness that antinomianism, honourable and necessary as it is, cannot be the only mode of resistance. That myth cannot be evaded by fiat.

'At the molten heart of things everything resembles everything else', writes Edward St Aubyn of metaphor and its annealing. For his protagonist that means anguish, but the insight might be a source of gladness. It is not that in the fire of the mind everything resembles everything else but that it *admixes* with it, becomes it, as it pours off soot and the slag of meaning, semiotic runoff, setting into fantastic opacities. It is by metaphors that we might, not recover, but construct, myth. Mindful of political ambivalences, what we forge from placeness may – may not, of course, but just *may* – have some partial, contingent, contested radical use.

Our commitment is not to primality, to any imagined deep-time depth. If deployed, landscape must be something that we choose to *do* – a way, per Jesi, to participate in reality – in fidelity to liberation.

The Island, they once called it, but it is a strip of shingle and sand tethered to the coast. The military had a secret base. This place is notorious for bygone death rays, radar towers, UFOs, the mouldering knoll-sided pagodas of an industry and statecraft of speculative apocalypse. Orford Ness is littered with battle rubbish, engines like discards of invasion, sculptures of themselves in rust. Shacks are overrun, wind, grass, birds. You pay a ferryman to cross the water – reality is not subtle – to trudge like mendicants in Hell.

The laboratories fell apart under the sun years ago. '[T]he closer I came to these ruins', Sebald wrote of his own then-illicit approach, 'the more any notion of a mysterious isle of the dead receded, and the more I imagined myself amidst the ruins of our own civilisation after its extinction in some future catastrophe'. As if that's a contradiction. The catastrophe is here, and these, like those of Covehithe church up the coast, are ruins by design. The policy is called 'managed decline'. A nationally sanctioned becoming-eerie.

In nineteenth-century Brazil, Mike Davis notes with cataclysm empathy, 'millenarianism in the *sertão* was also a practical social framework for coping with environmental instability … sermonising apocalypse but practicing energetic self-help'. Why not? It is not as if there are not many far worse strategies. Change that last conjunction, in fact, from 'but' to 'and' or 'so'. The sermons are inextricable from the struggle itself.

For a new chiliasm of the Left.

We could make sacred masks out of the military trash in the sand, if it helps, masks like those 'burning at our gate' in the eleventh, harshest verse of Jini Fiennes' 'Suffolk Song Cycle', masks that 'glare' and that '[w]ith sightless sense interrupt'.

Interruption could hardly be more urgent.

Lines of dead trees, lichened concrete in the bird sanctuary, drowned houses off the coast. Everything means what it means and means more than it means, too. Today, everything is a metaphor for the end, for hope, and for hopelessness.

On the other side of the world, bats are falling out of a sky that is cooking them alive, and we don't pretend that doesn't matter and we don't pretend that everything will be alright. Against the yaysayers, undefeated despair is militancy. Richard Seymour has it precisely right: 'it is the catastrophists,' he says, 'the doom-mongers who believe in the future.'

For the Catholic leftist Herbert McCabe, it was in the triumph of liberation for which he strove, the post-ruptural Kingdom of God, so close to communism itself, that 'there will be no more Eucharist, no more sacramental religion, no more faith or hope'. To hope against hope is not merely to contest all the dreg-like hope unearned: it is prefiguration. It is to live with an eye on the horizon where hope will be no longer needed.

In this baking flood-prone place the horizon is very clear.

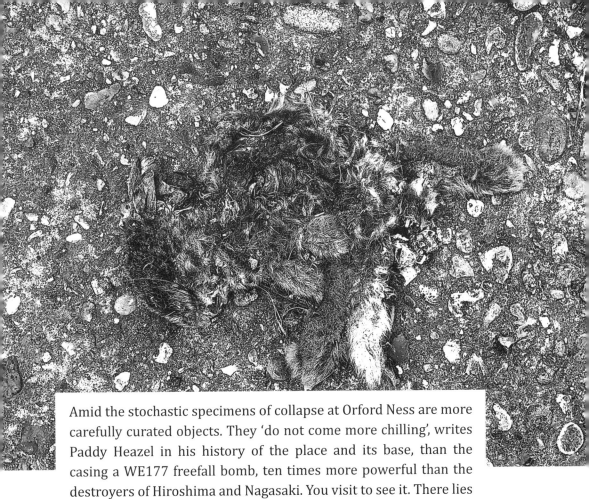

Amid the stochastic specimens of collapse at Orford Ness are more carefully curated objects. They 'do not come more chilling', writes Paddy Heazel in his history of the place and its base, than the casing a WE177 freefall bomb, ten times more powerful than the destroyers of Hiroshima and Nagasaki. You visit to see it. There lies its husk.

This is a landscape of relics. Mummied roadkill hares. The local saints – Julian, Pega, Guthlac, Witburga, Tova. '[O]f St Gilbert two pieces,' runs one ancient and meticulous list of sanctified dead parts from a Norwich church, 'of St. Euphemia the like, of the innocents the like, of St. Stephen four pieces, of St. Wulstan one piece, of St. Leger one piece'. And so, grimly and lengthily, on.

It took strenuous propaganda on the part of the twelfth-century monk Thomas of Monmouth for the cult of Saint William of Norwich to flourish. William, the 'poor ragged little lad', Thomas told, was tortured and murdered by Norwich Jews in grotesque mockery of Christ's passion. The tale of course was obfuscation, the defence of a down-at-heel knight for the murder of his creditor, by posthumously claiming that his victim was the ringleader of the child-killers. For the historian E.M. Rose, in indicting a whole community, the story was a key generative text of the blood libel,

215

with all the anti-Semitic murder that followed. It was a projection, an ushering-in of mass death by means of the smearing of the dead themselves, in the name of a dead boy, pornographically depicting his imagined death-mocking death.

Monmouth's tract was lost for years. But the repressed returns, of course. The man who unearthed the document in 'a small dank building in the churchyard' in 1890, who translated it and introduced it, was the seminal progenitor of the modern ghost story, that key eeritician, Montague Rhodes James himself.

'For James, who was both a horror writer and a conservative Christian,' writes Mark Fisher, 'the fascination for the outside is always fateful'.

If a Norfolk raven croaks above a house it portends death. As does a dog howling at night below a sickroom window. Bees swarming on a dead tree are death, too. Four crows in the road are death, an unmelted wick in a guttering candle is death, a candle burning at all in a shuttered room, the sound of a cuckoo heard from bed, a snake in the house, all mean death.

As, in East Anglia, does a certain post-morten softness. A cadaver that is too slow to enter rigor, that is recalcitrantly not-relic enough, is traditional presentiment of more mortality to come. In this place, death itself can be a sign for death. Death inadequately enacted invoking metadeath.

In 2013, the vicar Tony Higton – officiating chaplain for RAF Marham, erstwhile director of the CMJ, the Church's Ministry amongst Jewish People, once called 'Mary Whitehouse in a dog collar' for his traditionalist fervour during the Church's sexuality wars back in the 1980s – began work on a new project. Along with his wife Patricia Higton, herself a reader in the church, the 'high-profile West Norfolk clergyman', one Christian outlet enthused, inaugurated 'a web campaign calling Christians to take Eschatology (the doctrine of the End Times) seriously'. The site is regularly updated, navigating the traditional much-mocked tea-and-biscuits moderation of Anglicanism with the urgency of doomsday augury.

'There is', it warns, it assures, 'an escalating fulfilment of the biblical signs of the end'. Hence its assiduous evidence-parsing for impending armageddon.

'You're living in a nihilistic death cult', writes Seymour. He's talking of the fetishised machinery of the border, but that is not the cult's only mystery. It is not long since Corbyn's cordial refusal to pledge that he would enact pointless nuclear mass murder, like that imagined with the dead bomb, was a political scandal.

In these Higtonian end times, capitalism oscillates between disavowal and death-avowal. In the 2007 council climate-change strategy, 'Tomorrow's Norfolk, Today's Challenge', the crises to come are itemised as if by some bureaucrat St John – floods, destruction, sickness and death, the ruination of heritage, crop-failure, pestilence. Then, immediately, are cited those familiar commercial opportunities. '[H]otter, drier summers will help make Norfolk more favourable as a tourism destination'.

Welcome to terminal beach.

Like those crows in the road, the guttering candles, like the unstraight sowing of seed in an East Anglian field, they say, #EFDS is a harbinger of death. 'EcoFascist Death Squads', a dream of the online Deep Green right.

'[C]limate denial is integral to rightwing thinking', Rebecca Solnit will come to write in a few months time, and her words will be reassuring, and they will be quite wrong. The overt avowed hecatomb logic of genocide will increase in volume along with the temperatures. So too will the ranks of its enthusiasts, brayers of a long-sedimented drive.

'Long live death!' the fascist slogan goes – death of the enemy, the untermenchen, the unclean and rootless, the weak and feminine, the snake in the garden, and death, too, of the world, and ultimately, even, perhaps, of the self. There will be supremacist suicide cults, embracing all doom, including their own. Already, Pentti Linkola, the notorious, lugubrious doyen of fascist green thanatology, is clear on these matters: '[i]f there were a button I could press, I would sacrifice myself without hesitating, if it meant millions of people would die.'

It is not hard to imagine the semiotic bric-a-brac of the annihilationist myths to come. Such hothouse-Earth fascisms will festoon themselves, of course, in their pitiful solar symbols. They will maunder, of course, about Evola and solar civilisation, about the sun wheel, the sun cross, about the black sun and the *sol invictus*. They will be entranced by Albert Speer, by the theory of 'Ruin Value', by the tenets of the central importance of bequeathing to deep time suitable reich memorabilia, monumental and adequately impressive ruins.

They will pine, that is, as fascisms always have, to be a supremacist eerie. A crust like dried-up spittle. An absence proclaiming the triumph of death.

East Anglia is eroded by the sea. Out of *le blues*, with fury and without surrender, must come a contestation, to bring to this moment of disaster capitalism and fascist eerie a ruin communism, hope against hope.

In the converted chapel at Westleton, among all the piled-up books for sale, a tattered old volume fell open in your hands. At its end were ancient advertisments for more such lost volumes: *An Experiment with Time*, you read; and *Nothing Dies*. You fanned yourself with the pages.

They call it Silly Suffolk, sometimes, then quickly stress that the adjective is mutation of the old word 'seely'. That what it means is *holy*, for all that hallowed ground. But seely has many meanings. *Pious* and *good* and *blessed, holy*, yes, *happy* and *lucky*. But it also means *deserving of sympathy*, and *pitiable*, the *OED* informs. It means, *worn-out* and *crazy. Observant of due season*. It means *in danger of divine judgement*.

East Anglia, in its due season, facing vastation.

They executed the ungodly so often in Norwich that one old map marks out 'Ye place where ye Heretickes are custumably burned'. In 1589, they put Francis Kett – grandson of he of the rebellion forty years before – to flame, for denying the divinity of Jesus. One scandalised critic glossed his democratic theology of mortal flesh thus: 'Christ Jesus is not God, but a good man, as others be'. But as Dewey D. Wallace points out of Kett's heresies, 'eschatological motifs are far more prominent than denial of the Trinity', and '[c]entral to his eschatology would seem to be the notion that redemption is future and imminent'. Only when he ushers in the Kingdom will the son of man become God.

McCabe's beyond-hope draws near, in the hands of a self-actualising humanity. Kett could hardly more clearly be, as Wallace so shrewdly puts it, a 'link in that strange connection between bizarre religious notions and incipient rationalism', nor 'further confirmation of the significance of the passage from specifically eschatological eccentricities to radicalism'. Amen. Even his enemies marked his piety. At the stake, one allowed with grudging admiration, Kett 'went leaping and dauncing ... clapping his handes, he cried nothing, but blessed be God, blessed be God, blessed be God'. There are new ways to die, to move, to be in the body.

In the broads, in the corridors of reeds, a shimmering split the surface and made it gleam. A snake swimming. Another strange, alternate animal motion. It crossed right before your prow, the most beautiful thing that there has ever been. It thrust its head up out of the water as it went. It glared skyward, just as if it was staring down the sun.

RICHARD SEYMOUR

The Social Industry and the 'Lone Wolf' Phase of Fascism

What makes fascism dangerous is its molecular or micropolitical power, for it is a mass movement: a cancerous body rather than a totalitarian organism.

Gilles Deleuze and Felix Guattari, *A Thousand Plateaus.*

I

Fascism without fascism. In an age in which things are unclear, tendencies yet to congeal, political substances yet to find their settled form, we have to resort to contradiction. Theory must be as indeterminate, and speculative, as reality itself: a roll of the dice.

There has not been a better time to be a fascist since 1945, and yet there is no sign of a mass fascist party or paramilitary movement forming, let alone of a potential revolutionary-nationalist capture of state power. There are fascists, but this is not the classical fascist situation. The present political sequence is marked by a string of far-right successes. 'Lone wolf' attacks from Thomas Mair to Robert Bower. Trump, Bolsonaro, Jobbik. And the consolidation of an alt-right subculture. For all this, though, what is most clear is how unlike the past our current dilemmas are.

Historical fascism was, as anti-colonialists, Black internationalists and Trotskyists intuited, a concentrated expression of the imperialist will-to-power. Or, from the perspective of the Algerian Front de libération nationale's journal *Résistance Algérienne*, 'colonialism when rooted in a traditionally colonialist country'. Historiographical breakthroughs, from Ute Poiger to Mark Mazower, have substantiated this connection. German fascism is incomprehensible without its colonial drive, in rivalrous emulation of the British. Italian fascism cannot be apprehended without studying the genocidal application of General Douhet's 'Total War' doctrine in Libya, and the invasion of Abyssinia. And Franco's re-colonisation of Spain could not have succeeded without the prior pacification of the Rif rebellion in Morocco, from whence his 'reconquista' was launched.

That particular garrisoned version of global white-supremacy is dead, probably forever. Today's world-system, still formed by racial capitalism and policed by imperial violence, is now organised as a legal framework of nation-states enmeshed in the institutions of liberal globalisation. Notwithstanding Donald Trump's challenge to the 'globalists', these institutions are not yet seriously endangered. There is no immediate prospect of a return to the autarkic context of interwar capitalism, with its pressures towards interimperialist war.

The centralised systems of racial sovereignty known as slavery, segregation, apartheid, concentration camps and 'ghettos' are unlikely to return even under the securitarian and border crackdowns of liberal states: the American carceral-state is exceptional in its scope. Race-making under neoliberalism follows a more capillary logic. Sexual morality and demographic regulation are unlikely in the future to return to the format of pre-war patriarchy: indeed, the emerging anti-liberal Right can be understood partly as a reaction against patriarchal decline. Despite the hauntological anticommunism of the new far-right, moreover, the prospect of a revolutionary challenge to capitalism of the sort that Mussolini's *fasci* and Hitler's stormtroopers sought to crush, appears remote. There is no equivalent today to the civil war that characterised European societies from 1914 to 1945. As Dylan Riley argues in the

New Left Review, interwar fascism was built out of mass political participation, a 'thick' civil society that simply doesn't exist today.

Which is not deny that many of the traditional sources of fascism still obtain. Capitalism remains a crisis-driven system. Middle-class discontent continues to fuel reaction. Imperialism ongoingly produces new constituencies of armed right-wing murderers, from Vietnam to Iraq. The stalemate of the liberal state and the crisis of representation presents the opening for new far-right tendencies. The crisis of traditional gender relations and the torment of sexuality galvanises, as similar crises have before, the lurid masculinism and homosocial bonding of the far-right. The question, however, is what are the *novel* social and cultural sources of fascism in the twenty-first century?

What is particularly visible in today's far-right is its networked nature. In place of traditional fascist cadre organisations, there are online labyrinths, ephemeral street movements, flash mobs, brands and microcelebrities, electoral campaigns, milieux in which fascists and fascist ideas circulate freely but are not yet dominant. We see the logic of the swarm, the online shitstorm, the troll, spill over into meatspace. There are loose and deliberately ambiguous relations between followers and leaders, organisations and 'lone wolves', far-rights and alt-lights. Where symbols like the swastika or the iron cross once embodied a 'leading idea' with which millions identified, what Paul Gilroy once called 'logo solidarity', now Pepe the Frog (or the St George Cross, or the ISIS black flag) represents a memeified version of the same in vastly different circumstances. Recent right-wing mass killers, from Alek Minassian to Brenton Tarrant, have used the language of memes to express identification and belonging. Alberto Toscano has spoken of the 'intensely *superstructural* character of our present's fascistic traits', referring to the crisis of capitalist politics. Might one just as well say that these traits are *substructural*? If fascism doesn't present itself in a finished form at the molar level, is it nonetheless fizzing away at the molecular level? Can we sensibly speak, as Deleuze and Guattari did, of 'micro-fascisms', knowing how necessarily indeterminate such a concept must be? Indeed, given recent shifts in the scale of political action, from the rise of nanotechnologies to the digitalisation of capitalism, ought we now speak of 'nanofascisms'?

II

Consider Donald Trump, the ungainly global mascot of the new far-right. A real-estate salesman and television personality who built his brand and electoral campaign on Twitter, he is in no sense the leader of a fascist regime. Captive to a liberal state, attaining at best a pragmatic comity with large capital, he has struggled to define a viable policy agenda. He effects, not a radical statist concentration of power, but tilts and escalations in the administration of American imperialism, bionatalism, racist-carceralism, and the judicial consolidation of what left theologian William Connolly calls the 'evangelical-capitalist resonance machine'. Even in this respect, his record is patchy, as shown by his willingness to sign off on a bipartisan prison reform bill, streamlining sentences and saving taxpayer money.

Nonetheless, among his unique selling points is his hitherto scandalous ambiguity with regard to actually-existing-fascism. In the *Salvage* double-negative, he is 'not not a fascist'. From former Klan leader and neo-Nazi David Duke to 'white power' demonstrators in Charlottesville, Trump's refusal to offend these energetic parts of his base seems entirely kneejerk: 'his actual default position', as Bannon put it. When, following a series of death threats targeting Jews, Trump implied that Jews themselves might have made the threats, he was seemingly unreflexive in his reiteration of a far-right trope. When, a mere two days after the murder of Heather Heyer in a vehicular assault by a neo-Nazi on a crowd of antifascists, Trump found both 'blame' and 'very fine people' on 'both sides', he was likely dialling down his instinctive sympathies. Trump's affinities, that is, appear to be *spontaneous* and unmediated by historical knowledge, formed more by the culture industry than by reading the copy of *Mein Kampf* he allegedly kept by his bed.

Trump is as automatically attuned to the unconscious fascist potential in American society and mass culture as are alt-right trolls. A successful fascist agitator, Adorno remarked, meets the unconscious of his audience simply by turning his own unconscious outward. He 'resembles them psychologically', thinks in stereotype, participates in 'the brotherhood of all comprising humiliation', and is distinguished only, but spectacularly, by his ability to express latent ideology without inhibition. Thus Trump. The operational equivalent of 4chan, as writer Dale Beran put it, he is a labyrinth with no centre, a flow of swastikas, snuff footage, war porn, trolls, racist cartoons, antisemitic jokes and leaked celebrity nudes, his promises as empty as memes. Not a conscious fascist leader, let alone commander of a fascist apparatus, but a spontaneous conductor for the microfascisms of his audience. There will be others with more historical consciousness of their role.

Liberal astonishment about the 'return' of fascism, as though it had ever entirely gone away, reflects a blind-spot about its own potentials. Fascism, as Nikhil Singh put it in a perceptive essay on its 'afterlife', is a 'deviation of *democratic* regimes'. Far from being the 'monstrous Other' of liberal-democracy, it might be better understood as its 'doppelgänger'. It engorges the exclusionary will-to-power already discernible in liberal societies, from the internal frontiers policing racialised minorities to the martial expansionism through which liberal states routinely outwit their domestic constitutional constraints. Nor, we can only speculate, does it persist only in the macro-political organisation of states, parties and grand spectacles. Rather, it is scattered in micro-political enclaves, in atomic relations of force in friendship and kinship groups, in unconscious identifications, routine forms of authority, submissiveness, sadism and manipulation all capable of crystallising and congealing given an appropriate catalyst. It is essential to address fascism at this level, rather than satisfying ourselves that the classical fascist situation does not hold, and the classical fascist mass party is not marching to power, precisely in order to orient ourselves in the ambiguous political situation that we are in.

'What set fascism in motion yesterday', Félix Guattari warned in his rebuttal of post-war triumphalism, 'continues to proliferate

in other forms, within the complex of contemporary social space.'
Liberal society may be blind to the fascist potential, the microfas-
cism, that it incubates. Is the Left, as Guattari insisted it was, likewise blinded by its 'molar' preconceptions?

III

Today's networked far-right is a resonance machine. In the era of
Bush *fils*, Connolly's 'evangelical-capitalist resonance machine'
described a mutually confirming, catalytic relationship between
anti-democratic forces. Deploying the Deleuzian concept of resonance thus, he described how distinct social logics became enfolded
in, magnified and potentiated one another. The fruits of this alliance,
crystallised in the Republican Party, are nowhere more evident
than in the judiciary, where the legal far Right are militant for both
capitalism and conservative Christianity. An analogous relationship
of mutual catalysis can be found in the networked far Right.

We see, on the one hand, how much attention and profitability
far-right spokespersons bring to the digital platforms which host
them. Donald Trump, it was estimated in 2017, was worth $2
billion to Twitter. Not only had he built a political career in this
volatile medium, but he accounted for most of its revenue. On the
other hand, when Facebook reluctantly followed Apple, Spotify,
and YouTube in terminating Alex Jones' Infowars accounts over his
claims that the Sandy Hook massacre was a false flag, it became
very clear just how much profitable attention they had enabled him
to generate, when the Infowars site lost half of its 1.4 million daily
visits. Jones's profits, $5 million in 2014, depended on advertising
to a large fanbase mostly built online, chiefly for male supplements
such as 'Super Male Vitality' and 'Caveman'. After the ban he was
left begging fans to send in donations, to help him fight the beast.
His co-dependent relationship with his online platforms is likely
to become more apparent now that the courts, handling a civil suit
filed by Sandy Hook families, have demanded to see his accounts.

The major online platform brands, under tremendous pressure, are undertaking some reluctant moves to curb the worst of its far-right product. Infowars is just one egregious node in a volatile online ecology of far-right cultures. But a similar series of moves recently befell Tommy Robinson, former member of the fascist British National Party, and founder of the racist street gang, the English Defence League. PayPal stopped processing his donations in November 2018, YouTube cancelled his advertising revenues in January 2019, and Facebook banned him in February 2019. This will have been a significant financial blow. Robinson, while in prison for endangering the prosecution of child sex offenders, had been able to use his Facebook and Twitter accounts to raise £20,000 worth of Bitcoin donations. He was also generating revenues from advertising on his YouTube account, which had 270,000 subscribers and whose individual videos received millions of views. To put this in monetary terms, YouTube paid the average user $7.60 per thousand views in 2013, so Robinson's single most watched video alone would have garnered $15,200 at that rate.

Yet, the extraordinary success of far-right 'personalities' such as Stefan Molyneux, Gavin MacInnes and Richard Spencer, is thus far mostly untouched by bans. And it is extraordinarily lucrative. Molyneux, over a period of five years, made £1 million in Bitcoin donations thanks to his online presence. And the more money they made, the more valuable they were to the social industry. There is no reason to assume the majority of these far-right microcelebrities will suffer, either financially or in terms of publicity. Jones was, after all, explicitly targeted for making tasteless claims that damaged the media he operated on, not for his politics. Mark Zuckerberg was clear that he saw no reason for Facebook not to host far-right material, even Holocaust denial, if some users wanted it. Zuckerberg recanted. And under considerable pressure from Washington over the social industry's contribution to the 2016 presidential election outcome, most platforms are taking steps to mitigate their economic involvement with the far-right. YouTube now says it will ban overt Nazi material and Holocaust denial. Yet this will inevitably rely on algorithmic surveillance, and it will only target the crudest, most overt and unreconstructed forms of paleo-Nazism.

Most successful far-right figures, however deranged their politics, have proven adept at avoiding the kinds of statement that got Jones booted, are careful not to openly affiliate to Nazism, and moderate their speech to evade detection by the 'community standards' algorithms that are supposed to root out 'hate speech'.

If Twitter is now fuelled in large part by Trumpism – and the erotically imbricated reaction against Trumpism, #theresistance – YouTube has become the talk radio of the millennial far-right. It is the most linked source on alt-right websites, and a report by the investigative outfit, Bellingcat, found that YouTube was the single platform most credited by fascist activists for their 'red-pilling'. If, as Zeynep Tufecki has found, YouTube's 'up next' feature consistently points viewers toward more 'extreme' (generally, fascist or conspiracist) content, what sort of affinity does this betray? Are the 'parasocial' relationships, or libidinal bonds, that users form with far-right microcelebrities particularly selected for by the medium? If, after mass shootings, YouTube and Google consistently promote rightist conspiracy videos promoting a 'false flag' narrative, is the relationship between the emerging far Right and their online platforms anything other than incidental? Is theirs merely a mutual instrumentality, no different from the relationship between social networking sites and any other political tendency, or are they symbionts?

IV

To even consider this, one has to clear away the conceptual clutter. We are not speaking here of 'social media'. All media, all technologies, are social. Calling Twitter, Facebook and their equivalents 'social media' is like calling cigarettes 'friendship sticks'. They can be used in that way, but that is not what they're for. Rather, to take the appropriately Adornian detour, we are talking of a social *industry*. Among Adorno's critical contributions to antifascist thought was his concept of the 'culture industry'. In the dialectic of Enlightenment, the culture industry represented a step in the catastrophic subordination of life to instrumental reason at the service of capital. Since culture was effectively subsumed into the logic of capital, its rules of verisimilitude and legibility derived from capital, the 'borderline' separating it from 'empirical reality' had been obliterated. Integrating consumers 'from above', administering them as objects of sales techniques that became indistinguishable from artistic technique *per se*, it imposed an underlying production-line uniformity on culture. The individuality of cultural products was pseudo-individuality, a variation on a limited range of templates, reinforcing a narrow repertoire of mental habits.

This, arguably a simplification and exaggeration of the integrative trends in mass culture, feels almost clairvoyant as regards the social industry. For it is not merely a new *mediation* or *augmentation* of sociality, but its mass production along sophisticated algorithmic lines. It is sociality as simulacrum: an image generated by digital writing that does not represent an underlying social link so much as produce one. We engage as 'users', much as one might 'use' crack. Or, in the insufferable neologism of the industry, 'produsers': both workers and addicts. When we spend more time interacting with screens than meeting people face to face, the simulacrum *is* our social life. And when the entire process is subordinated to the production of revenue-generating data, the timeline, the feed, is a production-line. *Pace* Jonathan Beller, looking is not labouring: but it is an inducement to labour. To contribute to the feed, to clickthrough, to scroll. The social industry requires of us, who are neither customers nor paid workers, constant work. Its techniques for integrating over three billion people into an unprecedented, rapidly mutating system of surveillance, and goading them into incessant production, are based on a model of addiction. However crudely reductionist that model is, in its emphasis on delivering a 'dopamine hit', it nonetheless works. Whether we are surfing waves of approval, or anxiously hitting refresh on a contentious thread, it is irresistible. Having secured participation, however, the social industry permits engagement only on the basis of a narrow set of protocols. Far more than cultural products, all tweets, statuses, vlogs, posts are fundamentally identical, riffs on a formula, the eternal recurrence of the same in an 'infinite' flow.

Social life is, thereby, programmed. It is reified in as much as relations between people appear as digital objects: 'likes', 'shares', 'retweets'. The protocols of the social industry form the written code, the constitution if you will, of an emerging technopolitical regime. Ideologically, they are inflected, as Alice Marwick's research suggests, by Silicon Valley neoliberalism. They are so designed, from the avatar to the 'like' function, as to focus users on the production of branded identities, celebrity and the pursuit of status in a competitive hierarchy. But they don't prescribe these behaviours; they don't argue for them. They bend social life around them; they are in the reality-shaping business.

Even this is not the whole story. For, the conscious ideology of the social industry, the curious mixture of Gingrichism and Clintonism that pervades northern California, is not necessarily consubstantial with its ideological effects – or, to be more precise, its contingent politicisations of the unconscious.

It is not simply that the machine *engages* the unconscious. Even the most rudimentary machine does that. Joseph Weizenbaum's experiments with ELIZA, the computer programme that simulated Rogerian therapy, demonstrated that people will readily form transference relationships with a bot that by today's standards is extremely crude. Rather, it *digitises* the unconscious, in its very mechanisms of accumulation and control. The information collected on users is extraordinarily precise, including length of time scrolling, hovering over a particular post or comment, typing, how many words and characters were typed, watchtime, click-throughs, and so on. These metrics, social-industry spokespersons affirm, say a great deal more about our real wants and propensities than our articulate claims or demands. They know us, in a crucial sense, better than we know ourselves. And, aggregated, analysed and algorithmised, the data shapes what we see so we remain riveted. They work because we work; they harness passions and pleasures we know nothing of, and we provide them the means to more accurately play us. The social industry has produced something like Lacan's 'modern calculating machine', 'more dangerous than the atom bomb', which can always outplay a human being because it can work out the 'sentence that, unbeknown to him and in the long term, modulates a subject's choices'. A Freudian robot, as Lydia Liu puts it. A machine that is to us as Deep Blue is to a club chess player, guessing our moves long before we considerthem.

This is the social industry: the unprecedented subsumption of social life under the logic of computational capital. An early stage in the evolution of a more sophisticated machinery, which is likely in the future to incorporate augmented reality, integrated with 'smart city' technologies, and involving far more extensive surveillance and real-time manipulation capacities. A machinery that is already complexly interwoven with state bureaucracies, university and corporate research, intelligence services and various sectors of media, entertainment, gambling and amusement capital. An equipment that fuses with the existing culture industry and advertising sectors to produce, in Guy Debord's terms, a new diffuse spectacle. New fusions, subsidised by venture-capitalist profits, are likely to continue to appear.

The question is this. If the social industry shows a tendency to promote far-right content, if Google elevates 'false flag' conspiracy theories, if YouTube sends users along a conveyor belt toward 'extreme' content, if Twitter can help make the political career of the first 'alt-right' president of the United States, what signals is the machine picking up on, magnifying and reflecting back to us? YouTube's recommendations system, for example, acts on the basis of the clickthroughs and watchtime of its users. If it directs us to Nazi material, or 9/11 Truth videos, this is because this material is somehow riveting for its viewers. And what, you might ask, is so addictive about an hour-long Prison Planet rant about 'libtards'?

V

These are not the questions we expected to ask when the social industry made its breakthrough. A mere five years before Trump's election, the industry was experiencing its utopian moment, fuelled by massive industrial gains made possible by ubiquitous smartphone ownership. In this moment, the globalising zeal of traditional Washington briefly coalesced with the emancipatory hopes of Occupy, Anonymous and Pirate Parties. The Clintonites in the White House expected the industry to further US commercial interests, modernise its industrial base, and destabilise geopoliti-cal rivals. The cyber-utopians of the Left, however, staked a claim on the technological future in which networked flows of informa-tion would bypass hierarchy, destroy the old informational monop-olies, reduce the costs of political participation, and afford novel, 'rhizomic' principles of association. At the peak of the Occupy movement, for example, Guy Aitchison and Aaron Bastani pointed out that the emerging networks had delivered results by challeng-ing and outflanking traditional institutions. Information and social coordination need not be so hierarchical or centralised.

They were not *entirely* wrong about the potentials they identi-fied, but such potentials were not the whole story, and their politi-cal valence was not as it seemed. Far from bypassing hierarchy, the social industry is nothing but hierarchical systems of informational control wherein – generally under the rubric of 'free speech' and 'privacy' – the little Napoleons of the industry assert a monopoly on all data generated by users. While seriously weakening traditional forms of ideological control, throttling print media, and catalysing a crisis of representation, they have laid the foundations for more sophisticated controls. While reducing the costs of communica-tion and political participation, they have also reduced the costs of disaffiliation, infiltration and disruption. Their proprietary algo-rithms were designed to advance individual networking, not collec-tive organisation. Insofar as they are harnessed by organisations, Paolo Gerbaudo has shown in his excellent book *The Digital Party*, they tend to favour a form of leadership principle, wherein largely passive supporters have a consumer relationship to a charismatic personality, and are engaged on the basis of thin forms of 'partici-pation' and 'feedback'.

Moreover, occluded in the utopian moment was the profoundly

anti-social dimension of the social industry. One of the paradoxes of the industry is the way that it lubricates a form of sociality without sociality: a connection that is also a disconnection. This is not to reiterate the sentimental Levinasian idea that the face-to-face is the ultimate situation in which one encounters the other. One of the emancipatory potentials of modern communications technologies is precisely that we need no longer depend on a 'primary proximity' to form a social bond. Rather, it is because the whole industry is based on the model of addiction. Indeed, it might be said that addiction, wherein we can get enjoyment seemingly without laborious social mediation, is foundational to the current paradigm of capitalism. Whether it is gaming and amusement, infotainment, gambling, pills, 'male supplements' or the social industry, capitalism promises to satisfy our wanting while allowing us to evade the other.

Sociality may appear to be the substance of the social industry. It is just a 'platform', after all, existing to facilitate interaction. But the most important layer of interaction is not between users and other users, nor even between users and screens, but between users and the Freudian robot. A robot which solicits our engagement by showing us an edited stream of messages ostensibly written by other users. They could in principle be entirely the work of bots, for all the difference that it makes to our libidinal relationship with the machine. Indeed, the frequency with which users engage in behaviour that would be deemed shameful in offline life, indicates that perhaps on some level we don't believe the other users are real. What matters, what keeps us there, is not the presence of other users in the form of written traces, ghosts in the machine, but that little fix of *jouissance* when we're bored, anxious, depressed.

This is where the social industry exacerbates long-term trends in late capitalism, toward the disintegration of the social bond, and the domination of competitive atomism. The industry models user relations along the lines of a constant struggle of all against all, of billions of micro-enterprises, little celebrities, vying for flows of attention. The system's 'rewards' – 'likes', 'shares' and so on, with monetarisation possible at the higher reaches of popularity – are metrics for attention, which is struggled over as a scarce resource.

There is no spontaneous solidarity among users: quite the opposite. There are only temporary alliances that can turn, on a dime, to enmity. The more-or-less ruthless will-to-power induced by such a machinery can always be rationalised, moreover, on the grounds that it's 'only the internet'. Besides which, the 'logic of aggregation', as Jeffrey Juris calls it, means that minute individual actions of little consequence can accumulate into collective action of enormous consequence. In such a social system, the aggression, hate and will-to-domination that is usually restrained in daily life, is more permissible: encouraged, even. The economically incentivised hunger for approval gives added force to conformist propensities, and empowers those who would police social conformity. Moreover, in such a system, a certain degree of paranoia is logical, since you can never be sure who to trust, and are always in danger of becoming the object of the kind of quasi-randomised crowd furies that you might otherwise participate in. These are among the tendencies we might call 'microfascisms'. And they are clearly implicated in another salient dimension of the social industry which is its tendency to generate raging (and highly profitable) culture wars. With users working diligently to cultivate a self-image responsive to a stock market-like flux of sentiment and attention, they are easily drawn into moralised battles, strategies of anathema that rigidify existing cultural differences. The social industry doesn't just atomise, it also segments. Cultural lines which were as mobile and porous as weather fronts become hard borders in a balkanised terrain. The modern alt-right has been the major force to congeal from such wars, from #gamergate to #birthergate.

Given the consequences of these patterns of social breakdown 'offline', this is worrying. A spate of research has shown that, alongside the rise of social inequality and a crisis of masculinity, the prevalence of such competitive, dog-eat-dog atomism is a major contributor to the rise of mass shootings in the United States. The measurement of social breakdown is, of course, necessarily value-laden, and rests on such dubious metrics as 'social isolation', typically ascribed to the mentally unwell, or, in the case of Ichiro Kawachi's study of violent crime, 'social capital'. Nonetheless, it seems relatively uncontroversial that such breakdown exists: indeed the social industry, while exacerbating the trend, offers itself as a remedy to this trend. Among its reported clinical manifestations is a marked increase in the prevalence of paranoia and persecution fantasies. And if, as Stephen Frosh argued, paranoia is a way of being adapted to modern, surveillance societies, that goes many times over for the users of the social industry, who really are being watched, who can never be sure of the good faith of interlocutors, and for whom the unpredictable rewards and punishments built into the machine are impossible to make sense of.

We can see how paranoia and the sense of persecution can be politicised by looking at, for example, the formation of Men's Rights Activists (MRAs) communities, galvanised by their belief in an oppressive sexual regime lorded over by the potent 'Chads' and 'Stacys'. MRAs, alongside fascists and jihadists, have been well represented among recent 'lone wolves'. They represent a militantly reactionary response to the fraying of the conditions of social reproduction, scapegoating the accomplishments of feminism for growing precarity and the breakdown of the 'good life'. But they are also one case in the broader trend of rising conspiracist paranoia. Such conspiracism, though it has its 'alt-left' declinations (think of the leftists drawn to 9/11 Truth, or exaggerated versions of the 'Israel Lobby' thesis), overwhelmingly conduces to far-right ideologies.

With the postmodern 'waning of historicity', as Toscano dubs it, has come a general epistemological crisis. The declining authority of politicians, journalists and experts is widely remarked upon. But the sciences are also afflicted by a notorious 'reproducibility crisis', in which the results of experiments are increasingly difficult to replicate. This is in part due, according to Philip Mirowski, to the growing privatisation and commodification of scientific practice. The basis for authoritative knowledge has been eroded, and the major culprit in each case is the subordination of knowledge to the logic of capital. The social industry is part of this trend, inasmuch as it has fuelled the infotainment-based, clickbait-driven crisis of journalism: a sort of stock market of memes, driven by transient amusement, ephemeral passion. Sensationalist infotainment is not *intrinsically* more appealing than any other format for delivering information. True, the idea that being informed should be fun, rather than work, is an appealing one. But the persuasiveness of this idea derives from the underlying conditions of near-universal commodification. Choices in a market are made in micro-seconds. Do I click on this link, watch this broadcast, buy this newspaper? And while there are other proven ways to build and keep audiences, clickbait and sensation are cheaper to produce, more congruent with capitalism's interest in serving consumers rather than citizens and, precisely because of its *jouissances*, ideologically more effective. However, the market-driven degradation of information is not limited to the production of news. Google once proposed a similar, stock-market-like system for the scientific research, wherein investors would bid for the best research ideas. This, as with the social industry's devastation of print journalism, would only have accelerated trends already underway.

In the gap produced by the collapse of authoritative knowledge, small groups of amateur sleuths, citizen journalists, have taken to reconstructing the 'truth' on the basis of extravagant theories from 9/11 Truth to, for example, #Pizzagate. The latter, originally purveyed by a fascist publication, asserted that a pizza parlour in Washington DC was serving as a front for Hillary Clinton to traffic in child sex slaves. The claim went viral, helped along by the social industry's 'logic of aggregation', and resulted in a string of vigilantes turning up to investigate: one of whom, heavily armed, took control of the premises from terrified staff, before eventually giving himself up to police. Confronted with such paranoia, we might recall Ernst Simmel's claim that antisemitism is a flight from psychosis. That is, the delusion is not the symptom but an attempted self-cure. It is a way of being adapted to a society afflicted by a crash in meaning. It is both infotainment, delivering the narcissistic thrill one gets from outsmarting both 'sheeple' and 'elites', and critical theory for the meaning-bereft.

The social industry, as relentlessly productive as it is, continuously secretes this clickbait-theory, in the form of memes, infographics, short videos, and interactive games, and generates surges and frenzies supporting its distribution. If, in so doing, it tends to signal boost Islamophobic paranoia, Sandy Hook revisionism, 'white genocide' theory, and so on, it is hardly out of editorial malice. Rather, the question is how it puts to work, as the spur to attentional flows, paranoia, fantasies of restitution and revenge, desire for domination, the authoritarian need to be right, the capacity to humiliate, approval-seeking ingroup conformity and converse tendencies toward malice and social sadism. All of these tendencies are simply part of the quiddity of late capitalist life, what might be considered ordinary fascist *jouissances*. Or, as Foucault put it, the 'fascism in us all ... in our heads and in our everyday behavior, the fascism that causes us to love power, to desire the very thing that dominates and exploits us.' Arguably, what the programmed sociality, the simulacrum of sociality produced by the industry, brings to this situation is that it activates, aggregates, and accelerates the flow of these microfascisms. It provides rallying points, points of congealment in routine memetic surges of attention, points where political subjects are convoked.

These surges spill over into meatspace. The logic of the online shitstorm, wherein the aggregation of sentiment produces transient excitement and empowerment, devolves into flash mobs, make-shift occupations, demonstrations at short notice, and perhaps just enough mobilisation to tip electoral outcomes. It has even, given what we know of the online recruiting practices of ISIS, supplied much of the kinetic force for an *ad hoc* theocratic state. Yet it may be the phenomenon of the 'lone wolf' that raises the most troubling questions about the future of the networked far Right.

VI

Fascism is eschatotropic. Wherever it starts, it bends toward apocalypse. This is not to say that all Armageddonophiles, even on the far Right, are necessarily fascist. Rather, since it is a 'swindle of fulfilment', in Bloch's phrase, fascism and apocalypse have an elective affinity, a kinship of meaning, and tend toward mutual reinforcement.

There is no fascism without the cult of heroism, as Umberto Eco writes, and the '*Ur*-Fascist hero craves heroic death'. The achievement of fascism, Deleuze and Guattari insist, is to liberate a popular desire for suicide: its 'crowning glory' the death of the very 'people' whom it summons into existence. Anthrax, deadly pathogens, 'organised executions of multiculturalist traitors', weapons of mass destruction, atomic weapons turned against 'cultural Marxists'. Compulsively, performatively, Anders Behring Breivik's 'manifesto', *2083*, rehearses these scenarios with palpable erotic delight. Bypassing the institutions ostensibly captured by 'cultural Marxists', Breivik intended his murders in Oslo and Utøya, with gun and bomb, to rally his allies to a continent-wide race war. Starting with 'military shock attacks' like his own, he imagined it cresting toward the nuclear obliteration of the enemy.

In enthralled imitation, the Christchurch mass murderer Brenton Tarrant sought to turn himself into a meme presaging global race-war by live-streaming his massacre of fifty Muslims. His manifesto was a self-consciously memetic document, packed with Easter eggs for lulz-hungry admirers on the gamers' site, 8chan. Within weeks, yet another 8chan-embedded fascist killer had struck, this time at a Synagogue in San Diego, leaving yet another meme-packed manifesto. Like the incel killer Alek Minassian's cheerleaders, these killers were formed in and propelled by an online community of the lone-wolfish. And they were ghoulishly entranced by the prospect of annihilation. Like their alt-right co-ideologues, they evoked a last stand against a fantasmatic 'white genocide'. With this fantasy in the foreground, they pursued what Tarrant called 'heroic' death in murderous 'service to some grand crusade'. As Pankaj Mishra put it, the religion of whiteness has become a suicide cult.

Nor is this just the fantasy will-to-the-end of the 'lone wolf'. Millenarian tendencies are, of course, politically polyvalent. They appear in the English Civil War, early modern Catholic mysticism, the American revolution, the Zionist movement, twentieth century communism, and among certain Evangelicals who see in Trump a potential John the Baptist figure. As Catherine Keller has argued, any politics of counterapocalypse that doesn't take its own messianic drive seriously, ends up mimicking its opponent. Nonetheless, if ever the apocalypse was fervently and unconditionally willed, and even brought to the point of being materialised, it has been as a consequence of fascism. The Falangist slogan exhorted: 'Long Live Death'. The Ustasha chiliastically gloried in the 'bones, blood and spirit of martyrs'. Nazi war policy, as Adam Tooze has shown, was substantially driven by their apprehension of an apocalyptic war with Jews, from Operation Barbarossa to the Wannsee Conference. Faced with defeat, the Nazis embarked on a scorched earth policy to eradicate German churches, museums, state records, anything that constituted the historical memory of a 'German people'. Goebbels proclaimed: 'Germany must be made more desolate than the Sahara.'

The concept of the heroic, death-seeking, right-wing 'lone wolf' is, nonetheless, particularly geared toward an End Times crescendo. 'Kill me,' Minassian shouted at armed police after his vehicular assault on pedestrians in Toronto. 'I have a gun in my pocket. Shoot me in the head'. 'I've done my job', Darren Osborne told police after ploughing a van into a crowd at Finsbury Park mosque, 'you can kill me now'. Breivik, before being apprehended by police, was mulling over whether to shoot himself in the head. Dylann Roof, before embarking on his massacre at a black church in Charleston, left suicide notes for his parents. 'Pray that I become a martyr,' German ISIS killer Riaz Khan texted his recruiter, before attacking passengers on a train with an axe and knife. Alexandre Bissonnette, the Quebec mosque killer, had spent months planning his suicide, and researching mass shootings and suicide attacks. 'Kill me,' Florida mass shooter Nikolas Cruz begged police, 'Just fucking kill me.' This desire for a culmination, a final showdown, to be done with life, resonates with the original strategic intent of the 'lone wolf' concept.

The beginnings of the far-right 'lone wolf' lie in Vietnam and the Civil Rights era. As Kathleen Belew's history of the US 'white power' movement shows, the Vietnam War had forged a realigned far Right. For most of its history, white supremacy was an openly respectable policy in the US. The Ku Klux Klan, through three 'waves', had been a vigilante white-supremacist movement with mainstream support, which acted as a parapolitical auxiliary to state power. But the Klan scene that emerged post-Vietnam and in the post-Civil Rights state, was different, indicative of a new insurrectionary subculture. On the one hand, the alliances that white-supremacists had with politicians, police and the judiciary had been dislocated, and they now encountered the Federal government as an enemy. On the other, they had just gleaned invaluable direct combat experience, killing communists in Vietnam. Many of them cheerfully put this experience to work during the Greensboro Massacre in 1979 during which, with the connivance of local police, members of the Ku Klux Klan and the Nazi Party shot and killed members of the Communist Workers Party in the streets. The new alignment put Klan members, neo-Nazis, fascists, Christian Identitarians and anti-tax activists in the same milieus and often the same organisations. And increasingly it was contemplating culminations, final solutions, genocides.

While the term 'lone wolf' was coined by the FBI, with a discernible trace of romantic admiration, it was from within the Knights of the Ku Klux Klan, the organisation founded by former Nazi student agitator David Duke and future Stormfront proprietor Don Black, that the idea of was formulated. Louis Beam, Grand Dragon of the Texas Klan, had killed with distinction in the Vietnam War, organised militias to attack Vietnamese migrants on his return, and was charged twice with bomb attacks on leftist headquarters. But he recognised that any formal armed hierarchy could be too easily infiltrated and dismantled. 'Leaderless resistance' was an idea first advanced an ex-CIA agent, Col Louis Amoss, for the purposes of anticommunist struggle in Eastern Europe. It entailed the dispersal of armed force into tiny 'phantom cells' of ones and twos, who would act without instruction from a leadership. Beam was impressed. An ardent anticommunist, he foresaw a dark night of Federal 'tyranny' over the white race comparable to communist dictatorship. 'Patriots', should they wish to resist, would need a new division of labour between a propaganda arm which disavowed violence, and armed individuals who would commit in the privacy of their minds to insurrection. Ironically, whether he knew it or not, by adopting the idea of 'phantom cells' Beam was partly emulating the Viet Minh, his victorious opponents in Vietnam.

This was a tactic borne of political isolation and millenarian impatience. In previous waves of fascist terror, from Ustashe assassinations to the Bologna massacre, the far right had significant institutional and sometimes even popular support. Not so the 'lone wolf'. One of its most vocal advocates after Beam was neo-Nazi Tom Metzger, who launched the brand organisation, White Aryan Resistance (WAR) in the same year that Beam's article was publishing. Adopting Beam's rationale, it self-consciously eschewed formal membership, inviting supporters to identify with its precepts and act on them. For Metzger, the ideal would be to have mass paramilitaries take on the government: 'the SS did it in Germany ... we can do it right here in the streets of America'. The necessity of the 'lone wolf' arose from the fact that most whites were 'brain dead', a 'herd'. He was deeply impressed with the organised firepower of jihadist networks striking on US soil, and their ability to provoke escalating conflict. As with Breivik, Metzger's hope was that the demonstrative violence of individuals would provoke an apocalyptic race war, a final struggle in which whites would be forced to take sides.

VII

There is a marked gap between the formulation of the concept and its increasing appearance as a political reality. While the glamour of 'patriotic' insurgency struck a chord in the new insurgent subculture of the far-right, strikingly few 'lone wolf' attacks actually took place. Most of those that occurred were carried out by organised white power groups.

Mark Hamm and Ramón Spaaij have documented a spike in 'lone wolf' incidents in recent years. Between 2001 and 2013, there were forty-five lone wolf attacks carried out by forty-five individuals in the United States. By comparison, between 1940 and 2000, they count 171 attacks carried out by thirty-eight individuals. An important nuance to register here is that none of the recent attackers were repeat offenders. In counterterrorism idiom, they are 'chaos' killers rather than 'career' killers. Their attacks almost all had a certain finality about them, and most of the attackers either killed themselves or made little effort to evade capture. Recent lone wolf activity has mainly been far-right in source, but can in no obvious way be attributed to the strategic guidance of Beam and Metzger, not least because of its necessarily disorganised, disaffiliated nature. The perpetrators have more in common with those carrying out almost-daily mass shootings in the US, than with the hardened fascist cadres that Beam and Metzger hoped would listen to their words. Moreover one is struck, looking at the recent spate of killers, by the apparent *thin-ness* of their formal political and ideological commitments. This applies both to lone wolves and organised combatants. ISIS recruits who are religious novices, training for jihad with 'Islam For Dummies'. Individuals like Darren Osborne, 'red-pilled' and turned into racist murderers in a matter of weeks. Mass killers like Roof and Minassian, forming their ideologies almost entirely on the basis of engagement with online right-wing subcultures. ISIS recruited for both Caliphate-building and overseas attacks by putting to work the logic of online swarms, exploiting the social industry's affordances through hashtag-jacking, memes, Hollywood-style video clips, interactive games. A propaganda campaign very different from the elaborate theological and jurisprudential output of Al-Qaida.

The question is what constellation of circumstances converted reactionary pipe-dream into quasi-accurate description? To the extent that this trend has appeared outside the United States, it may reflect an Americanisation of the far-right. Breivik's cut-and-paste manifesto, drawing largely from the John Birch Society wing of US conspiracism, is some evidence of that. More generally, the 'war on terror' era saw a marked transition in the ideological orientation and leadership of successful far-right groups. The inherited hostility to the US and Israel, on racist grounds, was displaced by a new geopolitical axis guided by a new, imagined struggle for civilisation against Islam. Vlaams Belang, the English Defence League and even the Front national under Marine Le Pen's leadership, like Breivik, all tended to align themselves with the ideological obsessions of America's islamophobia industry. And this is now a highly profitable sector of media production in the social industry. Whereas far-right gangs once had to carry out robberies and forge money to fund their operations, they can now monetise racism provided they outmanoeuvre the 'hate speech' algorithms. This is the dark underside of old, liberal Washington's ambitious Silicon-led globalisation project.

Americanisation or not, however, that doesn't by itself explain why anyone answers the call to spontaneous, reactionary murder. If an ISIS spokesperson urges supporters to kill, using the nearest available weapon from a knife to a vehicle, why does anyone take it up? And why does anyone act on far-right propaganda, incel paranoia, islamophobia industry infotainment, conspiracy theories, with armed, murderous heroics? The popular conceptual short-cut to describe this phenomenon, is 'stochastic terror', a term that was coined anonymously online and has since become widely used in news commentary. Much as climate change produces 'stochastic' weather events, so the diffuse ecologies of online reaction reliably produce terrorist violence, even if the specific occurrences are unpredictable. This captures something about the way effects are produced through the social industry. Algorithms administer, not populations of individuals per se, but data populations. They anticipate a distribution of x effects over y population, given a certain stimulus. The problem is that, like the dud concept 'radicalisation', 'stochastic terror' assumes that jihadist or far-right propaganda is extraordinarily efficient at producing its own audience.

It may be that the social industry helps such propaganda find its audience. For this industry, as Geert Lovink enigmatically puts it, 'calculates with and not against the apocalypse'. In a striking early analysis of the social media strategy of ISIS, the security intellectual J. M. Berger argued that the group was succeeding because it turned Twitter into a 'metronome of apocalyptic time', a 'carrier wave for millenarian contagion'. The messaging of the Islamic State pivoted on its apprehension of an end times battle, al-Mahama al-Kubra, which in Islamic eschatology is to take place in Dabiq, a Syrian town that fell under ISIS control. The appeal of this narrative to ISIS's online supporters Berger attributes, in part, to the unique properties of the medium. In millenarian experience, there is a combined sense of temporal acceleration, social contagion and subjective immersion in an exceptional situation. When major upheavals, military victories, political upsets, appear to be coming 'out of nowhere', it lends itself to the sense that the normal rules don't apply, and licences extraordinary action. Such, indeed, must have been the experience of ISIS supporters on Twitter during its upswing. ISIS accounts were hyperactive, posting incessantly about doings, achievements, victories. They were prolifically productive, too, of easily shareable and digestible content: first-person shooter footage, video games, snippets of battles or executions, iconic images of the black flag flying over fields of flowers, and short Q&A sessions with jihadi leaders. They exploited successful hashtags to make their content go viral and, having discovered their latent community of support, they carefully identified potential recruits and virtually surrounded them, bombarding them with intimate interpellations, such that they were extruded from the saeculum into the realm of 'apocalyptic time'.

This, then, may also offer some clues as regards the acts of disorganised violence that fly out of the social industry's culture wars like sparks from a furnace. 'Apocalyptic time' is the time of the industry. It is the accelerating temporal experience of a machinery that is ever cresting toward yet another climacteric. Merely by dint of the way it connects data point to data point, aggregates sentiment in a flash, produces ever more complex 'stochastic' effects, it ensures that those who are predisposed to it, who hunger for the clarifying and simplifying violence of the end, will find their eschaton. Even without the focused efforts of recruiters, it bathes users in interpellations that reach them just as efficiently as a voice whispered in the ear. And the routine political shocks to which it now contributes are sufficient to create a sense of miraculous possibility. Yet, whence that hunger? What ignites the desire for an end in the first place? Inevitably, news coverage, scholarly articles, books and think-tank reports zero in on the mental health problems of perpetrators. In the case of killers who aren't Muslim, and thus don't come with a ready-to-hand Orientalist story of incorrigible barbaric Otherness, there has been a tendency to resort to mental illness as if this was a sufficient condition for their outbursts. Many of the 'lone wolves' are indeed demonstrably unwell. The stereotype of the 'lone wolf', the socially isolated, depressed, paranoid, unemployed older white male, is not totally inaccurate, at least in the United States. However, as the contemporary obsession with 'wellness' indicates, we are ubiquitously unwell. Anxiety and depression have measurably increased. And the social industry's power in part derives from its ability to monetise this distress, as a ready-to-hand remedy, a stopgap for the dysfunctional effects of neoliberal capitalism. The question is how pervasive mental distress becomes contingently politicised.

How does the 'red pill' become the attempted cure for subjective desolation? Why, when a subjective black hole appears, should it be the semiotic fragments of fascism, rather than some other content, that it gluttonously consumes? What accounts for the consolatory or compensatory power of racist, jihadist, masculinist, or fascist propaganda? What, to repeat an earlier question, is so enthrallingly addictive about this product, for many more users than have ever contemplated killing? And what happens when the 'stochastic' event, the spontaneous 'lone wolf', is subject to the logic of aggregation? We have seen armed standoffs between American reactionaries and the US government, from Ruby Ridge to Amon Bundy. At what point might we see the armed shitstorm? These are questions that beg for further research, and which I simply pose here, without trying to answer them.

These are early days in the social industry, and early days in the networked far-right resonance machine. We cannot say for certain how this machine might morph or falter in the face of opposition. Traditional Washington, mounting a fightback against Trumpism, is leaning hard on the social industry to crack down on 'fake news' among other nebulous entities. The industry's major brands may have peaked in terms of their ability to capture attention, and being overtly associated with the far-right, however profitable, risks significant user defection.

Nonetheless, despite everything, the social industry looks like an overwhelming success, economically, culturally and politically. Its ability to lure billions of users into a novel and dystopian form of sociality has yet to be seriously challenged. There is no indication, even amid backlash, that the machine will stop working. And this machine makes fascists.

TROY VETTESE

A Marxist Theory of Extinction

The Tragedy of Common Environmentalism

The same year the British parliament passes the 1773 Inclosure Act, the Tahitian sandpiper is extinguished as a species.

The Sixth Extinction, destroyer of worlds, is the annihilation of countless ancient and irreplaceable branches of the tree of life. Coeval with the birth of capitalism, the onset of the the Sixth Extinction began half a millennium ago, and is now proceeding at a furious pace comparable to the desolation of the last great die-off sixty-six million years ago. From the perspective of earthly life, capitalism differs little from colliding with a massive meteorite. E.O. Wilson, an influential naturalist, predicts that half of the world's flora and fauna will be extinguished by the century's end. Recent studies have estimated that mammalian species are disappearing one hundred to one thousand times faster than the natural rate. The drivers of the Sixth Extinction are myriad, but habitat-loss is its foremost cause, followed by poaching, though climate change will certainly play an increasingly important role. At least one mammal has already been extinguished by climate change, the Bramble Cay melomys in 2016, when rising ocean levels inundated this rat species' low-lying island home in the Great Barrier Reef.

Mammals, however, are only a tiny percentage of the animal kingdom, which is overwhelmingly invertebrate. Small creatures, like San Francisco's Xerces Blue butterfly (gone in 1941), have borne the brunt of the cataclysm: as many as 130,000 invertebrate species have vanished since the early-modern period, some seven per cent of all animal species. Yet apart from notable efforts like *Extinction* by Ashley Dawson and *Tragedy of the Commodity* by Brett Clark, Rebecca Clausen, and Stefano B. Longo, Marxists have neglected the debate over extinction, ceding the field to an unholy alliance of neoliberals and racist Malthusians.

The dominant framework for thinking about extinction, as well as many other environmental problems, has been the 'tragedy of the commons'. Garrett Hardin, a biologist, coined this phrase in 1968, using it as the title of a short essay he published in *Science*. It described an imaginary commonly-held pasture, where unscrupulous herders grazed more cattle than the grass could endure. 'Ruin is the destination toward which all men rush,' he concluded, 'each pursuing his own best interest in a society that believes in the freedom of the commons. Freedom in a commons brings ruin to all.' In this framework, what is rational for the individual – cheating – is irrational for the group, a contradiction that can only be suspended through the implementation of property-rights. Hardin invoked other examples where overuse degrades a commonly-held resource, such as free parking, campgrounds, pollution and fisheries. In the latter instance, 'maritime nations ... bring species after species of fish and whales closer to extinction' because of the 'freedom of the seas'.

'The Tragedy of the Commons' remains a canonical text of centrist environmentalism. Perhaps because the text is invoked more often than read, or perhaps because of taboo, it is often left unsaid that Hardin's allegory is extremely brutal, even fascist. Most people know that he advocated privatisation to remedy the tragedy of the commons, and a few more know he also suggested user-fees, but what is less-often discussed is the third proposal of 'coercive' population control, coupled with the dismantling of the welfare state. In his mind these issues were conjoined because state assistance might support 'the religion, the race, or the class ... that adopts overbreeding as a policy.' Later, he rearticulated the 'overbreeding' of undesirables as the 'passive genocide' of whites.

Such sentiments were not mere momentary lapses of judgement. As an ardent white supremacist, he advocated population control for people of colour (but not for whites – he himself had four children) and restrictions on immigration to the US (especially from Latin America) to obviate the creation of a 'chaotic Norte Americano Central'. He expounded these ideas until the end of his life in fascist publications like *Chronicles* and *The Social Contract*.

Hardin may have been one of the ugliest protuberances on the body politic of mainstream, white environmentalism, but he articulated the logical end of a shared ideology. In 1968, the year he published 'Tragedy of the Commons', it was revealed that the US government had sterilised thousands of Puerto Rican women over the preceding two decades, affecting a third of the population. On the mainland five years later, the involuntary sterilisation of two Black girls, Minnie and Mary Alice Relf, brought to national attention that the federal government annually underwrote the sterilisation of 100,000 to 150,000 poor people as a condition for further welfare assistance. As many groups supported coercive population control, they hesitated to criticise these outrages, a stance that alienated Black and Latinx social movements for a generation. Subsequent debates over immigration only worsened matters. In the 1970s and 1980s, Zero Population Growth, the Sierra Club and prominent businessmen co-founded the Federation of American Immigration Reform (FAIR), a group designated by the Southern Poverty Law Center as a hate group. FAIR focused on fighting Mexican immigration: one of its major early campaigns sought to prevent the counting of undocumented migrants in the 1980 US census, to starve welfare programmes of funding. Hardin sat on FAIR's board of directors.

The tragedy of the commons, for Hardin, was naturally transnational in scope. In 1974 he wrote 'Living on a Lifeboat', where he compared nations to lifeboats and refugees to people who 'fall out of their lifeboats and swim for a while in the water outside, hoping to be admitted to a rich lifeboat, or in some other way to benefit from the "goodies" on board'. In 1987 he told a journalist from the *New York Times* that he opposed aid to Ethiopia during its recent famine because the country 'has far too many people for its resources.' Despite the prevalence of this kind of rhetoric, environmentalists have never properly atoned for their xenophobia, nor forsaken hateful prophets like Hardin. Herman Daly, a founder of ecological economics and contributor to essay collections with Hardin, recently told an admiring Benjamin Kunkel in the *New Left Review* that he still desired coercive population-control, and that 'I don't believe in open borders.' Now, when an increasingly unstable global climatic system drives refugees from their homelands, Hardin's genocidal *Weltanschauung* must be expunged from the Left's environmental discourse.

No doubt Hardin was odious, but what's worse is that he wasn't very clever – he's no Carl Schmitt of US environmentalism. The 'Tragedy of the Commons' has gaps big enough to drive a herd of cows through. His fascist fable isn't historical or ethnographic, nor it does accurately describe how commons function or how they break down, flaws that Elinor Ostrom pointed out decades ago. That such an exercise in common sense earned her the Bank of Sweden prize demonstrates how entrenched Hardin's model is in economics, but Ostrom was hardly Hardin's only critic. Neoliberals, a clever bunch, recognised early on that the tragedy of the commons was an insufficiently rigorous framework, but were content to have it remain as fig-leaf covering their more nuanced work in environmental economics that still attracts too little scholarly attention. Nowadays, the only sincere fans of Hardin are naïve centrist environmentalists and neo-Nazis.

From a neoliberal perspective, a species should only be preserved – even if it is privately owned – if it is profitable, only if the market decrees it. Although conservative economists pen paeans to the market's sagacity in husbanding scarce nature, neoliberal economists are much blunter. From the point of view of capital, organisms have no intrinsic value – even the last few individuals of a species – but are merely different capital assets in a varied and constantly changing portfolio. This characterisation of nature as capital comes from Canadian fisheries economist, Anthony Scott, whose insight has been picked up by other neoliberals like Friedrich Hayek and Dieter Helm (Oxford don and chair of the Natural Capital Committee). This logic is laid out clearly in Hayek's *Constitution of Liberty*, where he argued 'from a social as well as from an individual point of view, any natural resource represents just one item of our total endowment of exhaustible resources, and our problem is not to preserve this stock in any particular form, but always to maintain it in a form that will make the most desirable contribution to total income.' Yet, it was another Canadian fisheries economist, Colin Clark, who laid out the logical terminus such arguments in the starkest fashion in the 1973 article 'Profit Maximization and the Extinction of Animal Species'. 'Roughly stated,' he wrote, 'the following are shown to be both necessary and sufficient conditions for extinction under present-value maximization: (a) the discount (or time preference) rate sufficiently exceeds the maximum reproductive potential of the population, and (b) an immediate profit can be made from harvesting the last remaining animals.' For Clark these two factors mattered much more than whether a creature were privately or commonly owned; privatisation was no salve for extinction.

Although neoliberals have hardly hidden how they view nature, as just another asset, it has taken the Left far too long to realise that this is where the centre of debate lies. Capital's control over flora and fauna is not as a special branch of the economy requiring its own theory, but just as industrial as the manufacture of steel and microchips. This insight is elaborated by Kenneth Fish in his *Living Factories* – perhaps the best book in Marxist animal studies. Fish characterises genetically modified organisms (GMOs) as 'factories – living factories. Microbes, plants and animals, indeed life itself, was, through techniques of genetic engineering, being harnessed as a fore of industrial production.'

GMOs, however, were only an extreme case of what capital seeks to do to all life. That is, capital erases distinctions separating organism from machine. 'For all the technological mastery marked by the coming of the machine, then,' observes Fish, 'the significance of the factory for Marx lies in how it approximates a living organism, that most natural of beings.' Marx's comments on the factory being an 'organism', that it is 'dead labour' that comes 'alive' when attached to a 'force of nature', is less a metaphor than a near-literal description of machines as capitalist beasts of burden.

Subsume and Extinguish

Trochetiopsis melanoxylon, a 'dwarf ebony' plant endogenous to Saint Helena, becomes extinct in 1771. That year Richard Arkwright opens the first water-powered textile factory in Cromford.

Once Marxists see that capital seeks to transform flora and fauna into machines, then it becomes easier to see what capital's relationship to nature is, and how the Sixth Extinction is an inherently capitalist problem. Perhaps the most useful Marxist tools are 'formal' and 'real subsumption', both described in the 1864–6 *Economic Manuscripts*. Formal subsumption occurs when 'production processes with a different social determination are thereby converted into the production process of capital'. If in the pre-capitalist era an individual owned the means of production (for example., a yeoman farmer) or was bound to a superior through dense social ties (for example, a guild apprentice or serf), capitalism replaces these relationships with ones mediated through money. Yet, the work process changes little if labour is only formally subsumed. 'Despite all this,' Marx remarked, 'the change indicated does not mean that an essential change takes place from the outset in the real way in which the labour process is carried on ... capital thus subsumes under itself a given, existing labour process, such as handicraft labour, the mode of agriculture corresponding to small-scale independent peasant farming.' Its basic form is cottage industry: the weaver works when she wants and at the pace she wants, often at home, meeting the capitalist infrequently for wages or supplies. This does not imply that that formal subsumption is innocuous. As it is difficult to increase productivity without machinery, greater surplus value can only be increased absolutely by prolonging the working day.

Real subsumption begins when the capitalist introduces machinery, transforming production through the 'conscious application of the natural sciences, mechanics, chemistry, etc.' Instead of the worker using a tool with her hand as during formal subsumption, the worker now uses a machine powered by a 'force of nature' (*Naturkraft*), like hydropower or coal. These changes allow the concentration of labour and increase productivity, facilitating the deskilling and devaluing of workers, but, perhaps more significantly, it forces workers to toil at the machine's pace and thus the pace set by the capitalist herself.

Marx's conception of subsumption is dynamic: formal subsumption often comes first, but once machine-made commodities begin to compete with hand-made, then handicraft workers will likely be destroyed as a class. 'History discloses no tragedy more horrible than the gradual extinction of the English hand-loom weavers.' Most Marxists tend to hover here, out of concern for the hand-loom weavers and their unfortunate successors. Yet, just by slightly shifting one's perspective, it becomes possible to see what happens when capital extends its reach into the kingdoms of flora and fauna.

One can begin in the pre-capitalist stage of nature-human relations, say, between fur-bearing animals and indigenous peoples in North America. While people hunted deer, otter, muskrat, and most lucratively, beaver, it was illogical to hunt all such animals. This is because the hunters' needs were easily sated, it would take considerable effort to find the last surviving muskrat, otter or deer, and there would be no more for the future. Extinctions were thus rare in pre-capitalist societies (though mega-fauna extinctions thousands of years ago may be exceptions). Yet indigenous peoples' relationship with fur-bearing animals changed once they became part of the world-market during the seventeenth century, a historic shift detailed by Richard White in his classic study, *The Roots of Dependency*. Insatiable demand from European milliners for furs spurred early corporations like the Hudson's Bay Company (founded in 1670, eight years after the last dodo was killed) to fan out across the North American continent. Corporations and merchants contracted out hunting to indigenous peoples, transforming beaver fur into a commodity that could be exchanged for kettles, beads, guns, horses, and knives. At this stage, however, indigenous trappers were only formally subsumed by capital, working when and where they wanted. Surplus value could only be increased absolutely, so capitalists tried to find more trappers and encouraged trappers to kill more beavers. Though they hunted more, the needs of many indigenous peoples were modest. Not for the first time, capitalists resorted to trading addictive commodities, alcohol in this instance, to expand the market. Eventually, too many animals were killed and crises ensued. Trappers could either travel inland or switch to other species, but these solutions remained within the realm of formal subsumption. Fur farms eventually would become a possibility, but this marked a leap to real subsumption.

Real subsumption occurs once capital masters a plant's or animal's biological functions, allowing it to be manipulated like any other machine. It is now possible to raise productivity, allowing capital to squeeze more relative surplus value from workers. Aquaculture illustrates the shift from formal to real subsumption: as populations of many fish species have crashed since the 1990s, there has been a shift to raising fish as livestock. Farmed fish are fed more frequently and richly than they would eat in the wild to fatten them faster. Their size can be further increased through hormonal treatment that can accelerate growth; hormonal treatment can even change a fish's sex, which could be advantageous if there is pronounced dimorphism in a species. Genetic intervention, via selective breeding or genetic engineering, is also possible, like the trademarked AquAdvantage salmon of AquaBounty Technologies. Within the factory setting of aquaculture, labour becomes more efficient, say, through the automation of feeding to replace hand-feeding. The scale of production can be expanded by concentrating fish far beyond what would be possible in the wild, with all of the attendant problems this brings in terms of waste and disease. The latter can be partially mitigated by plentiful resort to antibiotics, while the former can be a burden imposed on others.

One can distinguish three intermediate forms between formal and real subsumption, which could be termed 'ranching', 'kidnapping', and the 'factory in the jungle'. Ranching occurs when it is cheaper for a capitalist to only partially subsume the life-processes of an organism. For example, the Texas longhorn cattle were prized during the late nineteenth century because they could fend off predators with their impressive ossein headgear and were hardy enough to survive off prairie scrub. Their life cycle was almost feral until the animals were rustled and driven to the railheads in Kansas. The longhorns' hardiness was a 'free gift of nature' that lowered costs; it was useful to capital until it became more profitable to subsume more aspects of cattle, so they grew faster or bore more muscle. Eventually, such artificial creatures reached proportions where they needed to be kept in feedlots, rather than let out on the range. Fish hatcheries were similar to the longhorn's pattern, as fingerlings are bred and then introduced into rivers or lakes to replenish original, decimated populations. While their births are unnatural, the fish look after themselves for most of their lives, and capital requires labour only at the end to catch, kill, and commodify. This was a half-way step to aquaculture.

Kidnapping is the mirror-image of ranching, because opposite moments of a creature's life-cycle are subsumed: that is, adolescence rather than birth. An illuminating case study in *The Tragedy of the Commodity* traces this process in the tuna trade. As tuna cannot reproduce in captivity, fishers try to capture and cage wild juvenile tuna so they can be fattened for the market. Thus, it is a mix of formally-subsumed fishing and really-subsumed aquaculture. Of course, this hybrid form only hastens a species' decline, as it allows little opportunity for reproduction. Due to a combination of overfishing and kidnapping the Mediterranean tuna population steeply declined during the 1990s and 2000s. Globally, populations of various tuna species have dropped seventy-four per cent since 1970. This figure obscures regional variations and it is worst in the Pacific Ocean, where blue and yellowfin populations have completely collapsed to only two or three percent of their historic populations.

In the third intermediate variant, the jungle factory, the life-cycle of the hunted organism remains wild, but hunting undergoes real subsumption. Formally subsumed fishing endured for centuries in British waters because it was generally not very effective, though the hunting of several cetacean species in the North Atlantic was exceptionally lethal. As late as 1882, the influential biologist Thomas Huxley could declare in his inaugural address of the London Fisheries Exhibition that 'probably all the great sea fisheries are inexhaustible'. Yet only eight years later, scientists expressed concern for declining fish stocks due to the rapacity of steam-powered trawlers, a technology then less than two decades old. In the twentieth and twenty-first centuries, real subsumption of oceanic hunting was taken to ludicrous extremes. Whalers and fishers pilot powerful boats more like battleships than the modest schooners in the age of sail. They are armed to the teeth with exploding harpoons, satellites measuring surface temperatures, 'fish-aggregating devices', sonar and spotter-planes. Slaughter and butchery can take place on the ship itself and, thanks to massive freezers, these floating factories can stay at sea for months. The brutal efficacy of industrialised trawling, a hobby horse of the *Economist*, has forced even that mouthpiece of *bien pensant* neoliberalism to concede that 'modern fishing is really analogous to mining: fish are pulled from the sea faster than they can be replenished'.

Vegan Communism

Karl Marx died 14 March 1883. A hundred and fifty-one days later, the last quagga died in a Dutch zoo.

An analysis of formal and real subsumption, as well as their intermediate forms, reveal specifically capitalist mechanisms of extinction. Capitalists may try to proceed from formal to real subsumption once a species' numbers become depleted, but the life cycle of the creature may be too delicate to bear capital's embrace, like tuna. Capital may not even bother if there is a suitable substitute available, such as the Texas Longhorn that replaced the bison. If a creature is controlled via real subsumption, then it is not threatened by extinction except if it is dissolved through cross-breeding as aurochs were, in 1627. Once intensive husbandry such as salmon aquaculture or feedlot cattle begains, capital will attempt to increase relative surplus value by increasing productivity. Just as a nineteenth-century factory worker's productivity increased by operating steam-powered machines of greater horsepower that consumed ever more coal, the real subsumption of nature allows the concentration of *Naturkraft*. The massive, artificially sustained population of livestock, numbering near fifty billion, rely on fossil-fuelled crops to be kept alive in such numbers. They are living factories, which is why researchers from the Worldwatch Institute count livestock respiration as greenhouse gas pollution – as if it were expelled by machines – noxious vapours that compose fifty-one per cent of total emissions.

Real subsumption has allowed the expansion of animal industry, and it is this process that overwhelmingly propels the Sixth Extinction. Animal industries require more than four billion hectares, almost half of the Earth's inhabitable surface. Such a huge amount of land-theft has already caused countless extinctions, but more will come if the meat industry doubles, as it is projected to by 2050. It's not much better in the sea, because many popular fish, especially tuna, are voracious carnivores, making it about as strange and inefficient for humans to eat them as if we munched on a tiger-salad sandwich. For every 1,000 tonnes of tuna biomass (about two adult fish), a tuna feedlot operation requires fifty to sixty tonnes of fishmeal per day. Such food is growing scarce as aquaculture and tuna-kidnapping grows, forcing capital to plumb ever greater depths and trawling the mesopelagic layer hundreds of metres deep, cutting new swathes of extinction. In this way, it's possible to see the effects of the intermediate forms. Ranching increases pressure on other creatures, as the commodified animal takes massive amounts of space, while kidnapping not only puts pressure on both the subsumed animal and the surrounding ecosystem, and the third form, the jungle factory, accelerates the decay of any mode of production that only formally subsumes nature. All these forms of subsumption must be reversed if there is to be any hope to halting the Sixth Extinction. This means giving back at least half of the Earth, including half the sea, to nature. Right now, only a sixth of the world's landmass has any protection, and only a twenty-fifth of the sea.

Marxists should fervently oppose capital's ruthless domination of nature, of turning all the world into a factory, mall, or garbage dump. Through subsumption capital estranges both humans and other creatures from their species-being – from how they should naturally live. The Left must reject the neoliberal *Weltanschauung* that nature is just another form of capital: rather, the Left must endeavour to support nature's self-actualisation too. What this might look like it is too early to say, given the dearth of Marxist work on the topic; but at the very least more space must be made for wild flora and fauna, and this means livestock must be reined in. While the analysis sketched out here applies to plants as much as it does to animals, given the wastefulness of converting grain to animal flesh and milk, avoiding animal products at least minimises one's complicity with the subsumption of nature. Becoming vegan is the simplest and most effective action an individual can take to reduce one's environmental impact, though of course, no Marxist would be content with mere 'lifestyle' politics.

Whatever form the future's communist society will take, its emergence must be complemented by the abolition of animal industries, to be replaced by community-run organic vegan agriculture, so that humanity treads lightly in the global biosphere. Socialist mastery over nature, as the technophile Left advocates, would not halt the Sixth Extinction. Instead, humanity's relationship to nature should be guided by humility, empathy, and restraint. It is the Left's concern whenever any creature is subsumed within capital's maw to be enthralled or extinguished, dooming half of creation to oblivion.

PETER DRUCKER

#MeToo and Queer Experience

Thirty-seven years ago, Christopher responded to an old-fashioned print ad that I had placed.* He wrote me a letter, and we talked on the phone. When we arranged to meet in person, I knew he was older than I was. But somehow I had failed to imagine what he might look like – for example, that he might be balding. When I saw him, he did not correspond to my image of a possible sexual or romantic partner. We sat and talked, and he seemed very nice and bright and loving, but still…. And then he reached out and touched my hand. His touch was electric. That was the real beginning of everything. That moment lit a flame that for me, thirty-seven years later, has never gone out.

#MeToo is often about individual stories, but the relevance of this one may not be immediately clear. But it is relevant. We look differently at sexual encounters now, fortunately, thanks to #MeToo. Consider for a moment, if you would, how you feel about this story knowing that both Christopher and I identify as male, and how you would feel about it if I were female. The gender identity and sexual orientation of the people involved in a sexual encounter

---

* I would like to thank Christopher Beck, Johanna Brenner, Penelope Duggan, Anne Finger, Maral Jefroudi, Gary Kinsman and Holly Lewis for comments on an earlier version of this article, the editors of Salvage for comments on a subsequent version, and the participants in the workshop where I presented the paper at Historical Materialism 2018 in London. I need to stress, more than usually, that none of these people necessarily agrees with my arguments or conclusions, for which I alone am responsible.

make a difference in assessing the reality or the risk of harassment or violence involved in it.

The #MeToo campaign, focusing on men's sexual harassment and abuse of women, has shown how pervasive it is. It has also trained a spotlight on some men accused of sexually assaulting or harassing other males. Gay men, like straight men, can be rapists and harassers. That they are themselves victims of straight male supremacy don't stop them from being privileged, selfish or violent. The attention to this scandalously neglected dimension in the wake of #MeToo is a good thing. But currently the spotlight on male-on-male abuse relies on an analytical grid that has been borrowed, generally unchanged and unexamined, from the analysis of heterosexual abuse.

Women and queer people share an interest in resisting violence that emanates from, and reinforces, sexist gender roles and a family system dominated by cisgender straight men. But the queer dimension of #MeToo risks being obscured – particularly when #MeToo statements implicitly suggest, as Jess Fournier has argued, that 'men are only perpetrators or "male allies", never survivors'. Moreover, as Noah Michelson has pointed out, eliding the differences between male-on-female and male-on-male abuse 'potentially diminishes – and thereby potentially dishonors' queer stories.

Beyond this, there are other queer dimensions of #MeToo that require a complex intersectional frame that integrates class and race with sexuality as well as gender. The analysis needs to point not primarily towards ways of stopping individual men from misbehaving, but towards ways of eliminating the structural inequalities that empower some men to abuse women and others. We also need to distinguish tactics that enlist the state usefully (on balance) to resist oppression from tactics whose reliance on the state reinforces entrenched power structures. Here I want to focus on three issues in particular: age difference; affirmative consent; and the illusion of queer-straight equality.

Age Difference

LGBTIQ people have different experiences of childhood and youth than straight people. Virtually nobody growing up needs to be taught that heterosexuality is a normal phenomenon. The over-whelmingly majority of children have a male and a female parent, who were at some point a sexual couple. Children exploring non-straight sexual desires, or non-conforming gender identities, face a different reality: a strong sense of being different, and at times of feeling completely alone. Images of queer people in the media lack the familiarity and immediacy of images that comes from one's family. And for working-class and racialised kids, even they can be difficult to relate to.

This means that many LGBTIQ young people depend on older queer people, who they have actually met and can form some kind of bond with, to give them a picture of what it can mean to be queer themselves. Even queer people who remain close to their parents generally need to supplement their family of origin with a 'chosen family' that includes older LGBTIQ people. In a heteronormative society, young queers' reliance on older queers is to some degree structural and inevitable.

For some young queer people – certainly for many gay men of my generation – the process of forming bonds with older LGBTIQ people may sometimes include sexual relationships with them. In the past such relationships were often criminalised, even where homosexuality as such was not. In Britain after decriminalisation in 1967, in Canada after 1969, and in the Netherlands for most of the twentieth century, the age of consent for gay sex was twenty-one, while the age of consent for straight sex was significantly lower. Police often did their best to catch gay men having sex with a partner under twenty-one, as a way of criminalising homosexuality in general. Even where ages of consent have now been equalised (as in the European Union as a whole), age difference in queer relationships is often viewed with suspicion.

Within LGBTIQ communities as elsewhere, women in particu-lar are sensitive to the dangers of abuse that age difference can entail. Yet lesbians too are aware of the importance of older women as sexual models. Meg Christian's song 'Ode to a Gym Teacher', recalling her girlhood crush on 'a big tough woman, the first to come along / That showed me being female meant you still could be strong', was an anthem at one time for many lesbians. Prominent Canadian lesbian writer Jane Rule met her life partner when Rule was twenty-three and her partner thirty-eight. I'm particularly sensitive about this issue because, like Rule, I was twenty-three when Christopher and I met, and he was thirty-eight. Today, now that I'm sixty and he's seventy-five, people rarely perceive any age difference between us (sometimes I wish they would). But it was different when we met. I suspect that my parents, who at first weren't thrilled about my being gay, thought that my sexual orientation was somehow Christopher's fault. (If so, luckily, they got over this long ago.)

This affects the way queers view sexual aggression, especially when there's an age difference. Precisely because young LGBTIQ people can have such a compelling need for older queers' examples and affection, abuse can have a particularly painful sting of betrayal. But there is also danger in policing young people's sexuality in ways that deny them agency. In defending young people's right to say no, we should also defend their right to say yes, without which the right to say no is virtually meaningless. The long history of witch-hunts against LGBTIQ people that began with charges of abuse of young people should drive this point home for us. As queer activist Masha Gessen has written, as a woman she wholeheartedly welcomes #MeToo, but 'I am also queer, and I panic when I sniff sex panic ... Sex panics in the past have begun with actual crimes but led to outsized penalties and, more importantly, to a generalised sense of danger.' Gessen reminds us of Gayle Rubin's warning that 'a period of renegotiating sexual norms ... tend[s] to produce ever more restrictive regimes of closely regulating sexuality'. These more restrictive regimes can pose a special threat to young queers.

Queer teenagers still have to fight to express and act on their queer desires. Even today in supposedly tolerant societies, the law is often one of the obstacles they have to contend with. Accounts of male-on-male abuse exposed during #MeToo have revealed that the age of sexual consent has sometimes been raised in recent years. In some US states where the age of consent was sixteen or lower forty years ago, it is now seventeen – exceptionally high by international standards. For a sixteen-year-old queer person with homophobic parents, criminalising any sexual contact they might have with a nineteen-year-old adds burdens to the already burdensome pursuit of a queer life. Ages of consent this high need to be vigorously opposed.

Our focus should be less on chronological age, and more on conditions that empower young people to explore their sexuality safely, freely and in an informed way. I have argued, including in my book *Warped*, for a nuanced approach to the capacity for sexual consent, even among young teenagers. This is not an argument for the kind of uncritical celebration of 'boy love' that some gay men indulge in, entranced with tales of such relationships in ancient Athens or the eighth-century Arab caliphate. The intergenerational same-sex relationships common in many different cultures across millennia were embedded in very different sexual cultures, where the desires of the younger partner were not necessarily a major concern. The last century, however, offered more genuinely liberating legal frameworks for intergenerational relationships. In Soviet Russia in the 1920s, courts relied on medical opinion in formulating a flexible conception of 'sexual maturity' instead of an arbitrary age of consent. In the Netherlands between 1991 and 2002, an older person having sex with someone aged 12 to 15 was legally exempt from prosecution unless a complaint was made by the younger partner, the younger partner's parent or guardian, or a child welfare agency. I have argued that these two examples could be drawn on to legally define 'readiness for different sexual acts in a flexible and differentiated way, with the young person's own awareness and initiative given priority over "expert" opinion'.

We need to hope, as JoAnn Wypijewski wrote almost twenty years ago in her review of Judith Levine's *Harmful to Minors*, that 'children might learn to find joy in the realm of the senses, the world of ideas and souls, so that when sex disappoints and love fails, as they will, a teenager, a grown-up, still has herself, and a universe of small delights and strong hearts to fall back on'. Unfortunately, the trend has for decades been in the opposite direction: towards greater paternalism and tighter restrictions on young people's sexual self-determination.

ᚷ

Sanctified Tyrannies

Especially among queers, the fight against abuse needs to look beyond an obsession with youthful innocence and older predators. Power differentials derive from age are entangled with wealth and power accumulated by birth or career. Some of the male abusers of men exposed in recent months have specifically gained power in the fields of art and sports. Stars and teachers are often surrounded by a celebrity aura that seems (for a time) to sanctify abuses of power that would seem grubbier in a factory or office. But the dynamics are fundamentally the same: perpetrators, without regard to the pleasure, indifference, distaste or revulsion of their target, are able to dangle promises of advancement, or threats of ruination, as a means to sexual conquest.

There are crucial differences among the victims in such cases, however, which journalistic accounts neglect. Male assault and harassment of women and trans people make all women and trans people feel less safe in public and hold them back in waged work. Often sexual harassment is part of an attempt to drive women and trans people out of workplaces, occupations or managerial positions where they are unwanted. Some of the recent decline in women's representation in blue-collar occupations, as the *New York Times* has reported, is due to sexual harassment. For lesbians, who are even more dependent on paid work, sexual harassment of this kind threatens their economic survival. Straight male homophobia also sometimes takes the form of sexual baiting in the workplace.

By contrast, gay men's sexual harassment of other men is rarely, if ever, an attempt to drive men out of workplaces. Men's position in the arts and sports in particular is secure and uncontested. So if employers in these fields fail to effectively combat sexual harassment by gay men of other men, they are not contributing to a hostile climate for men in general. This forms a contrast with the US prison system, for example, where a pervasive culture of male-on-male rape – an integral part of a viciously punitive, racist system of mass incarceration – clearly does create a hostile climate for young men. It also contrasts with women's situation in the US in particular, where the law rightly holds that employers that fail to effectively combat sexual harassment of women perpetuate a climate of discrimination. By failing to make this distinction, media accounts of abuse underplay the qualitatively distinct threat to women and trans people, and obscure how much is at stake for them.

The upshot is that sexual assault and harassment of men by other men, irrespective of age, is almost always embedded in class and other hierarchies. Yet analysis of this is generally foregone in news stories, which tend to focus on the age and sexual proclivities of, especially older, gay men. These stories never seem to ask where the actors' union reps were while abuse was happening, or query the intense reverence for teachers, coaches, celebrities. As long as these sanctified tyrannies are not addressed, focusing on individual perpetrators can only have a limited impact in reducing abuse.

Affirmative Consent
The 'yes means yes' standard of affirmative consent holds that a sexual act is only permissible, at any stage, with the explicit consent of all parties. It has been adopted for universities in New York and California, and written into law in Sweden. Many feminists support it as a weapon against sexual abuse.

The merits of affirmative consent as a safeguard against male abuse of women are a subject of legitimate debate. I will not intervene here in that debate. But queer experience suggests reasons to hesitate in same-sex cases. Here again I need to appeal to personal experience, to the story of how Christopher and I met: according to a strict interpretation of affirmative consent, Christopher should not have touched my hand. He should have asked first. If he had, I'm afraid that I would have said no. When I think of the possibility of Christopher's not reaching out and touching me, I'm devastated by the thought of what might not have been.

For me, that experience says something about the value for queers, after centuries of repression, of unanticipated, unauthorised desire. So many of people's desires these days are shaped by the sexualised images – mostly, still, heterosexual images – with which we are continually bombarded. Sexual orientations are explicitly chosen earlier on average than in the past. As a result, our desires are restricted, bounded, by all sorts of expectations. Despite supposedly greater social tolerance for LGBTIQ identities, studies show that male teenagers who identify early as straight are less likely to experiment with same-sex encounters today than fifty years ago. To the increasingly entrenched virtual taboo on non-sexual touching, due to a fear of abuse and the growing sexualisation of society, has been added a particular taboo on same-sex touching, due to the increased rigidity of sexual orientation. This taboo denies the way sexual orientation shifts in the course of a lifetime, and denies its subjects the chance for real boundary crossing and new experience.

The taboo also has bloody consequences in view of the congealed legacies of homophobic prejudice. In the recent past in many US states, homophobic murderers could escape conviction for their actions by restoring to the 'gay panic' defence. They claimed to be so traumatised by a sexual advance that they were no longer responsible for their actions. So while, in many countries around the world, women are in prison today for killing their abusers in self-defence, gay and bisexual men have been effectively subject to extrajudicial execution because of non-violent, non-coercive sexual advances, which were viewed as abuse.

Given this, what are the implications of affirmative consent for queer desire? Of course, in any situation, for whatever reason, no means no. And even in the absence of violence or coercion, sensitivity and care for the other person's pleasure are vital in any sexual encounter. Men in particular, as #MeToo has reminded us, need to be less fixated on their own impulses and more alert to cues, verbal and non-verbal. The fact that many #MeToo accounts take place in the grey zone between obvious assault and 'bad sex' shows that many men still have a lot to learn.

Should a queer person, though, never make a sexual advance to a person of unknown sexual orientation without a clear invitation? Should a trans or intersex person never make a sexual advance to someone who hasn't clearly signalled openness to sex with a trans or intersex person? What would all this mean for 'the seduction of homoerotic desire', to which, the Chinese scholar Chou Wah-shan has written, the 'straight world is itself never immune'? Of course there's nothing wrong with asking. Words can be sexy. But in queer settings, a single, tentative touch can sometimes overcome barriers to transgressive desire that words alone might not.

For many women, burdened by straight men's neediness, demands and entitlement, overcoming barriers to desire might not be the highest priority. But for many queers, female and male, encouraging same-sex advances may be just as vital as fending off unwanted ones. Criminal law cannot do full justice to these competing imperatives. So criminalising misconduct (short of assault) is not the best starting place for queer sexual politics.

Make-Believe Equality

Many of the same principles that apply to women's charges of sexual assault and harassment should apply when men make similar charges. Studies have shown that false accusations of this kind are rare. Given how long victims have been shamed, ignored and silenced, they deserve the benefit of the doubt. Male victims are just as entitled to recognition and redress as female ones.

What's at stake in #MeToo, however, is not only individual guilt, but also the structure of oppressive systems. If we want to effectively fight male-on-male sexual aggression, we need to take account of the somewhat different social organisation of sex between men. When news stories mention gay and straight perpetrators in the same breath, acknowledging no salient differences between them, it plays into what Lisa Duggan has called 'homonormativity'. This is a set of attitudes suggesting that LGBTI people can be fully equal – if and only if they conform as closely as possible to heterosexual patterns, preferably marrying, adopting or giving birth to kids and forming respectable nuclear families.

Coverage of #MeToo seems to take place largely in this make-believe world of already achieved gay–straight equality. Even when reporters are unaware of past prejudice and would consciously reject it, such coverage risks implicitly evoking age-old stereotypes of gay men as powerful, privileged, predatory paedophiles. This was the stock in trade for generations of anti-gay prejudice, not only on the right but also – especially where Stalinism and Maoism held sway – on the left. The evidence for this notional gay power and privilege has always been slim to nonexistent. Studies show that gay and bisexual men on average have lower incomes and are less likely to occupy positions of authority than straight men – not to mention trans people, whose economic situation is in general dire. Yet media representations of lesbians and gay men as privileged and prosperous both helps produce the dominant image of the neoliberal queer, and keeps old prejudices alive and well. Even young LGBTIQ people can be haunted by these lurking spectres – not least because of the still widespread prevalence of violence against queer and trans young people in schools, on the streets and in their families. Far from oblivious to imagery of predatory gay men, young queers are all too sensitive to it. Not only because they might actually experience abuse, but because every instance of abuse gives new life to gruesome images. Because of this, many gay men are reluctant to ever call perpetrators of abuse gay – a reluctance that, however driven by fear of oppression, also reflects a denial of the unruliness and dark side of desire.

Today, images of predatory, powerful gays serve as a stick driving queer men in the direction of homonormativity, tacitly reproaching them for failing to conform to norms of monogamy and domesticity. They reinforce, even where laws overtly prohibit discrimination, the structure of the heteronormative family, the omnipresent cult of heterosexual romance, and the still powerful norms of masculinity and femininity that haunt sexual and gender nonconformists. They also, implicitly, reinforce the fallacious idea that prejudice would disappear if only all LGBTIQ people behaved well. This pressure weighs powerfully on queer psyches. Heterosexual hegemony and the gender binary are far more powerful than the mainstream media acknowledge.

To analyze same-sex abuse adequately, therefore, we need to probe the different dynamics of different sexual and gender identities. Much more reflection is needed about why some men are victimised, and how they are viewed if they admit to being victimised. As Joy Castro has perceptively suggested, 'the articulation of an experience of victimisation pushes one into a feminized role (thus provoking the doubt that's always deployed against women qua women)'. One of the most traumatic aspects of abuse for male survivors is the way it can lead them to doubt their masculinity. While straight male victims can panic at the thought that their abusers perceived them as gay, gay and bisexual victims can reproach themselves for being too passive and thus somehow effeminate. Studies have shown that revulsion at effeminacy is still all too widespread among cis gay and bisexual men. By contrast, female victims seem to worry that they were too visibly, alluringly feminine, and thus somehow brought abuse on themselves. All victims risk blaming themselves, contributing to their sense of shame and their silence – but in gender-specific ways. Combating survivors' shame and enabling them to speak out requires understanding these dynamics.

In short, queers cannot simply be folded into a general struggle against sexual abuse. Our struggle against abuse needs to be part of our ongoing fight for queer sexual liberation. For decades now, we have suffered from the reduction of liberation to equality with straights in straight-defined institutions, and from the reduction of real equality to juridical equality. It is time to renew the call that some courageous lesbian feminists made in the early 1980s for a new sexual politics. At least for queers, it is time for a politics that is alert to danger but gives the same priority to pleasure and desire – the desire that can catch fire at a moment's touch.

SARAH GREY

Not Today

I

In a river valley, sirens' wails reverberate. They hit a sheer rock face, the aluminum wall of an old factory, the steel beams of a bridge, then water.

Back when the mills were running, sirens mounted on water towers and smokestacks brought the women out onto their porches, the prayer in their eyes the same in Polish, Slovak, Arabic, Yiddish as they looked down to the steep-staired sidewalks, through trees and over roofs to the water: an accident at the mill? An explosion in the mine? Who? Please, God, not today.

Every day sending fathers, sisters, husbands, children down the icy stairs with a packed lunch into danger. Every day not knowing. Every night a sigh of relief when the shift ends, welcoming them home, maybe a little beer on their breath from a stop on the way up the hill. Every night a prayer of thanks.

These things happen when you work with molten iron, coke, steel. When everything is hotter and heavier than anything you could imagine existing in hell. They happen when you delve deep into the earth in tunnels that subside sometimes, when sometimes houses sink down to the second-floor windows. Sometimes fingers disappear into sewing machines or jigsaws. You learn to live with not knowing. You learn to pray. Please, God, not today.

II

Prayers reverberate too. All through the valleys, all along the rivers
and atop the hills, jutting out over roads carved into cliffs: songs,
bells, chants, choirs, calls to prayer in every tongue. Even the bosses
step out of their Fifth Avenue mansions to sing sober Protestant
hymns in sober Protestant cathedrals.

The houses of worship are built to compete with the mills'
scale and majesty. Skilled stoneworkers carve the words of God in
Hebrew, Armenian, Russian. Worshipers pass beneath tile mosaics
or gilded onion domes. Pennies of grandmothers and small children,
not easily spared, buy a cornerstone from Jerusalem for the shul.

No one says a survival prayer crossing this threshold.

A day off is a rest from small survival prayers. In such places
one can pray out loud, with others, and watch the prayers swirl
up and out of the stained-glass windows to mingle with the other
prayers and be blown down the Allegheny, down the Monongahela,
to merge into the great Ohio.

III

There comes a day when the mills quiet. The city continues,
somehow. It prays for the dead: the millworkers and miners, the
strikers shot by Pinkertons, the vitality bled out of its soil by the
men who bought and sold it.

Some houses of God grow quiet too, congregants grown old,
children and grandchildren off to find work in other cities. The
elders pray for them now, not for themselves. Their congregations
are small enough to share the grand houses. At Wilkins and Shady,
at Tree of Life, there are three. They show up faithfully, if not always
promptly, and the stained glass swirls like their prayers.

Squirrel Hill continues with more vigor than the mill towns.
On a ridge between universities, it protects its own. The houses
are old: red brick with green lawns or tangled ivy. On doorframes

mezuzahs, rainbow flags, sometimes both. Jewish life is old here too, stretching back to days of robber barons. This is where Jews came together to make change and declare solidarity with the Christians and Muslims and Hindus around them. Here, in 1885, Reform rabbis debated the Pittsburgh Platform, that proposed a new, modern, anti-Zionist Judaism based on the 'divine nature of human spirit' and offered to 'extend the hand of fellowship to all who cooperate with us'. They looked to the future here, and then built it, here, in the most diverse neighborhood in western Pennsylvania.

Outside young women in backpacks pass – international students tired from a long Friday night in the dorms. They'll eat pancakes at the 24-hour Eat'n'Park on Murray Avenue while the elders pray. Prayers still fly thick in the air in this neighborhood.

IV

Even in American gun culture, the AR-15 stands out. Enter a shooting range and the safety earmuffs tight and heavy against your skull will dampen the bang-bang-bang of Glocks and rifles so that, after a few minutes' exposure, you stop jumping. They will not protect you, though, against the aural assault of the AR-15, which sounds as though the air itself is exploding. Its booms are slow and deliberate, meant to be felt deep inside the body, to induce panic in its prey. They are unmistakable.

There are no sirens mounted on the roof at Tree of Life. No one expects death to happen here. The sirens come later. At first there is only the strange shattering boom. The neighbors are confused. But SWAT team officers with machine guns of their own gesture frantically at them – get inside, get inside, stay down.

Inside, their prayers interrupted, the elders hide in a dark closet and hold their breath. The man with the gun is shouting between booms, something about Jews, hard to understand him.

Eleven elders die.

V

Pittsburgh has its civil religions, too.

Its greatest secular saint lived around the corner from Tree of Life. Fred Rogers, mild Presbyterian minister, puppeteer, and host of Mister Rogers' Neighborhood, was known on these streets. He tipped his student waitresses generously and inquired about their studies, their journeys from Indonesia and China. Everyone had a story about him. When chaos reigned he calmed the city: quietly desegregating television, standing up against greed, helping children understand why a hijacked plane had flown over their heads on its way to death in 2001.

Those who leave the city tend to keep the faith.

It is the United States' two hundred and seventy-fifth mass shooting of the year, but this one is different. Those who know Squirrel Hill have a hard time articulating why. It can happen anywhere, we all know that – our children rehearse hiding from mass shooters in their classrooms, crowding into closets much like the elders did. But this is Mister Rogers' neighborhood, we sputter, tearful in our black and gold.

On Wilkins Avenue a vigil forms. There are signs: at least as many invoke Mister Rogers and his cardigan as mock the false sympathy of the man who has left the White House to intrude upon the city's grief. A reporter stands among the crowd, marveling that the mourners are singing, can we get the mic on that? A woman steps toward him, intent, hair flying in the wind: 'We are praying. We're praying. We're Jewish. This is how we pray.' And then her group is past him, leaving the cameras behind as the crowd follows. Prayers of grief and survival prayers swirl among their feet, down, down toward the hospital where Jewish doctors and nurses extract bullets from the shooter's body.

VI

If they had some kind of protection inside the temple maybe it could have been a much different situation.

While the bodies are still in the temple, the families still being informed, Trump talks to the cameras. The worshipers should've prayed under the muzzles of guns, he says. The way schoolchildren study under the eyes of police. They should have been more careful, should have armed themselves. Should have uttered survival prayers with every step, should not have expected any place to be holy.

But, he announces, he's coming to Pittsburgh to pay his respects. He chooses the day of the funerals. The mayor pleads for understanding: the city wants tight security at the funerals. No one feels safe praying now. Hosting a presidential motorcade takes resources and planning, he says. So many armed guards to post. Ask the families what they want, he says.

That's not Trump's style. He intrudes. Squirrel Hill gathers again, on the steps of Mister Rogers's church. There is shouting. There are tears. The Trumps walk in with flowers and place stones on the white wooden stars of David hastily erected on the synagogue lawn. The rabbi receives them with sombre grace: no shouting, no tears.

The motorcade rolls to the hospital. The people in the streets turn their backs. Inside, the Trumps pose for photos. To the first responders they hand out brass souvenir coins embossed with 'Make America Great Again' and 'Donald J. Trump' in three places.

VII

Maybe there would have been nobody killed, except for him.

Him is Robert Bowers, 46, owner of 21 guns and a Gab account. He grew up and still lived half an hour away from Squirrel Hill, in Baldwin, out in the South Hills, near the airport and Kennywood Park. One of those dozens of working-class river-valley boroughs that line the edges of the city. Baldwin, 'home of the Fighting Highlanders', has ten churches, but no synagogues.

Since the nineties, Bowers had kept a shotgun by his door. He refused to pay federal taxes. In this he echoes the earliest settlers of the South Hills, 7,000 of whom mustered here in 1794 for the Whiskey Rebellion. Whiskey was effectively a form of currency then; when Treasury secretary Alexander Hamilton taxed it, local farmers, most of them veterans of the revolution, revolted. Like most American history, there was a component of racism, too: they wanted federal protection against the Indigenous residents whose land they'd claimed. President Washington led the crackdown himself. It was one of the first real flexes of US federal power. Some people around here never got over it.

Bowers loved Jim Quinn, 'Quinn in the Morning', a local right-wing radio host whose billboard ads show him lighting a cigar from a flame in the barrel of a miniature AR-15. Bowers had been railing against Jews and Muslims online for months. He blamed Jews for the presence of Muslims and fixated on HIAS, a Jewish nonprofit that aids refugees.

As the Saturday morning prayers rose up, he made his decision. 'HIAS likes to bring invaders in that kill our people. I can't sit by and watch my people get slaughtered. Screw your optics', he posted. 'I'm going in.'

PAIGE MURPHY

Militating, she goes.

Cabins were

    concrete,

        were a church,

           a built

               body,

                  were the desert,

                     were 1848,
                     were not that moment,
                     were preceding it,
                     were before
                     a desperate plea to numerate

Militating grave to grave,
the graves in Yucatan,
the graves in place names,
the graves in years — a plea for presence

There is a dream of rapes past, previous futures
through the ring, yesterdays breaking up
disrupting today's getting together
Dream of bedrooms   horror   bad lace
broderie   bilous coughs   unwaged labour
The sheer force of her return to work the
day after   twenty three   twenty four   thirty two
fifty one years of memory   one thousand eight hundred and forty
eight   years of childhood
GOOD & BAD
knowing the latter to exist in absolute certainty
there is very very evil
it is true, vocally disassociate it-self, on account
of one   of two   twenty three   twenty four   thirty
two   fifty one
The secret is feverish and lives
in a bedroom,
in a wooden door
in a drained basin,
witches militate
drainpipes to unleash their rusted load
where it had sat in little puddles,
banalities   soap suds   a dream clean
of false hope   a dream cleansed of innocence,
only the promise of angels and hell
lies true, in a trap door
(behind you)

militating un even circles
both spheres

...of summer in the apartment
in the studio room
in the bedroom
in little submission?
there is evil in it

yes   yes

About the Contributors

JAMIE ALLINSON is one of the founding editors of *Salvage*. He teaches International Relations of the Middle East at the University of Edinburgh and is the author of *The Struggle for the State in Jordan* (I. B. Taurus, 2015). He is currently working on a book about counter-revolution.

IMOGEN CASSELS is the author of *Arcades* (Sad, 2018) and *Mother; beautiful things* (Face, 2018). Her poems have appeared in the *London Review of Books,* the *White Review*, the *Cambridge Literary Review*, *Blackbox Manifold*, *Stride*, *Erotoplasty*, and elsewhere.

PETER DRUCKER is a Fellow of the International Institute of Research and Education (Amsterdam) and the author of *Warped: Gay Normality and Queer Anti-Capitalism* (Brill, 2015).

SAI ENGLERT is a lecturer at Leiden University. He works on political economy, labour movements, Labour Zionism, and settler colonialism.

JULES JOANNE GLEESON is a communist from London. Her writing has featured in *VICE*, *Hypocrite Reader*, *New Socialist*, *Blind Field*, *'Identities'*, *JSTOR Daily*, Verso and Pluto Press' blogs, and *Viewpoint*, *Ritual*, *Commune* and *Tribune*.

SARAH GREY is a writer and editor based in Philadelphia. She grew up in Cheswick, Pennsylvania, and attended Chatham College. More of her writing can be found at sarahgreywrites.com.

J. N. HOAD is a communist, DIY transsexual and *femmes de lettres* in the North West of the UK.

SOPHIE LEWIS is a writer and queer communist theorist living in Philadelphia. Her first book, *Full Surrogacy Now: Feminism Against Family* was published by Verso in May 2019.

R. H. LOSSIN is a PhD candidate in Communications at Columbia University. Her dissertation, 'The Point of Destruction: Sabotage, Property and Speech in the Progressive Era', explores the role of property destruction in labor disputes. She has written essays and reviews for *New Left Review*, *Jacobin*, the *Nation* and the *Brooklyn Rail*.

MORGANE MERTEUIL is a feminist activist based in Paris, who has been active in the defence of sex workers rights. She coordinated, with Stella Magliani-Belkacem, Felix Boggio Ewanjé-Epée and Frédéric Monferrand, the collection of Marxist-feminist essays *Pour un Féminisme de la Totalité* (Editions Amsterdam, 2016).

CHINA MIÉVILLE is a founding editor of *Salvage*. He is the author of various works of fiction and non-fiction. His most recent book is *October: The Story of the Russian Revolution* (Verso, 2017).

PAIGE MURPHY is a poet, prison abolitionist and hysteric living in London.

KEVIN OCHIENG OKOTH is an independent writer and researcher living in London. He writes on imperialism and twentieth-century anti-colonial struggles.

RICHARD SEYMOUR is a founding editor of *Salvage*, an author and a broadcaster. His latest book is *The Twittering Machine* (Indigo, 2019).

KATYA TEPPER works out of the lived experience of chronic autoimmune illness, considering how the body processes and translates its environment. They have exhibited work at White Columns, NY, Atlanta Contemporary, ATL, Red Bull Arts, Detroit, among others.

TROY VETTESE is a post-doctoral fellow at Harvard University, where he studies neoliberal environmental thought.